The Educational Thought of
W.E.B. Du Bois

The Educational Thought of W.E.B. Du Bois

An Intellectual History

Derrick P. Alridge

foreword by
V. P. Franklin

TEACHERS
COLLEGE
PRESS

Teachers College
Columbia University
New York and London

Published by Teachers College Press, 1234 Amsterdam Avenue, New York, NY 10027

Thanks to the *History of Education Quarterly* and the History of Education Society, *Educational Theory, The Journal of Negro Education, Kappa Delta Pi*, and the *Georgia Encyclopedia* for allowing me to use parts and revised versions of my essays in their publications for this book. Thanks also to the David Graham Du Bois Trust for permitting me to quote from unpublished materials in *The Papers of W.E.B. Du Bois*. And I am indebted to the Moorland-Spingarn Research Center for citations from the Anna Julia Cooper Papers and Charles H. Thompson Papers.

Library of Congress Cataloging-in-Publiction Data

Alridge, Derrick P.
  The educational thought of W.E.B. Du Bois : an intellectual history / Derrick P. Alridge ; foreword by V. P. Franklin.
      p. cm.
  Includes bibliographical references and index.
  ISBN 978-0-8077-4836-7 (paperback : alk. paper) — ISBN 978-0-8077-4837-4 (cloth : alk. paper)
  1. Du Bois, W. E. B. (William Edward Burghardt), 1868–1963.
2. Education—Philosophy.   3. African Americans—Education.   I. Title.
  LB875.D83A43 2008
  370.1—dc22
                                                                    2007045677

ISBN 978-0-8077-4836-7 (paper)
ISBN 978-0-8077-4837-4 (cloth)

Printed on acid-free paper

Manufactured in the United States of America

15   14   13   12   11   10   09   08   8   7   6   5   4   3   2   1

Dedicated to Dr. Asa G. Hilliard III (Nana Baffour Amankwatia II)
Educator, Scholar, and Warrior

Contents

Foreword

Throughout his long and illustrious career, W.E.B. Du Bois was not only concerned about "the souls of black folk," he was also committed to their education. Du Bois approached "education" broadly, along the lines pursued later by historian Lawrence Cremin, who defined education as "the deliberate, systematic, and sustained effort to transmit or evoke knowledge, attitudes, values, skills, and sensibilities." During his early career as a historian and social scientist Du Bois believed that education, not just formal schooling, would be needed to solve the so-called Negro Problem. Schooling was needed for those who were denied it, and education was needed for those schooled in the ideas and practices of white supremacy.

Du Bois was committed to unearthing and disseminating scholarly truths about the history and cultures of African-descended peoples. At the same time, he was vehement in his insistence that African American men, women, and children be provided the same educational opportunities available to white citizens in the United States. Therein lay the basis for his well-known, but often misunderstood disagreement with Booker T. Washington, one of the leading black spokespersons at the turn of the 20th century. While Du Bois and Washington understood that the most gifted members of the African American community should provide the leadership, they differed on how that "Talented Tenth" should be trained. While Du Bois was willing to support literacy training and industrial education for the masses of African Americans who would have to work to survive and advance in American society, he opposed the industrial programs offered at Samuel Armstrong's Hampton Institute, Washington's Tuskegee Institute, and other secondary industrial schools because they were training the teachers and other leaders for the black community—the Talented Tenth. Du Bois firmly believed that the black Talented Tenth should receive the same schooling in institutions of higher education as the white leadership class. If college and university training was appropriate for the preparation of white leaders, it was needed just as much (or more) for the African American leadership.

Throughout his life Du Bois was a teacher and educator, as well as a scholar-activist, and he used his incomparable genius to produce speeches, publications, and other works to promote knowledge and understanding among peoples throughout the world. While several volumes of Du Bois's writings on "The Education of Black People" have been compiled and published, Derrick Alridge provides the first comprehensive analysis of Du Bois's educational thought, placing it in its appropriate historical and intellectual context. Alridge begins with Du Bois's own training and education in the United States and Europe, and makes it clear that Du Bois accepted the Progressive ethos which promoted the belief that social scientific research should be used to reform society and advance humanity at the dawn of the 20th century. Du Bois along with Jane Addams, John Dewey, Lillian Wald, and other progressives engaged in educational activities that sought to ameliorate the social conditions for children and workers who were victimized by unrestrained corporate capitalism. In *The Philadelphia Negro: A Social Study* (1899) and *The Atlanta University Studies* (1897–1911), Du Bois provided social scientific data and analyses that researchers and reformers would use throughout the century in formulating responses to deteriorating social conditions created by the rise of the urban industrial nation.

Many other African American educators and intellectuals shared Du Bois's emphasis on education for black advancement. Alridge discusses the educational beliefs and practices of Alexander Crummell, Anna Julia Cooper, Kelly Miller, and Nannie Helen Burroughs; and while each developed their own educational vision for African Americans, they shared Du Bois's commitment to providing improved educational opportunities for the black masses and elites. However, these opportunities decreased greatly in the 1930s during the Great Depression, and while African Americans in no way were responsible for the economic debacle, they were arguably its greatest victims. As "the last hired and first fired," black workers and their families came together to help one another survive those desperate times. Alridge provides an insightful analysis of Du Bois's economic and educational programs and proposals for dealing with the depressed and depressing social circumstances for African Americans. Du Bois offered a controversial proposal arguing that the segregated black institutions should serve as the foundation for collective black economic programs aimed at relieving the suffering in black communities. Through black cooperative enterprises, African Americans would be able to provide work and supply the goods and services needed for their survival and advancement.

Du Bois was not alone in promoting "social reconstruction" and emancipatory education for African Americans in the 1930s and 1940s. Through an examination of the educational ideas of Carter G. Woodson, Alain Locke, Mary McLeod Bethune, Charles H. Thompson, and Horace Mann Bond, Alridge shows how they were influenced by Du Boisian social analysis and laid the groundwork for future educational programs and social movements. In the early 1950s, however, Du Bois became a victim of the anti-communist crusades and his participation in the international peace movement led to his arrest, indictment, and trial as "an agent of a foreign power." While he was ultimately acquitted and exonerated of these charges, Du Bois was painfully disappointed by the lack of support he received during this ordeal from the black professional class. As far as he was concerned, he felt abandoned by the members of the Talented Tenth whom he had nurtured throughout his career. Alridge provides a superb analysis of how Du Bois's educational vision for African Americans and other oppressed peoples reflected the changing domestic and international context during the Cold War era. The advance of U.S. imperialism and governmental propaganda and censorship troubled Du Bois and led to his renewed emphasis on critical thinking, the freedom to learn, and education for liberation.

At the same time, Du Bois maintained his campaign for the promotion of the study of African and African American history not only for purposes of "race vindication," but as source of knowledge and inspiration for black youth and adults. As was the case with historian Carter G. Woodson, Du Bois opposed "the mis-education of the Negro" and through his promotion of Pan-African solidarity, Du Bois sought to educate African peoples about their past in order to prepare them for their future. Du Bois's "Afro-centric" approach to the study of world history predated the scholarly preoccupations with Afrocentricity in the 1980s and 1990s, and manifested itself in Du Bois's plans for the publication of the *Encyclopedia Africana*, which he believed was essential "not only for the emancipation of the American Negro, but for the emancipation of the African Negro and the Negroes of the West Indies, for the emancipation of the colored races, and the emancipation of the white slaves of modern capitalist monopoly."

Derrick Alridge's *The Educational Thought of W.E.B. Du Bois* is a major contribution to American and African American intellectual and educational history. Alridge provides the first detailed scholarly analysis of the full range of Du Bois's educational philosophy, placing it within the context of the larger social and intellectual movements in American society and throughout the African world. Well-documented and gracefully written, Alridge's important work fills one of the remaining gaps in our knowledge and understanding of the intellectual legacy of the leading African American scholar-activist of the twentieth century.

V. P. Franklin

V. P. Franklin holds a President's Chair and is Distinguished Professor of History and Education at the University of California, Riverside. He is also Editor of The Journal of African American History.

Acknowledgments

This book would not have been possible without the support of many individuals and organizations. To begin, I would like to thank the Association for the Study of African American Life and History (ASALH) for providing an intellectually stimulating, welcoming, and encouraging environment for me to develop many of the ideas that appear in this book. I would also like to thank the National Academy of Education (NAE) and the Spencer Foundation for awarding me a postdoctoral fellowship that helped me complete the archival research for this book.

I am also indebted to several mentors at Penn State University. Aaron D. Gresson has been an unswerving mentor; his friendship has been invaluable to me and his work in the sociology of knowledge has tremendously influenced my scholarship in intellectual history. James B. Stewart has been a steadfast supporter and co-conspirator in the study of Du Bois's thought, and it was he who inspired me to become a Du Bois scholar. Henry C. Johnson has been a supporter since my graduate school days. Aaron, Jim, and Henry have truly been my "guides to clear thinking." Thanks also to each of them for providing feedback on early drafts of this manuscript.

Thanks also to V. P. Franklin of the University of California, Riverside for his mentorship and support of my scholarship over the past decade. I am also indebted to him for providing critical feedback on this manuscript and for writing the foreword. Many thanks also to Ronald Butchart for his generous support and feedback on this manuscript and many other writing endeavors. Linda Perkins has also been an avid supporter who has provided great mentorship and valuable critiques of my work over the past few years. Thanks also to Wilson Moses for our many conversations about African American intellectual history at his home library in State College, Pennsylvania.

Many thanks to my friend and colleague Maurice C. Daniels, Dean of the School of Social Work at the University of Georgia (UGA). Our discussions and friendship over the past decade have helped sustain my energy as a scholar and provided me with great intellectual comfort and challenge. In writing this book I have tried to live by his maxim, which is "just do the work and let the work speak for itself."

Several peers contributed immensely to the intellectual environment within which this study evolved. Ronald E. Chennault has been a steadfast friend and supporter whose scholarly work in cultural studies influenced aspects of this study. Jerome E. Morris, friend and colleague at UGA, has done important work on African American youth and communities that has inspired and complemented my thinking on Du Bois and the education of black folk. Larry L. Rowley, a friend and fellow Du Bois scholar, has listened attentively to my interpretations of Du Bois over the past decade and provided intellectually rigorous critiques of my work. He also introduced me to a number of obscure sources that I found very useful. His intellectual tenacity inspired me tremendously. Phyllis Jeffers-Coly encouraged me to think beyond the bounds of academic disciplines and to find my voice in my writing. Her warm spirit and intellectual tenacity have always reinvigorated me when I needed a strong dose of "positive energy," as she calls it.

Also, thanks to my colleagues at UGA who provided much support. Many thanks to Diane Miller, a friend and colleague at UGA, who has been one of my greatest supporters. Her encouragement, editorial suggestions, critical feedback, and keen eye for detail made this a much better book and contributed immensely to the book seeing the light of day. Thanks to Judith Preissle, my program chair and former department head, for providing the intellectual space for me to grow and develop as a scholar. She has been a dear friend and an avid supporter. Thanks also to my friend Carl Glickman, who read an early draft of the manuscript and provided valuable feedback, and who has always been a source of great support. Thanks to my current department head, Ronald Cervero, for his generous support and intellectually stimulating conversations about Du Bois. Thanks also to UGA curriculum historian William Wraga for engaging me in many conversations on progressivism and education. Thanks to Dean Louis Castenell for his words of encouragement and support over the past decade. As dean of the College of Education at UGA, Dean Castenell has provided an energizing environment for me and other scholars to do our work.

Thanks to Ida Jones, historian and archivist at the Moorland-Spingarn Center; Uzoma Miller in Special Collections at Fisk University; and Danielle Kovacs at the University of Massachusetts for help locating materials in their respective archives. Thanks also to Nadine Cohen for her archival expertise and help at the University of Georgia library.

While it is impossible to list all the people who have supported me during the course of this project, I want to specifically express my gratitude to a few. They include Judy Alston, Deborah Atwater, Jihad Aziz, Yvonne Baines, Blannie Bowen, Joya Carter-Hicks, Leon Caldwell, Lubna Chaudhry, Vicky Crawford, Jack Dougherty, Tracey Ford, Chana Kai Lee, Catherine Lugg, Barbara Alvarado-Bartusiak, Catherine Lyons, Ronald Baxter Miller, Johnny Miller, Layli Phillips, Letha See, Linda Tillman, Vanessa Siddle Walker, Jackie Irvine, Russell Irvine, and Thomas Midgette. Thanks also to fellow Africana Studies scholar Corey D. B. Walker for his powerful scholarship and for sharing his insights on the African American intellectual tradition. Thanks also to Jim Garrison for helping me better understand Hegel.

Special thanks to Dwayne Wright and Kevin Williams, two of my former students who provided intellectual support and research assistance during their years at UGA. They continue to inspire me through their work as young intellectual warriors. Also thanks to several other graduate assistants, including Evetta Armstrong, Chang Bo, and Anthony Omerikwa, who provided library assistance during this process. Thanks to Brian Ellerbeck, Aureliano Vazquez, and the staff at Teachers College Press for their support and patience as I nurtured and worked through the ideas in this book.

Godspeed to Dr. Asa G. Hilliard III (*Nana Baffour Amankwatia II*) who recently joined the ancestors. I was blessed to have Asa provide me with feedback on an earlier draft of this manuscript. His wisdom enlightened me and thousands of others.

Finally, thanks to my parents, Dolphus and Sadie Williams and Govie Alridge Jr., who have provided the foundation of my life and scholarly enterprises. Thanks also to my mother-in-law, Delyour Wolfe, for her kindness, support, and encouragement throughout this process. Terrance Alridge, my brother and best friend, has given me unwavering support throughout the years. My son, Max, provided a respite from this work to enjoy the delights of fatherhood. I could not have a better son. Last, but not least, I send special thanks to Lori, my soul mate and wife, for reading and critiquing drafts of this manuscript and for tolerating my many days away from her to bring this project to completion. Her support, encouragement, and love have made this book possible.

Introduction

> No American university (except Negro institutions in understand-
> able self-defense) had ever recognized that I had any claims to
> scholarship.[1]
>
> —W.E.B. Du Bois

William Edward Burghardt Du Bois (1868–1963) was a renowned educator, a prolific writer and thinker on American educational issues, a preeminent scholar on the African American experience, and one of the most articulate voices for the downtrodden during his seventy-plus years of scholarship and activism. He was the first African American to graduate with a Ph.D. from Harvard, co-founder of the National Association for the Advancement of Colored People (NAACP), antagonist to Booker T. Washington and many others, and author of the seminal *The Souls of Black Folk* (1903), *The Phila-delphia Negro* (1899), and *Black Reconstruction* (1935), all cogent analyses of race relations and racism in America. No other African American or other American scholar has ever offered as comprehensive a set of educational ideas for black people as did Du Bois.

Despite his contributions, however, Du Bois has been for the most part neglected as an educational thinker in twentieth-century American history, and his educational ideas have been largely ignored by the fields of educational and intellectual history. When Du Bois is acknowledged, it is usually in the narrow context of his "great debates" with Booker T. Washington.[2] Moreover, existing scholarship on Du Bois's educational thought has tended to rely primarily on Du Bois's most popular writings on his best-known ideas. Missing is a comprehensive historical analysis of Du Bois's educational ideas, based on published and unpublished work, that provides a nuanced and complicated understanding of Du Bois's educational thought.

The Educational Thought of W.E.B. Du Bois: An Intellectual History examines the educational thought of W.E.B. Du Bois from 1895 to 1963. A central argument of this study is that Du Bois was a pragmatic educational theorist who developed original ideas and adopted and adapted many ideas of his time to forge educational strategies aimed at improving the social, economic, and political conditions of African Americans. Like many other intellectuals—particularly those who lived long lives—Du Bois expressed

1

ideas that were at any given time concrete, clear, and consistent but that, examined over the course of his lifetime, were also pragmatic enough to meet the complex and changing educational needs of African Americans.

This study seeks to move scholars beyond the overly simplified, binary discussions of Du Bois as an advocate of classical/liberal arts education and the antithesis of Booker T. Washington and vocational/industrial education. Instead, it engages a more multifaceted Du Bois who revised, rethought, and updated his educational ideas throughout his lifetime to address pressing problems facing African Americans of that period. In doing so, this work situates Du Bois within an African American intellectual tradition and places him within the context of African American educators of his day.[3] As such, this study falls within the tradition of historians such as Earl Thorpe, Harold Cruise, V. P. Franklin, William Banks, August Meier, Wilson Moses, Linda Perkins, Jerry Watts, Sterling Stuckey, and others who have identified and explicated an African American intellectual tradition in their work.[4]

A DU BOISIAN JOURNEY

The origins of my journey toward the study of Du Bois's educational thought date back to 1992. On April 29 of that year, riots broke out in South Central Los Angeles after the acquittal of four white policemen who brutally beat African American motorist Rodney King. The acquittal of the four policemen by a predominately white jury detonated an explosion of deep-seated tension in Los Angeles, as numerous African Americans and Hispanics took to the streets to protest and riot in response to the acquittal.

For many African Americans, the Rodney King decision exposed the enduring racism that continued to fester beneath the surface of American life. The riots reflected many black Americans' loss of faith in the American judicial system and the failure of past civil rights efforts to improve social and economic conditions enough for African Americans. Such feelings of despair during the early 1990s were exacerbated by a recession in 1992 that disproportionately affected blacks. High black unemployment, the deterioration of the urban areas in which many blacks lived, and the poor quality of education that many African Americans received as a result of a lack of funding and inadequate resources for inner-city schools undergirded the anger felt by many African Americans.

When the Los Angeles riots broke out, I was a young and enthusiastic high school history teacher in a working-class high school in South Carolina. Sixty percent of the students in the school were white, 30 percent were black, and 10 percent were Hispanic or Asian. Shortly after news of the riots reached the school administration, the history teachers were notified that our classes could watch the events unfolding on television because of their historic significance. However, we were instructed not to discuss the events in our classrooms because of the racial tensions that might arise between black and white students.

A few days later, after things had calmed down somewhat on the streets and in the media, I engaged my students in a discussion about the Rodney King verdict, the riots, and the racial tensions that surfaced during and after the riots. My African American students expressed their disappointment in the jury's decision, but most stated that they expected the decision. Most of my white students also expressed disappointment in the verdict, but focused their discussion on the rioting that followed.

Throughout the spring, I struggled with our discussions of the events surrounding the Rodney King verdict. I was only a year and a half old during the Watts riots in 1965 and four years old when Dr. Martin Luther King Jr. was assassinated in 1968. No previous event that I could remember had evoked as much racial tension, or had so vividly illuminated the persistent racial divide that continued to split the country, as the events of spring 1992. As a result, I often found myself at a loss for the words that would allow me to engage my students about these events and lacking a conceptual lens through which to discuss the issue in a meaningful way.

A year later, as a graduate student, I read W.E.B. Du Bois's *The Souls of Black Folk* (1903). While reading *Souls*, I was captivated by Du Bois's poetic, lyrical, and descriptive articulation of the state of race relations during the early 1900s. As a former teacher, I identified with his rich descriptions of the conditions of black life and education while he was a teacher in Tennessee. I felt awakened by Du Bois's powerful concept of "double-consciousness," which described blacks' attempt to maintain their own culture and sense of self within a society that sometimes despised blackness. Du Bois's description of the "veil of color" resonated with my life as I recognized how the veil was ever-present for me as an African American male growing up in the post–Civil Rights era. Finally, Du Bois's statement that "the problem of the twentieth century is the problem of the color-line" encapsulated my awareness that while progress has been made, racism remains a pervasive problem in contemporary America.

After reading *Souls*, I devoured many of Du Bois's other works, including *The Suppression of the African Slave Trade to the United States of America*, *John Brown*, *Black Reconstruction*, *Dusk of Dawn*, and *The Black Flame* trilogy, among others. These texts provided me with a lens through which to consider the contemporary problems of race, the struggles of my generation, and the challenges of my students. I remember thinking that if I had read and understood Du Bois prior to 1992, I might have been more effective in teaching my students about race, poverty, and class after the riots.

I often reflect on the events of 1992 and my subsequent reading and understanding of Du Bois's ideas in my work. I am ever-cognizant of the power that ideas have on society and of how ideas can provide insight into

our understanding of the past and present. As a historian of education interested in improving the education of all children, I believe firmly that "ideas
have consequences" and that studying the history of ideas can provide us
with lampposts to illuminate our present and future.[5] As a result, I have
undertaken a comprehensive study of Du Bois's educational thought and
sought to illuminate Du Bois's educational ideas as a means of identifying
better possibilities for our present and our future.

A CONTEXT OF IDEAS

This study is not intended to be a biography of Du Bois and does not present
a point-by-point chronology of his life. Several historians already have offered noteworthy biographies of Du Bois.[6] As an intellectual history, this study
is concerned primarily with Du Bois's *ideas* as expressed in his writings,
speeches, research studies, and novels, all of which provide insight into his
thinking about the education of African Americans. As such, this work examines Du Bois's educational ideas within the intellectual and historical
currents of his day and chronicles the development of his educational ideas
over time. Such an approach replaces simplistic and one-dimensional interpretations of Du Bois with a more complex and nuanced understanding of
his educational thought.

To help contextualize Du Bois's educational thought, this study examines briefly the ideas of a number of other African American educators of Du
Bois's day. Du Bois, for instance, influenced and was influenced by such African American educators as Alexander Crummell, Carter G. Woodson, Anna
Julia Cooper, Kelly Miller, Alain Locke, and Charles H. Thompson, among
others. The work of such thinkers fostered an intellectual environment and
produced a constellation of ideas that stimulated and interacted with Du Bois's
own thinking about the education of African Americans. Juxtaposing the ideas
of other African American educators with Du Bois's thought is a critical step
in understanding Du Bois, as it brings to light a broader vision of black educational thought and illuminates the role of such thought in developing an African American intellectual tradition in the twentieth century. While it is beyond
the scope of this study to provide a comprehensive or exhaustive examination
of the thought of African American educators, in future work I hope to offer
a more comprehensive examination of these ideas.[7]

Historical events and social context play an important part in shaping
any individual's thinking. Thus, I have given considerable attention to the
historical events of Du Bois's lifetime and aspects of Du Bois's personal life
to show their influence on his thinking. Du Bois's early years growing up in
Great Barrington, Massachusetts; his education and life at Fisk University,

Harvard University, and the University of Berlin; his personal experiences living in Jim Crow society; his participation in a number of racial uplift and civil rights organizations; and historic world events such as the two world wars, the Cold War, and the burgeoning civil rights movement all played important roles in shaping his thinking.

In studying Du Bois's educational thought, I discovered that Du Bois did not leave a cohesive educational philosophy or educational road map for African Americans. However, he was a prolific scholar who left numerous works that provide insight into his educational thought and philosophy. Some of his most popular writings and speeches on education were published in *The Education of Black People: Ten Critiques, 1906–1960*, edited by Herbert Aptheker. This volume is important because Du Bois himself chose his favorite essays on education, providing us with an overview of what he believed was most important in his educational thought.[8] Equally significant is Eugene Provenzo's edited volume of Du Bois's educational writings, *Du Bois on Education* (2002). Provenzo's volume contains several of the essays included in Aptheker's book, but Provenzo also includes a few obscure and often overlooked essays not included in Aptheker's collection.[9]

While the essays in Aptheker's and Provenzo's volumes represent only a fraction of Du Bois's writings on education, their depth and breadth provide a broad overview of Du Bois's educational ideas, and an ample book on Du Bois's educational thought could be written from the essays in these two volumes alone. However, Aptheker's and Provenzo's volumes did not intend to provide analyses of Du Bois's educational thought, leaving a gap in the scholarship on Du Bois. As a result, there has been a need for an analytical and comprehensive historical examination of Du Bois's educational ideas, which this study seeks to provide.[10]

Du Bois also espoused his views through a variety of other outlets, including research reports, journals, newspaper articles, books, pamphlets, research prospectuses, speeches, correspondence with other scholars and friends, unpublished writings, and other kinds of documents that are not represented in Aptheker's and Provenzo's volumes. These sources, along with his most popular educational writings, help to bring Du Bois's educational views to light and provide a vision of a Du Boisian philosophy of education.

COMPLEXITIES AND CHALLENGES

Bringing to light Du Bois's educational thought has not been a simple task. Studying the ideas of such a complex thinker as Du Bois presents a number of dilemmas and challenges. Because Du Bois lived such a long life, wrote across so many disciplines, and produced such an extensive body of literature, it is sometimes difficult to ascertain his views. A survey of Du Bois's thought reveals great fluidity in his thinking, in which he readily adjusted and revised his opinions on social and educational matters in response to changing times.

A testament to the multiple and divergent readings of Du Bois's thought may be found in the various labels scholars have attached to him. He has been called an Afrocentrist and a Eurocentrist, a radical and an accommodationist, an integrationist and a separatist, and a capitalist and a socialist. In various periods of his life it would be fair to say that Du Bois supported elements of all these perspectives, at times changing or even contradicting aspects of his thinking. Historian Wilson Moses cogently sums up the ways in which one may consider the complexities of Du Bois's thinking over time:

> While some scholars argue that Du Bois changes his thinking quite a bit, another approach might be to recognize patterns of consistency accompanied by patterns of evolution. Or it might be correct to say that his personality did not change, while some of his ideas did. Or you might say that he continued to put old wine in new bottles. On the other hand, you might say he changed radically and fundamentally on some issues. Or you might say that while he believed himself to be changing, he was a real stick in the mud. Or you might say all or some combination of the above, in which case Du Bois would be like most people who live past 40.[11]

In Moses's view, complexity and conflict are elements of human nature that are virtually inevitable. Moreover, reconciliation often arises out of this very complexity and conflict. In this view, Du Bois was a consummate pragmatist and dialectician who modified his educational views to fit the emerging and changing realities of African American life. For example, during the early 1900s Du Bois vigorously supported classical/liberal education as the most effective educational curriculum to uplift African Americans from the lower social, economic, and political levels of society. By providing training in the humanities, law, and the sciences, Du Bois believed, classical education would give African Americans the wherewithal to dismantle segregation, elevate black culture, and refute views of black inferiority. Eventually, however, Du Bois revised his view and concluded that a synthesis of classical and vocational education would provide the optimal educational strategy for black advancement.[12]

During the early 1900s, while Du Bois was advocating classical education, he also called for the establishment of a "talented tenth" whose purpose was to uplift the black masses. The talented tenth was Du Bois's ideal of a black leadership cadre consisting of the most educated and intellectually gifted. Classically trained, they would become the standard-bearers of the race and lead African Americans to the promised land of equality.

However, by 1930 Du Bois had revised his view, incorporating a technologically advanced form of vocational/industrial education into his educational philosophy. When Du Bois revised his thinking on educational curriculum, he was also forced to reexamine his concept of the talented tenth. Du Bois's support for a form of vocational education as a component of his revised educational views meant that the black masses, rather than a select few, would have the potential for and responsibility of leading their people. Moreover, by 1930 it became clear to Du Bois that the talented tenth were using their educational advantage largely for their own self-advancement while neglecting the black masses. In the 1940s, he began advocating the education of the black masses for leadership, a model that he called the "Guiding Hundredth."[13]

These are only a few examples of the ways in which Du Bois revised and reconciled his thinking on educational and other matters. Such fluidity in his views makes his thinking elusive, at times forcing me to question whether I am conveying Du Bois's ideas as he intended them. Such inevitable frustrations in studying Du Bois have taught me the valuable lesson of not attempting to pigeonhole Du Bois into any one category, but rather to forthrightly acknowledge the variations in his thinking and to seek out the influence of and connections to an African American intellectual tradition in education. I was continually reminded of this fluidity in Du Bois's thinking as I searched for the educational ideas he left us.

I must also note at the outset that Du Bois believed that education alone was not a panacea for solving the problems of African Americans. Discriminatory institutional structures and laws, racism, unbridled capitalism, and other entities outside of education, Du Bois argued, were major culprits in maintaining blacks' inferior status and needed to be addressed alongside education to improve black life. As a result, Du Bois tended to analyze the conditions of black education and develop his educational ideas within the larger context of black life rather than at the micro level of the school. Therefore, this study examines Du Bois's educational ideas within the larger social, economic, and political contexts of black life.

Over the past several years, friends, colleagues, and critics have offered helpful critiques of my interpretations of Du Bois, sometimes agreeing with my work and other times challenging my interpretations. For example, while a number of scholars have commended me for helping to advance the discourse on Du Bois beyond the Du Bois/Washington debates, others have criticized me for privileging the later and post-1920s Du Bois. Similarly, while some have criticized me for being overly cautious so as not to make Du Bois a hero for our present time, others have repeatedly cautioned me about the potential of my analysis to become presentist. I have welcomed such critiques, as they have prompted me to rethink certain of my premises and interpretations and have helped strengthen many of my arguments.[14]

It will be evident to most readers that I greatly admire Du Bois and many of the ideas he developed over his lifetime. Having said that, this book is by no means intended to present Du Bois as a hero or messiah who was without flaws. Throughout this study I try to point out the weaknesses in Du Bois's ideas as I see them. In writing this book, I had both an academic and a general audience in mind. While I hope this book engages the academic community, it was also written to reach a lay audience that may not know much about Du Bois or his times. Therefore, in addition to historians and other academics, I hope that teachers, educators, students, the "folk," and all those concerned with the education of African American people will read and glean some insights from this book. Finally, I make no claim to present a definitive history of Du Bois's educational ideas; rather, I hope to initiate an ongoing exploration of the educational thought of an extraordinary African American educator of international importance.

STRUCTURE OF THE BOOK

This study's four parts and ten chapters are organized chronologically and thematically around Du Bois's educational ideas and proactive agendas in response to blacks' social, economic, and political plight during his lifetime. Part I examines the development of Du Bois's educational thought throughout his formal schooling in Great Barrington and at Fisk University, Harvard University, and the University of Berlin. Part II explores Du Bois's educational ideas as they emerged within the Progressive Era environment of the late nineteenth and early twentieth centuries. Part III examines Du Bois's educational thinking during World War I and the Harlem Renaissance. Part IV analyzes Du Bois's educational thought within the context of World War II, the postwar period, the Cold War, the modern civil rights movement, and independence movements around the world.

PART I

Development of a Mind, 1868–1895

The mid- to late 1800s through the first two decades of the twentieth century represented a period of racial strife in the United States, as African Americans attempted to carve out a place for themselves in a society experiencing great technological advancement, massive industrialization, and rapid social change. During this period, blacks struggled to catch their stride on the road to freedom. It was within this context and through his own educational experiences that the seeds of W.E.B. Du Bois's educational thought were planted. Du Bois's educational experiences in Great Barrington, Massachusetts; Fisk and Harvard Universities; and the University of Berlin exposed him to many ideas that would find their way into his developing educational thought.

CHAPTER 1

The Education of W.E.B. Du Bois

The historical context into which Du Bois was born and the era in which he pursued his formal education held both promise and challenge for black Americans. Some of the freedoms that enslaved blacks dreamed of came to fruition after the Civil War, while other hopes and dreams were dashed by broken promises, compromises, and deeply entrenched views of white supremacy and black inferiority. These events would mold and shape Du Bois in his youth and tremendously influence the development of his thinking about black education.

THE WORLD OF DU BOIS'S YOUTH

After the Civil War, the "Radical Republicans" in Congress, comprised primarily of Northerners who supported abolition, moved quickly to disenfranchise former Confederates in the Southern states and secure rights for the freedpeople. In 1865, Congress created the Freedmen's Bureau to provide freed blacks with material relief and aid and help them adjust to the U.S. economic and social system. In 1866, Congress extended the life of the Bureau and expanded its authority to make decisions regarding the formerly enslaved African Americans in the South.[1]

When Congress extended the life of the Bureau, it included a provision for education and a half-million-dollar appropriation for school repair and building rental. It is estimated that the Bureau spent almost $4 million on school buildings to provide educational opportunities for the freedpeople. Until the Freedmen's Bureau was closed in 1872, it provided assistance to black Southerners, collected data on the conditions of black life, and supervised societies and organizations involved in black schooling. Because of Bureau Commissioner Oliver Howard's and Bureau Education Commissioner John Alvord's own religious leanings, the Bureau favored the work of evangelical societies in the freedmen's education movement.[2]

While the Freedmen's Bureau legislation helped improve the education and schooling of many blacks, the U.S. government and Southern whites continued to ignore the immediate social, economic, and political needs of the freedpeople for such necessities as land, protection, and jobs. In addition, the Bureau's accommodating posture toward Southern whites compromised efforts to provide the freedpeople with a good education and fostered a white-dominated educational system that blacks were nevertheless encouraged to accept.[3] In addition, under presidential Reconstruction (1865–1866), legislatures throughout the South passed Black Codes that restricted blacks' rights. Such codes included vagrancy laws that forced blacks to work whether they desired to or not. Those who refused to work could be arrested. Other Black Codes prevented blacks from testifying in court unless they were testifying against other blacks. Under the Black Codes, blacks were also fined for violating curfews, possessing firearms, and giving seditious speeches.[4]

Discrimination also occurred in Bureau labor practices in which government agents succeeded in pushing black workers back onto their old plantations. For instance, some Bureau officials were sympathetic to planters and ignored the freedpeoples' grievances against them. In other instances in which Bureau officials attempted to act on freedpeoples' complaints regarding labor and pay, the Bureau did not have the support of the military to enforce their decisions. The planters' attempts to restore a form of the old slavocracy and some Bureau officials' refusal or lack of power to enforce laws to protect black Southerners helped restore white control over black labor.[5]

Despite some of the problems the Bureau created for blacks, many blacks also gained legal rights and obtained education during the Bureau's years in the South. Congress passed the Reconstruction Act of 1867, which divided the former Confederate states into five military districts. A military commander headed each district and was charged with protecting life and property. Under the Civil Rights Act of 1866, Southern states were required to draft constitutions that would enfranchise black voters and ratify the Fourteenth Amendment. Four years later, the Fifteenth Amendment was passed, declaring that U.S. citizens' right to vote could not be abridged or denied by the United States or any state on the basis of race, color, or previous servitude. Subsequently, the Civil Rights Act of 1875 provided further guarantees to black citizens by prohibiting racial discrimination in jury selection and in public places and accommodations.[6]

Confronted by such liberal laws and measures, some Southern politicians and landholders sought to resurrect the "Old South." In 1866, the Ku Klux Klan was founded in Pulaski, Tennessee. Originally the Klan was merely a social group of ex-Confederate soldiers. However, it soon developed into a band of terrorists who attacked and murdered blacks, harassed black teachers and whites who sympathized with blacks, and vandalized or destroyed black schools and churches throughout the South. Other groups such as the Knights of the White Camellia and the White Brotherhood also engaged in acts of violence against blacks in an attempt to protect and preserve what they viewed as the Southern way of life and to stop black men from voting. Such groups saw black enfranchisement as a threat to their position of privilege and believed it was their duty to preserve white hegemony over blacks.[7]

Congress eventually responded to the backlash of the Klan and other terrorist groups by passing the Enforcement Acts of 1870 and 1871. These acts gave the President authority to appoint an election supervisor to prevent fraudulent voting practices and intimidation of voters. The Acts also gave the U.S. district attorney authority to use the federal courts to prosecute those who violated these laws.[8] Despite the federal government's attempts to stifle the Klan and similar groups, the social situation for black Southerners deteriorated during the 1870s and 1880s.

Perhaps the most telling sign of things to come occurred after the election of Rutherford B. Hayes in 1876. In courting white Southern votes during his presidential campaign, Hayes promised the South a "hands-off" policy in black–white relations. In 1877, Hayes made good on his promise by removing the remaining federal troops from the South. Popularly known as the Compromise of 1877, Hayes's deal with the South signaled the reality of political change for black Southerners and helped embolden the courts to revisit some of the progressive legislation passed during the heyday of the Radical Republicans. In 1883, for instance, the Supreme Court declared unconstitutional much of the Civil Rights Act of 1875, which prohibited racial discrimination in jury selection and guaranteed equal accommodation in public places. The Court stated that the federal government could protect citizens against the discriminatory practices of states, but not of individuals.[9]

The prevailing social thought and ideologies of the time had a great influence on the discriminatory practices and racism directed toward blacks during the Reconstruction and post-Reconstruction eras. Historian George Fredrickson points out that "race thinking emerged for the first time as a central current in Western thought" during the nineteenth century, but that American racial prejudice could be traced back to slavery in the seventeenth century. Historian Roy Harvey Pearce also argues that nineteenth- and twentieth-century views about nonwhites, particularly Native Americans, can be traced back to seventeenth- and eighteenth-century European thought, which promoted Christianity and Western enlightenment over non-Christian and non-Western cultures and civilizations. For many whites, the prevailing view that black and other nonwhite races were inferior provided a rationale for the enslavement and mistreatment of Africans, African Americans, and Native Americans during the nineteenth and early twentieth centuries.[10]

During the nineteenth century, many white politicians used theories of evolution to justify viewing the black race as backward and uncivilized. For instance, they used Charles Darwin's idea of natural selection, proposed in his *On the Origin of Species* in 1859, that posited that certain species achieved dominance over others as a result of conflict and competition. Many whites also used philosopher Herbert Spencer's idea of "survival of the fittest," proposed in *Principles of Biology*, to argue that organisms that achieve dominance over other organisms were the ones best adapted to their environment. Building upon Darwin's and Spencer's ideas, some whites argued that

African Americans did not need equal rights because they would eventually become extinct after Emancipation. Others called for black people to be deported and returned to Africa. With this intellectual and ideological foundation in place, it was not difficult for nineteenth- and twentieth-century Americans to apply Western European ideas of civilization and savagery to nonwhites in order to justify nonwhites' status as second-class citizens, or even subhumans.[11]

Nevertheless, even after Reconstruction there remained a ray of hope for African Americans. During the 1880s, some Northern politicians continued to promote black equality by advocating educational opportunity for all citizens. Senator Henry Blair of New Hampshire, for instance, argued for the need to improve education in the South. He pointed out that the South's abysmal educational system did not even provide basic elementary education to its citizens; in many cases children received only a few years of education. To address the problem, Blair proposed that the federal government spend $77 million over a period of eight years on schools in the South. The Blair Bill, as it was called, also required participating states to commit to the education of their citizens by providing extensive funding for education and schooling. After much discussion and resistance from many Southern senators, the Blair Bill was defeated in 1890.[12]

During the mid- to late 1800s, some white and black educators formulated an educational agenda that they believed was most suitable for African Americans. Given African Americans' needs to make a living and the need for a labor force in the South after Emancipation, a number of white educators promoted vocational and agricultural education for blacks. General Samuel Chapman Armstrong was one of the most influential of these promoters. Influenced by his father's work with Hawaiians as Minister of Public Instruction in Hawaii from 1848 to 1860, Armstrong saw the need for sustained and dedicated work among black Southerners. Just as his father viewed the Hawaiians as savages, Armstrong believed that blacks were "backward," uncivilized, and childlike and that they needed the guidance of whites to uplift them from their savagery. Armstrong believed that freedpeople needed education that instilled in them the values of thrift, self-help, cleanliness, and independence. Such values, Armstrong argued, would act as a stabilizing force to counter innate black immorality and laziness.[13]

Armstrong eventually put his philosophy into practice by opening a manual training school called Hampton Institute in 1868. Hampton's primary purpose during its early years was not to spend a great deal of time beyond reading, writing, and arithmetic, but rather to "civilize" blacks and instill in them a respect for labor and training of the hand. The school's philosophy held that if blacks dedicated themselves to labor, their character would deepen and they would gain greater self-respect.[14]

The Hampton Idea, as it became widely known, was dedicated to training black teachers in the ethics of hard work and the "dignity of labor." Armstrong intended for these black teachers to spread the Hampton Idea in order to supply a source of labor for years to come. During the late 1800s and early 1900s, other white educators such as Robert Ogden, J.L.M. Curry, and Thomas Jesse Jones carried on or revised aspects of industrial education for the purpose of developing a stable workforce and assimilating those formerly enslaved into Anglo-American culture. This ideological backdrop of white men advocating black industrial education would influence educational discourse among black educators at the dawn of the twentieth century.[15]

The ideas of social uplift and humanity's progress toward higher levels of civilization endemic in nineteenth-century thought found their way into Du Bois's school curriculum. At the same time, however, the realities of black life in America were unavoidably a part of his early education. During his youth, Du Bois experienced racism and had to come to grips with the lowly social and economic status of blacks, or what became known as the "Negro problem." Du Bois's education during the Victorian Era and Gilded Age, juxtaposed with the "Negro problem," would help lay the foundations of his early educational thought.

GREAT BARRINGTON, MASSACHUSETTS

William Edward Burghardt Du Bois was born on February 23, 1868, into a working-class family in the bucolic hamlet of Great Barrington, Massachusetts. His father, Alfred Du Bois, a mulatto of Haitian and French descent, abandoned Du Bois and his mother when Du Bois was a toddler. Du Bois's mother, Mary Silvina Burghardt Du Bois, and the Burghardt clan provided young Willie, as Du Bois was called, with an extended family structure during his formative and adolescent years. As a child living in a small Western Massachusetts town, Du Bois was shielded from many of the racial hostilities experienced by most African Americans and had a relatively idyllic childhood in Great Barrington. The town of Great Barrington had very few African Americans and the schooling young Willie received was primarily among whites.[16]

During Willie's early years, Mary enrolled him in Great Barrington's public schools. He quickly surpassed his classmates in academics, but noted later that he did not excel in football or marbles. Nonetheless, Du Bois remembered his childhood in Great Barrington fondly and in his autobiography noted that it was a "boy's paradise." He recollected: "There were mountains to climb and rivers to wade and swim; lakes to freeze and hills for coasting. There were orchards and caves and wide green fields; and all of it was apparently property of the children of the town."[17]

In addition to Great Barrington's natural amenities, Du Bois believed that the town was a model of democracy and noted that during the spring months the townspeople held public meetings to discuss public expenditures, education, and other civic matters. He also remembered the "ragged fat old man" whom the children called Baretown Beebe who descended from the mountains each spring to call for the discontinuation of the high school. Because the old man was a citizen and property owner, Du Bois noted that the stolid townspeople listened to him, but each year voted to retain the high school. For Du Bois, such recognition of a fellow taxpayer's right to speak represented the essence of democracy.[18]

Despite the fairy tale–like picture that Du Bois painted of Great Barrington, he also noted subtle social class distinctions. He observed that many of Great Barrington's citizens, including blacks, loathed the Irish Catholics, who lived in separate parts of town from the general population. He also recognized his own prejudices toward the Irish as a young man. "They did not belong to my traditional community and consequently I felt no comradeship with them. I think I rather assumed, along with most of the townfolk, that the dirty, stinking Irish slums were something that the Irish themselves preferred and made."[19] Du Bois also noted that the Irish, not African Americans, were on the lowest level of the social strata in Great Barrington.

Du Bois, however, would have his own encounter with racial prejudice in Great Barrington. He remembered, for instance, an event that brought the reality of the "color-line" to his idealized childhood:

> I remember well when the shadow swept across me. I was a little thing, away up in the hills of New England . . . In a wee wooden schoolhouse, something put it into the boys' and girls' heads to buy gorgeous visiting-cards—ten cents a package—and exchange. The exchange was merry, till one girl, a tall newcomer, refused my card—refused it peremptorily, with a glance. Then it dawned upon me with a certain suddenness that I was different from the others; or like mayhap, in heart and life longing, but shut out from their world by a vast veil.[20]

Du Bois noted that the greeting card incident was one of his first overt experiences of racism and that from that point on he was cognizant of the "vast veil" of racism.

By the time Du Bois entered high school, he began to earn his first wages to help support his mother and himself. One job entailed filling base-burning stoves with coal before school and sometimes after school and on Saturdays. During his high school years, Du Bois also delivered papers and served as a correspondent for the *Springfield Republican* and the *New York Age* and worked as a columnist for the *New York Globe*, *The Freeman*, and *New York Freeman*, a newspaper run by the black journalist and intellectual T. Thomas Fortune.[21] While much of Du Bois's writing during his period at the *Globe* focused on the social life of the Great Barrington black community, signs of his developing ideas about black racial uplift and education came through in his columns. For instance, in one column Du Bois encouraged the black men of the community to join the "Law and Order Society" of the town to enforce laws against selling liquor.[22] Such a view was likely influenced by Du Bois's mother's abhorrence of liquor and her puritanical instructions to young Willie not to drink liquor. Du Bois also called for black citizens to join a newly formed organization known as the Sons of Liberty whose purpose was to promote "advancement of the colored race."[23]

Du Bois also expressed the importance of education and literacy while writing for the *Globe*. In one column, he recounted a trip to Providence, Rhode Island; New Bedford, Massachusetts; and Albany, New York; and noted that while African Americans in these cities possessed some wealth, they had no literary societies. In another column, he praised Great Barrington blacks who formed a literary club called the Sons of Freedom for contributing to the uplift and advancement of the race.[24]

Du Bois's education in Great Barrington provided him with a solid foundation that would undergird his future training and his thinking about education. At the suggestion of his high school principal and mentor, Frank Hosmer, Du Bois enrolled in the classical course instead of the regular course at Great Barrington High. He took four years of Latin; three years of Greek, arithmetic, algebra, and geometry; and one year of English, ancient history, and American history. He also took courses in geography, physiology, and hygiene.[25]

Du Bois excelled in academics and often outperformed his classmates. He noted, however, that he was ashamed of the lowly performance of another black youth who, for a while, attended the school. Clearly, Du Bois realized early on that education was the key by which African Americans would open the doors to social advancement and believed even in his youth that African Americans had an obligation to excel in their schooling.[26]

In 1884, Willie graduated from Great Barrington High School with honors. He delivered a convocation speech on the abolitionist and socialist Wendell Phillips, perhaps choosing this topic because of Phillips's advocacy of black civil rights and his support of temperance. That Phillips received his law degree from Harvard may have played a role in Du Bois's desire to attend Harvard. Moreover, Du Bois was also likely impressed with Phillips's idealism and activism regarding his notion that the intellectual and scholar should play a central role in elevating the masses. In his address "The Scholar in a Republic," given at Harvard College in 1881, Phillips laid out a philosophy of leadership that placed responsibility on scholars to enlighten the masses. That Du Bois would espouse similar views later is of no great surprise, given that Du Bois would become immersed in the intellectual environment of Harvard.[27]

A college education, especially for a black man, was very expensive. The issue became even more complicated in March 1885 when Du Bois's mother died. However, after working for a year as a timekeeper on a construction site and receiving financial and moral support from community leaders such as Frank Hosmer and from surrounding churches, Du Bois headed for Fisk University in Nashville, Tennessee. In Great Barrington, Du Bois lived primarily among whites. At Fisk, he was soon to become immersed in the world of the black masses and elites.

FISK UNIVERSITY

Fisk University in 1885 provided fertile ground for the young New Englander to immerse himself in the culture and history of his people. Nestled in the hills of Tennessee, Fisk was a four-year black institution established to train leaders to "uplift their race." The townships surrounding Fisk were home to black Southerners fewer than three decades removed from slavery, which placed Du Bois in close contact with the residual conditions of the "peculiar institution" and the restrictions of the Jim Crow South. The change in scenery was both exhilarating and disconcerting for Du Bois. He recalled, "I came to a region where the world was split into white and black halves, and where the darker half was held back by race prejudice and legal bonds, as well as by deep ignorance and dire poverty."[28] He was, however, "thrilled to be for the first time among so many people of my own color or rather of such various and such extraordinary colors."[29]

Fisk also exposed Du Bois to African Americans from a variety of social backgrounds, including a number of aspiring and educated black women and men who would later make significant contributions to society. Otho Porter, Du Bois's roommate at Fisk, would later become a renowned physician in Kentucky. Classmate Maggie Murray would become the third wife of Booker T. Washington, and a "coarse-looking" fellow named Sherrod, "poor and slow," studied at Meharry Medical School and "became one of the best physicians in Mississippi."[30] Fisk's dynamic intellectual and social environment served as a training ground for Du Bois and his fellow students, and during the last two decades of the nineteenth century and the first decade of the twentieth, Fisk would provide African Americans with a cadre of young leaders who would challenge white supremacy and improve the plight of black people.

John Ogden, Erastus M. Cravath, and Edward P. Smith were white men who founded Fisk School to provide free education from the primary grades to normal school for black students. The school opened its doors on January 9, 1866. In 1867, the school developed a normal department to help train black teachers for the South. The curriculum in the normal department reflected that of many similar colleges of the day, leaning heavily toward the liberal arts and incorporating courses in U.S. history, natural philosophy, chemistry, and physiology. It also emphasized pedagogy-related courses such as reading, writing, penmanship, geography, sentence analysis, and arithmetic. Students studied Greek, Latin, French, German, mathematics, and natural science, and also received instruction in the Bible.[31]

Fisk's curriculum was similar to that of Great Barrington High School. While noting some limitations of Fisk's curriculum, Du Bois praised the instruction of his black and white professors. He stated that Professor Adam Spence was a "great Greek scholar by any comparison." He noted that Thomas Chase, with whom he studied chemistry and physics, had exemplary teaching skills and was superb at teaching his students about science and life. He also praised the instruction of his philosophy professor, President Cravath.[32]

Fisk's liberal arts curriculum and qualified and devoted faculty, Du Bois later reported, were instrumental in helping him develop an agenda and program for advancing the race. Moreover, it was in the Fisk environment that he began to develop his views of himself and his classmates as "race men and women," paving the way for his educational ideas regarding the talented tenth. He recalled:

> I replaced my hitherto egocentric world by a world centering and whirling about my race in America. For this group I built my plan of study and accomplishment. Through the leadership of men like myself and my fellows, we were going to have these enslaved Israelites out of the still enduring bondage in short order. It was a battle which might conceivably call for force, but I could think of it mainly as a battle of wits: of knowledge and deed, which by sheer reason and desert, must eventually overwhelm the forces of hate, ignorance and reaction.[33]

While developing his ideas about education within the halls of academe, Du Bois was ready to engage in the practice of education to "free the Israelites"—poor, disenfranchised blacks in Tennessee. For two summers, he taught school in rural Wilson County at School #5. The pay was a meager $28 per month in 1886 and $30 per month in 1887.[34] His paltry wage, he would later note, was of no significance, but the experience would stay with him for the rest of his life. Very early in his teaching experience, he realized the awesome responsibility that awaited him: "I trembled when I heard the patter of little feet down the dusty road, and saw the growing row of dark solemn faces and bright eager eyes facing me. . . . There they sat, nearly thirty of them, on rough benches, their faces shading from a pale cream to a deep brown, little feet bare and swinging, their eyes full of expectation."[35]

Du Bois realized the impact that education could have on black youth, many of whom had never traveled beyond the hills of Tennessee. Du Bois had pleasant, dreamlike memories of his experience: "We read and spelled together, wrote a little, picked flowers, sang, and listened to stories of the world beyond the hill."[36]

One of Du Bois's first goals in his new teaching job was to "extermi-nate" the 1857 revised edition of the *Webster New Speller*, also known as the "blue-back speller," that the school had used for generations. Du Bois seemed most disturbed by the rote memorization encouraged by the blue-back speller. Despite some tension among adults in the community over his attempts to eliminate the speller, however, Du Bois moved many of his stu-dents through the speller rather quickly and managed to eliminate it by the last day of the school year.[37]

In place of the blue-back speller, Du Bois preferred the "word-method" approach to teaching the alphabet. While he did not delineate how the method worked, he alluded to his approach by stating that the method showed "a pile of difference between the theory and practice."[38] This statement sug-gests that his method emphasized the practice of sounding out words and letters rather than memorizing words to learn to read. According to Du Bois, the outcomes of his pedagogical approach were successful:

> My reading class made rapid advancement in spite of the fear on the part of many parents that they would learn to read before they could spell. The Arith-metic class began to find out what they were studying and became interested; the class in Geography discovered they were living in Tennessee; while the class in hygiene were surprised to learn the heart was on the other side. But what-ever the pupils may have gained, it was little to what I acquired.[39]

Du Bois's early teaching experiences influenced his later educational thought, in which he emphasized educational strategies that would address African Americans' real-world problems. Du Bois realized that he would not have the luxury of being an abstract educational theorist or philosopher, but that his ideas must, at their core, help uplift black citizens from their social abyss. Teaching among his race during the summers of 1886 and 1887 helped prepare him for this task.

As editor of the Fisk student newspaper, *The Fisk Herald*, Du Bois pro-vided his fellow schoolmates with glimpses into the world he experienced during his summers teaching in the Tennessee countryside. In his essay "The Hills of Tennessee" he wrote:

> I like teaching. The school is small, but all are interested in their work, which makes the teachers' work very pleasant. I am the first colored teacher who has dropped in among these hills and hence am short of curiosity. But I get along very well with both white and black although I have had to swallow some large lumps of "sassiness" and even now some of the old farmers say they'll "de dad-immed ef they like sich a biggety nigger."[40]

Perhaps one of the most insightful works expressing Du Bois's ideas about education, written during his Fisk years, was his three-chapter novel, *Tom*

Brown at Fisk. Published in the *Fisk Herald* between December 1887 and March 1888, *Tom Brown* chronicles the lives of two characters, Ella Boyd and Tom Brown. Ella is a refined young lady who attends Fisk University and meets Tom while searching for a teaching position in the backwoods of Tennessee. Tom, on the other hand, is a rather crude fellow who has aspirations of furthering his education, but is tied to the obligations of helping his family make a living. After some prodding by Ella, Tom attends Fisk and becomes immersed in college life. At Fisk, Tom becomes more refined and obtains an appreciation for college life. At the end of the story, Tom becomes a successful businessman and a devout Christian and marries his former teacher, Ella.[41]

Several themes emerge from this story. First, Du Bois clearly demonstrated the value he placed on higher education. Second, through Tom, Du Bois demonstrated that black talent could be mined from the black masses and educated for leadership through higher education. Third, Du Bois's use of Ella as the teacher who helps Tom develop into a leader shows that even during his early years Du Bois saw women as an integral part of black advancement. Fourth, Du Bois's development of Tom from "a rather crude fellow" to an accomplished college graduate and businessman illuminates Du Bois's burgeoning notion of middle-class attainment for leadership in the talented tenth. Whether or not he realized it, Du Bois was describing class formation and the process by which blacks would obtain higher social and economic status.

While at Fisk, Du Bois's educational ideas regarding black leadership began to take root. In an unpublished student essay, Du Bois developed a profile of the type of leadership the black community needed to persuade the country and the world that blacks should be treated equitably. Focusing on Frederick Douglass's attributes as a skilled orator who spoke with eloquence and logic, Du Bois found perhaps an early prototype of his talented tenth. Du Bois stated, "When Fred Douglass appealed to the Caesar of the American people on behalf of a race despised spit upon and trodden under the feet of men, he had to be eloquent and thank God he was!"[42] Du Bois believed that he and his classmates must develop the oratorical skills of Douglass to represent their race and argue their case for racial equality before the leaders of the world.

Du Bois's evolving educational thought regarding African American leadership is evident in his letter of application for a scholarship to Harvard, dated 1890. He stated, "I hereby apply for a scholarship to aid me in my studies in the graduate department of Harvard College next year (90–91). I wish to study for the degree of Ph.D. in social science with a view to the ultimate application of its principles to the social and economic use of the Negro people."[43] Even before attending Harvard, Du Bois had begun to conceptualize an agenda for using social science as a method to address the "Negro problem." This is not surprising given the burgeoning Progressive ethos of the time, which advocated the use of social science to bring about social reform. Clearly, Du Bois saw himself as representative of the type of leadership needed for his race.

Du Bois also began to develop his ideas on race relations while at Fisk. In "An Open Letter to the Southern People," he called for greater understanding between blacks and whites and pointed to their shared interest in supporting Prohibition. Ignorance, Du Bois pointed out, had prevented the races from alleviating tensions between them. Du Bois opined: "We [Negroes] are not foolish enough to demand social equality or amalgamation, knowing full well that inexorable laws of nature regulate and control such movements. What we demand is to be recognized as men, and to be given those civil rights which pertain to our manhood."[44]

During Du Bois's Fisk years, he was cognizant of whites' fears of "race amalgamation" and was strategic in easing their fears by stating that African Americans were not concerned with race mixing or "social equality" in terms of integration into white society. Rather, they were concerned with being treated as men and provided the civil rights granted to all men. Furthermore, Du Bois saw the fair treatment and education of black citizens as intricately intertwined with the development of the South. Providing public education to both blacks and whites, Du Bois believed, would benefit the Southern economic system as a whole by producing a more efficient working class.

By the time he graduated from Fisk, the young New Englander had grown both intellectually and socially and had come to grips with many of the realities of being black in the United States. At Fisk, he learned that the black masses remained socially, economically, and politically shackled to a caste system not unlike slavery, but that systematic planning, appropriate education, and exemplary black leadership could unite and uplift the race. While Fisk represented the ideal curriculum for educating black leaders, Douglass and other "strong men" and women represented the type of leadership necessary for race uplift.

Looking to Germany for the quintessential "strong man" as a prototype for black leadership, Du Bois chose Chancellor Otto Von Bismarck as the subject of his commencement address. For Du Bois, Bismarck's uniting of a "mass of bickering peoples" in Germany was an example of what blacks needed in the United States. Douglass and Bismarck represented the attributes of intelligence, strength, and eloquence that Du Bois believed black leaders of his day needed to unify and uplift their race. Such attributes would serve as exemplars in his conceptualization of the talented tenth.[45]

HARVARD UNIVERSITY

In 1888, Du Bois realized his dream of attending Harvard University. With a $250 grant from the Price Greenleaf Fund at Harvard and recommendations from President Cravath and Professor Frederick Chase, Du Bois transferred to Harvard as a junior in the fall of 1888. Excited about furthering his education and enlarging his worldview, Du Bois nevertheless did not consider Harvard to be the beginning or the end of his education. With a great sense of confidence, Du Bois later noted that Harvard's teachers were not better than his Fisk instructors; they were just better known.[46] Du Bois's educational experiences at Harvard, as at Fisk, significantly influenced the young scholar and helped him further develop his ideas of race uplift. Access to the great libraries of Cambridge and Boston; interactions with scholars who conducted sophisticated work in history, philosophy, and political economy; and exposure to black Bostonian culture and life proved to be the ideal elements for advancing his education.

At Harvard, Du Bois studied under teachers such as William James and George Santayana in philosophy and Albert Bushnell Hart in history. Many scholars, however, assert that it was William James who most influenced Du Bois and his developing ideas. As William James's student, Du Bois was exposed to many of James's ideas and likely read James's writings about double-consciousness in his classic work *The Principles of Psychology*, published in 1890. James's works, primarily in the fields of pragmatic philosophy and psychology, so strongly influenced Du Bois that he later described James as his "guide to clear thinking."[47]

Du Bois also noted that James and other faculty members at Harvard had a profound influence on his work on race:

> I revelled in the keen analysis of William James, Josiah Royce and young George Santayana. But it was James with his pragmatism and Albert Bushnell Hart with his research method, that turned me back from the lovely but sterile land of philosophic speculation, to the social sciences as the field for gathering and interpreting that body of fact which would apply to my program for the Negro.[48]

James was also impressed with the young black New Englander. A decade or so later he mentioned Du Bois's talents in a letter to his famous brother, Henry James. Praising Du Bois's seminal work, *The Souls of Black Folk*, James wrote: "I am sending you a decidedly moving book by an . . . ex-student of mine, Du Bois, professor of history at Atlanta (Georgia) Negro College."[49]

The eccentric James was well known in academic circles and in Harvard Yard, and became associated with what was known as the Metaphysical Club. The Metaphysical Club consisted of intellectuals Charles S. Peirce, Oliver Wendell Holmes Jr., and Chauncey Wright, among others. They met periodically to engage in philosophical discourse about the issues of the day. The group believed that ideas could be used and adapted to address societal problems arising as a result of technological advancements, increasing immigration, and poverty. With the mission of using and adapting ideas to address social issues, the Metaphysical Club became an incubator of sorts for the pragmatic philosophy that would emerge during the late nineteenth century. Collectively, the group was instrumental in helping move American thought into the "modern" age after the Civil War and into the technological and industrial era of the twentieth century.[50]

James and his fellow philosophers challenged the rigid, established ideologies that reinforced the status quo and embraced those ideas that were transforming society during the late 1800s and early 1900s. They promoted a philosophy that interrogated ideology and subjected ideas to experience and rigorous scrutiny. Their approach was well received by a public that was increasingly heterogeneous and diverse as a result of increasing industrialization, urbanization, and immigration following the Civil War.[51] In his treatise on pragmatism, James stated that the pragmatist "turns away from abstraction and insufficiency, from verbal solutions, from bad *a priori* reasons, from fixed principles, closed systems, and pretended absolutes and origins. He turns towards concreteness and adequacy, towards facts, towards action, and towards power."[52] Pragmatists, as James, Peirce, and later John Dewey would become known, promoted a discourse of modernist thinking in which communities of scholars would test hypotheses and scrutinize ideas to solve social problems.[53]

The ideas put forward by James and others regarding pragmatism influenced the young Du Bois. In pragmatism, Du Bois found philosophical and speculative approaches with which to attack solidly held, but unproven and unscientific, myths and assumptions about "the Negro." Pragmatism's conceptual frame enabled Du Bois to challenge inherited absolutes and dualisms, and he was drawn to James's conception of truth as fluid and all experience as meaningful. Pragmatism would eventually become an integral part of Du Bois's early educational thought, providing a framework in which he promoted black education as a means of interrogating irrationalism and racism. Du Bois believed that African Americans could attack ignorance— the core of racism and discrimination—by undertaking a careful examination of scientific research and evidence. Thus, through black education both blacks and whites would be freed from destructive stereotypes based on misinformation and myth and become liberated from their own racism.[54]

Even before Harvard, Du Bois was exposed to the ideas of German philosopher Georg Wilhelm Friedrich Hegel. In *The Phenomenology of Mind* (1807) and *The Philosophy of History* (1837), Hegel presented an approach to history that Du Bois utilized as he mapped out a course of history for African Americans. Hegel argued that history was comprised of people and events moving together toward higher levels of humanity and human civilization. During this process, Hegel proposed, the unifying societies and peoples would encounter obstacles in the form of conflict.[55]

The conflict would result in humanity breaking apart, often by seemingly irreconcilable differences. In Hegel's *dialectic*, these apparent differences would eventually be resolved through compromise and reconciliation among the opposing entities, resulting in a higher synthesis annulling the differences while preserving them at a higher level of integration.

Throughout his life, Du Bois used Hegel's idea of historical development and emergence to call for African-descended peoples to take their place among the advanced races of the world. Du Bois also employed Hegel's dialectic to explain the nature of being black in America and European societies. He proposed that blacks synthesize and reconcile their "warring souls" as a means of resolving the double-consciousness of being an African American.

Evidence of Du Bois's grappling with the Hegelian dialectic while at Harvard may be observed in his incomplete and unpublished novel, *A Vacation Unique*. In this story, Du Bois wrote of two young black students who planned to spend their summer entertaining people to raise money for their academic expenses. Du Bois himself had spent a summer working as a bus-boy in Minnesota at a Lake Minnetonka resort. In this way, the youth in his novel represented a composite of sorts of Du Bois.

In the novel, Du Bois lamented the challenges the black youth would face in entertaining whites and navigating white society on their summer vacation:

> By becoming a Nigger you step into a new and, to most people, entirely un-known region of the universe-you break the bounds of humanity and become a a-er-colored man. Again you will not only be a Negro but a Negro in an un-thought of and astoundingly incongruous role. Having in this manner reached an entirely unique and strange position you will be in [a] position to solve in a measure the problems of Introspection and [the] Fourth Dimension, for you will have an opportunity of beholding yourself in your seaside and mountain (resort).[56]

In this passage, Du Bois speaks in rather cryptic language about the challenges the youth would have as black people interacting in a white world. In the remainder of the novel, he discusses the advantages of seeing the world from an African American vantage point and how that viewpoint offered an insightful perspective on race. *A Vacation Unique* provides an early and crude articulation of Du Bois's conceptualization of double-consciousness. The novel reflects what Du Bois observed as the dialectical positionality and so-cial tensions that African Americans experienced living in a world in which they were not accepted. The characters' ability to overcome these dialectical tensions reflects the Hegelian aspect of eventual transcendence, or what Du Bois called the "twoness" of being "a Negro in America."[57]

While at Harvard, Du Bois also began developing ideas that clearly fore-shadowed his views on classical and vocational education. In a largely over-looked essay, "Does Education Pay?," delivered before the Boston National Colored League in 1891, Du Bois laid out a curricular strategy for his race.

He argued that African Americans should not forgo a broad liberal education for the purpose of gaining practical work skills to make a living. For Du Bois, a broad liberal education and practical education for making a living were not mutually exclusive. He stated, "Never make the mistake of thinking that the object of being a man is to make a carpenter—the object of being a carpenter is to be a man."[58]

To demonstrate the importance of liberal education, Du Bois asked how subjects such as algebra, Greek, Latin, and philosophy might apply to everyday life. In responding, he addressed the concern among many African Americans of the time that a liberal arts education would not prepare them for the realities of making a living or help them obtain one of the few professional jobs open to black workers in a Jim Crow society. Du Bois provided examples of how algebra and other liberal studies would broaden the knowledge base of black workers such as bankers and bricklayers. Individuals throughout history, he argued, applied knowledge gained through a broad liberal education to everyday problems in life. He stated, "what Aristotle thought, what Phidias carved, what Da Vinci painted, what Bacon knew, what Leibnitz created, what Kant criticized, and how Jesus Christ loved" demonstrated how broad knowledge, acquired through liberal education, could lead to the creation of a better world.[59]

As part of his early thinking about the need for liberal education, Du Bois began to formulate a content outline of history that reflected his ideal of liberal education. He also presented what he believed was an ideal curriculum for African Americans. The curriculum included primarily classic readings in Western literature and history, such as William Cullen Bryant's translation of *Homer's Iliad and Odyssey*, *The Hebrew Bible*, Theodor Mommsen's *History of Rome*, Edward Gibbon's *The Decline and Fall of the Roman Empire*, Dante's *Inferno*, Johann Wolfgang Goethe's *Faust*, and selections from the writings of Herodotus, Aristotle, Plato, Sappho, Horace, Cicero, Tacitus, Voltaire, Rousseau, Carlyle, Emerson, and other Greek, Roman, and European thinkers.[60]

In addition to these historical and literary works, Du Bois encouraged African Americans to read publications such as *Century*, *Harper's*, *The Nation*, and the local weekly paper and to visit the many museums and libraries in Boston.[61] Du Bois's educational vision for black Bostonians was very similar to the education he received in Great Barrington and at Fisk and Harvard. During his Harvard years, Du Bois had not yet articulated a notable appreciation for African and other non-Western literature, cultures, and civilizations.

In June 1890, Du Bois received his bachelor's degree in philosophy, *cum laude*, from Harvard. One of several students selected to deliver a commencement address, he chose as his subject Confederate president Jefferson Davis. Again highlighting the leadership model of the "strong man" as the standard-bearer of progress and civilization, Du Bois praised Jefferson as a "typical Teutonic Hero" who "defied [disease], trampled on precedent, would not be defeated, and never surrendered."[62] Du Bois saw Davis, like Bismarck, as the type of leader African Americans needed to organize and uplift themselves.

In another address in 1890, Du Bois praised Scottish historian Thomas Carlyle's idea of strong leadership and cultural refinement. Du Bois was especially drawn to Carlyle's notion that a hero could be an intellectual, poet, or man of letters and that sacrifice was an important aspect of the hero. In his book entitled *On Heroes, Hero-Worship, and the Heroic in History* (1841), Carlyle identified various heroic leaders in history who had united their people. Reflecting on Carlyle's ideas on heroism and heroic sacrifice, Du Bois pondered the issue of sacrifice and black leadership. "Here comes the crucial point in every man's life—it is a real conflict—a stubborn contradiction which none can escape and at these crossroads the hero and the man part company."[63]

Du Bois observed that with sacrifice black leaders could live a "larger" life of manhood and womanhood, be men and women of letters, and be "surrounded by educational institutions, libraries, museums, art galleries, and theaters," which he described as "a perfect paradise for the scholar."[64] Du Bois's ideals of sacrifice and intellectual and cultural refinement were consistent with Carlyle's ideas. Thus, Du Bois's plan to identify and develop educated and refined African American race leaders or a talented tenth was likely influenced by Carlyle's conceptualization of the hero.[65]

Another document that provides insight into Du Bois's burgeoning educational thought while at Harvard is his essay "Harvard and the South: A Commencement Pact, 1891." Reminiscent of "An Open Letter to the Southern People" in its appeal to Southerners' failure to educate both blacks and whites, Du Bois strategically presented the destiny of the races in tandem. In the essay Du Bois encouraged Harvard to share its knowledge, through its students and graduates, with the South. He attempted to convince Southerners that the South's economic success depended on the type and quality of education it provided to its citizens and on its willingness to grant political rights to the working class. Du Bois refrained from blaming white Southerners for their past treatment of blacks, stating, "It must be noted that the problem is not primarily a moral one. Without doubt the moral integrity of the southern people has suffered from the institution of slavery."[66] The most pressing problem, Du Bois argued, was Southerners' abysmal economic status and failure to engage in industrial development.

To address the economic problem, Du Bois called for basic schooling and good education for blacks and whites and full political rights for the laboring class. A liberal or humanities education, he believed, would help educate black workers and leaders in the "correct economic ideas" of the industrialized and modernized world. Such an education would be broad and universal—the type of education that Harvard represented and that the South needed: "I mean that wider, freer Harvard—that spirit of intellectual breadth and liberty that seeks Truth for Truth's sake: that Harvard which, thanks be to God, in these days is getting nearer to the slums. In this spirit and in this spirit alone, we build a new South."[67]

Thus, Du Bois believed, at this early stage of his career, that a broad and liberal education that engaged and addressed problems confronting those in the slums was the most effective form of education for African Americans. Black and white citizens, he believed, could collectively make the South an industrial force if whites were willing to recognize black political rights. Du Bois's appeal was cunning in that he linked the South's economic future to the quality of its treatment of its black citizens.

After completing his B.A. at Harvard in 1890, Du Bois enrolled in a master's program in history at Harvard and began collecting data for a study on the African slave trade under the direction of Albert Bushnell Hart. In 1891 he delivered a paper before the American Historical Association entitled "Enforcement of the Slave Trade," which became the topic of his master's thesis. In June 1892 he received his M.A. in history, and this work would later serve as the foundation for his doctoral thesis.

Du Bois was not satisfied with studying only in the United States and had long desired to study at a German university. In 1890 he had applied for a grant from the Slater Fund for the Education of Negroes to study for a Ph.D. in Germany. After much urging and cajoling by Du Bois, former U.S. president Rutherford B. Hayes, chair of the Slater Fund, notified Du Bois in April 1892 that he would be awarded $750 for his first year of study, renewable for a second year.

For the son of Great Barrington, burgeoning "race man" of Fisk, and recent graduate of Harvard University, 1892 was a watershed year. He had successfully defended and presented his master's thesis and was headed to Germany. In August 1892 he arrived in Rotterdam. Two months later he would begin study at the Fredrich-Wilhelm III Universitat in Berlin, also known as the University of Berlin.

UNIVERSITY OF BERLIN

Founded in 1809, the University of Berlin was considered one of the great universities of Europe. Studying at a German university with some of the country's most renowned scholars at a time when Germany was experiencing heightened social and intellectual activity was an exhilarating experience for Du Bois. Du Bois immersed himself in German culture. While he often felt isolated at Harvard, Germany in contrast seemed to provide Du Bois with a more cosmopolitan worldview and encouraged him to adopt a more sophisticated view toward whites and racism. He would declare that:

> In Germany in 1892, I found myself on the outside of the American world, looking in. With me were white folk—students, acquaintances, teachers—who viewed the scene with me. They did not always pause to regard me as a curiosity, or something sub-human; I was just a man of somewhat privileged student rank, with whom they were glad to meet and talk over the world; particularly the part of the world whence I came.[68]

The political activity and progressive social reforms taking place in Germany would tremendously affect Du Bois's ideas for addressing the "Negro problem" in America. Under the training of professors Heinrich Von Treitschke, Adolf Wagner, and Gustav von Schmoller, Du Bois was exposed to a new way of thinking about black social problems beyond the detached methods he found in his Harvard education. Du Bois's German professors were in the thick of German politics and absorbed by the social problems of their day. They believed that systematic analysis and study of Germany's social problems would help produce solutions to these problems.[69]

Neither Von Treitschke, Wagner, nor Schmoller hailed from the discipline of philosophy in which Du Bois had focused much of his Harvard studies. Their study of social problems was situated within the field of political economy, a predecessor of sociology. Under Von Treitschke, Du Bois studied politics and was exposed to Von Treitschke's criticism of the "uncivilized" practice of lynching in the southern United States. Wagner likewise exposed Du Bois to his German nationalist views and offered a harsh critique of *laissez-faire* economics and the divisiveness it caused by polarizing rich and poor Germans. Less nationalistic than Von Treitschke, Schmoller also rejected *laissez-faire* economic liberalism in favor of a political economy grounded in research with clearly defined goals. Like his colleagues, Schmoller believed that the state should help dictate the role of the economy.[70]

Schmoller, it appears, had the most profound influence on Du Bois. In 1882, Schmoller began teaching economics at the University of Berlin. Between 1890 and 1917 he was a member of the German Historical School (*Deutsche Historische Schule*). He also served as president of the Association for Social Policy (*Verein fur Sozialpolitik*). These two institutions emphasized a scientific approach to the study of economics and society based on ethics. The German Historical School, however, focused more on empirical research, while the Association for Social Policy focused on implementing social policy based on scientific research.[71]

Du Bois remembered Schmoller as a scholar of the scientific method and a "teacher of men and molder of coming scientific thought." In his notes on his German student years, Du Bois wrote that Schmoller had a "Passion for statistics and precise hist[orical] information, but handles his facts easily like a master, so that he can handle any theoretical question and bring a lot of statistical evidence to back him up."[72] From Schmoller, Du Bois would discover a means of employing systematic scientific research on the Negro problem and social reform.

In 1893, Du Bois joined the Association for Social Policy, likely under the influence of Schmoller, and strengthened his belief that scientific research could be used to help bring about social reform for African Americans. Later, during the first decade of the twentieth century, Du Bois incorporated into his educational philosophy the idea of using scientific research to foster social reform. Germany helped provide Du Bois with the scholarly tools to address the Negro problem as well as to develop his own confidence as a leader of his race or a "race man."[73]

There is also evidence that while in Germany Du Bois further engaged Hegel's ideas as a means of understanding the dialectical positionality of African-descended people in white-dominated societies. For instance, in his unpublished novel *A Fellow of Harvard*, written while he was a student in Berlin in December 1892, Du Bois engaged the issue of double-consciousness and black leadership. Du Bois constructed a plot that is undoubtedly a composite of his own life. He noted: "The hero is a western born boy of N.E. ancestry—somewhat eccentric from childhood. His delight in school (in St. Paul) was to [pore] over a Harvard Catalogue & picture himself a fellow of Harvard."[74]

In a story line that mirrored his own experiences, Du Bois's protagonist, John Johnson, is awarded a scholarship to attend college and the townspeople encourage him to attend "college x," which is a veiled identifier for Fisk. Johnson becomes disgusted by the "narrowness" of college x and transfers to Harvard as a junior. Johnson devotes his time to his studies at Harvard and receives a fellowship to study in Europe, where he becomes a socialist. Johnson attempts to complete a doctorate in Europe, but fails because of the "unreadiness of his thesis." Johnson returns to the United States and accepts a faculty position at a black college in the South, where he is promptly identified as a radical for disagreeing with both blacks and whites on campus. Du Bois concludes the story with Johnson leaving the black university, publishing his masterpiece, having his work rejected by the public, becoming insane, and dying a "fellow of Harvard."[75]

Du Bois's story reveals much about his evolving thought on the challenges facing him as a future black leader. In the novel, the protagonist finds himself in conflict with both the black and white worlds. Despite his success in becoming a Harvard graduate, Johnson is not accepted by his people, leading to his demise. This perspective is significant because it reflects Du Bois's later notion that black leaders would have to maintain a psychological and sociological connection to their own culture in order to navigate white-dominated society. In Du Bois's novel, the protagonist dies as a result of alienation and disconnection from the black community.[76]

While in Germany, Du Bois took time away from his studies to see the country he had admired from afar. In his diary, one can sense his excitement as he prepared for a spring outing in 1893: "It was the 24th of March, Friday that I started—a beautiful day with clean blue sky and floods of the sweetest yellow sunshine imaginable. I arose at 6 ½ [6:30] and put the finishing touches to my packing."[77]

Du Bois also took time out to write to *The Fisk Herald* in order to extol the intellectual benefits of study in Europe: "Europe: the culminating point of human education. Let no man dare to call himself educated, let not one presume to think himself cultured until he has felt and realized this center of the world's civilization."[78] Future leaders of the race, Du Bois believed, should study the accomplishments of "great" societies and civilizations such as Europe to serve as an inspiration to uplift black culture and society. He encouraged Fisk students to see and study Europe in the vigor of their youth.

Writing in his journal in February 1894 on a Friday evening around 7:30 P.M., Du Bois again reflected on his experiences in Germany. He noted that he was "free from those iron bonds that bound me at home." He also reflected on how Germany had endowed him with new zeal to help his people "stand among the honored of the world." He proclaimed, "I will have a Philosophie Doctor from Berlin!"[79]

Unfortunately, Du Bois would not receive the German Ph.D. The Slater Foundation did not renew his grant for a third year, which he needed to complete course and dissertation requirements. Before leaving, Du Bois celebrated his twenty-fifth birthday in Germany. The itinerary for the day reflected the precision of thought of the determined young scholar. At 8:00 A.M. he was to have a breakfast of coffee and oranges, followed by time for reading. Later that evening, his notes reveal, he performed a solitary candlelight ceremony and offered a prayer to the *zeitgeist* or "spirit of the moment" in dedicating himself as the "Moses" of his people, whose duty was to lead the race. He stated, "These are my plans: to make a name in science, to make a name in literature and thus to raise my race."[80] Du Bois understood the challenges of his self-appointed role and reflected upon this new phase in his life and the reality of being "dropped suddenly back into nigger hating America."[81]

CONCLUSION

From 1888 to 1892, Du Bois obtained education and training that would greatly influence his thinking on the social, economic, and political problems of his race. This background shaped his view that education was essential in preparing African Americans for the conditions and problems they would face in society, and influenced his thinking about the types of education that were most beneficial for his race. From Fisk, he obtained a firsthand account of the ravages of slavery, discrimination, and racism on his people and began to realize that racism and misinformation about African Americans were woven into the fabric of American life. Also at Fisk, he began to develop his idea that strong leadership within the black race was necessary to unite the race for its own improvement. Education, Du Bois believed, could provide the appropriate knowledge base to train talented blacks for leadership in their quest for equal rights.

For Du Bois, Harvard University was the epicenter of American social thought. It broadened his intellectual repertoire and introduced him to the emerging field of sociology. At Harvard he became immersed in the intellectual climate of philosophical speculative thought and scientific historical methodology. Du Bois's Harvard years honed his appreciation for education and introduced him to research methods that he would later use in attacking the "Negro problem."

Du Bois's education in Germany opened his mind to new ideas about science and society. It introduced him to Europeans' attitudes about African peoples and their ideas about racism in the United States and exposed him to possibilities for the advancement of Negro civilization. Du Bois's experiences at the University of Berlin and in Germany more broadly also helped clarify his role in the uplift of Black people. In Germany, he developed a view of himself as a systematic scientist who could help bring about social reform for Negroes in America through careful and precise study of the "Negro problem."

Fisk, Harvard, and Berlin would have a tremendous influence on the development of Du Bois's educational thought. Together, these universities provided the foundation for the broad liberal education Du Bois believed African Americans should receive to challenge white supremacy and discrimination, solve their own problems, and uplift themselves to the level of other peoples and societies. As he moved into the twentieth century, however, Du Bois would have to adjust some of his ideas to meet changing circumstances and address other educational ideas that were promulgated by white educators as most beneficial for African Americans.

PART II

Educating and Uplifting the Race, 1895–1920

The period from 1895 to 1920 marked a time of highs and lows for African Americans. A few decades removed from slavery, African Americans would have to establish a strong social, economic, and political foundation amidst turbulent social change and the challenges of discrimination. During these years, African Americans made strides in obtaining greater literacy, a number of black colleges sprang up and a few entered their second or third decade, a few blacks were appointed to political office, and some blacks acquired wealth.

Despite such successes, the black masses remained second-class citizens and were denied equal social, economic, and political rights. During this period, Du Bois was at the forefront of initiating and sustaining the national discourse on solving the "Negro problem." At the center of his discourse was the role he believed education could play in improving the lives of black people.

CHAPTER 2

The "Negro Problem" in the Age of Social Reform

The world that the young Du Bois, a self-proclaimed "Moses," entered during the final decade of the nineteenth century was in a turbulent state of change. Increased immigration, rapid industrialization, migration from farms to cities, and massive overcrowding in urban centers brought an array of problems to the United States, including increased poverty, crime, and social and industrial instability. Within this context, Du Bois adopted and adapted the ethos of Progressivism to address the social, economic, and political problems of black people, or what was widely referred to as the "Negro problem."[1]

THE PROGRESSIVE ETHOS

The late 1800s through the early 1900s, commonly known as the Progressive Era in U.S. history, was a time when many middle-class white Americans tried to make sense out of a new and more complex world. The period was an anxious one for middle-class whites, who more readily came into contact with various ethnic groups and the social problems facing American society.[2]

Historian Richard Hofstadter asserts that Progressivism called for "orderly social change" and that social reformers were not interested in bringing about a revolution. In his view, Progressives believed that humans were innately good and that social reform, not a complete overhaul of society, was the best means to improve American society. Progressives' main objective, therefore, was to change existing institutions and create new ones to improve social life. Such improvements, they believed, would occur through institutional change, progressive social rhetoric, efficiency-based strategies, scientific investigation, and community-based development.[3] Historian Lynn Gordon similarly argues that the Progressive Era was a period of "optimism and energy" that "pervaded middle-class America. Progressives exuded confidence that human beings could ameliorate the deficiencies of national life, while remaining within a traditional framework."[4]

For Progressives, immigration, migration to the cities, and rapid social and industrial changes were potential threats to a stable society. In the first decade of the new century, 449,000 immigrants came to the United States. The number of immigrants to the United States peaked in 1907 at 1,285,000.

The number of Americans who were foreign-born increased from 10 million in 1900 to 14 million in 1910.[5] While the Progressive Era encompassed a period of comparative prosperity and jobs were created for many immigrants in urban centers, the working conditions in factories and industries were abysmal. For instance, about 1.7 million children under the age of sixteen worked full-time to support their families. Often, full-time work ranged from 10 to 15 hours per day. Many adults also worked long hours in crowded, unsafe, and unsanitary working conditions.[6]

As a result of the country's growing social problems, Progressives successfully lobbied for the passage of several laws to help address the problems. Organizations such as the National Child Labor Committee sought the passage of laws banning the employment of young children and limiting work hours for older children. Progressives also established social settlement houses to help immigrants adjust to their new lives. One of the most famous settlement houses was Jane Addams's Hull House, established in 1889 on Chicago's Near West Side. Hull House was a nonsectarian institution that provided citizenship lessons, English language training, and vocational skills and training to mostly immigrant populations.[7]

Through their social activism and publications, and particularly through the work of crusading journalists called "muckrakers," Progressives exposed the social ills of the day. Many Progressives felt that special-interest groups had stifled the voices of the people. They believed their mission was to inform the public of the country's social problems and expose instances of corruption. Perhaps the most popular of the muckraking exposés was Upton Sinclair's *The Jungle* (1906), which called attention to unsanitary conditions in Chicago slaughterhouses. The book alarmed the public and President Theodore Roosevelt so much that Congress passed the Pure Food and Drug Act in 1906, forbidding the manufacture or sale of improperly labeled products. Sinclair, an acquaintance of Du Bois's, was only one of many Progressive journalists who called attention to the social conditions of the period, resulting in the passage of a number of additional laws designed to protect the public interest.[8]

Despite the action and rhetoric of Progressive reformers, the Progressive Era was extremely difficult for African Americans. According to historian Rayford Logan, the 1890s and early 1900s, which he called "the Nadir," were characterized by a marked increase in racial tensions and a stiffening of segregation and white antipathy toward blacks. Increased racial tensions resulted in the solidification of Jim Crow laws that greatly restricted black life in the South and other parts of the country. In 1896 the United States Supreme Court sanctioned black oppression when it declared in *Plessy v. Ferguson* that the doctrine of "separate but equal" was constitutional. *Plessy* and Jim Crow laws provided governmental sanction for discrimination and prejudice that further entrenched the "Negro problem" in American society.[9]

The passage of Jim Crow laws during the final decade of the nineteenth century accompanied an increase in violence against black citizens. Between 1890 and 1918, some two to three blacks were burned at the stake, hanged, or murdered in other vicious ways every week in the United States. These lynchings were often festive occasions at which women and children were present to observe the highly ritualistic events that culminated in the sacrifice of black life. The lynchers viewed blacks as animals or subhuman. The large number of lynchings and the brutal, coldhearted manner in which black lives were taken reveal the depth of some whites' hatred for and fear of blacks during the period.[10]

To justify these acts of terrorism, a number of writers produced works that denigrated African Americans and presented them as a danger to whites and a threat to white European civilization. These works included Frederick L. Hoffman's *Race Traits and Tendencies of the American Negro* (1896); Charles Carroll's *The Negro: A Beast* (1900); and Robert W. Shufeldt's *The Negro: A Menace to American Civilization* (1907).[11]

Perhaps the most popular of the racist writings of the period were Thomas Dixon's trilogy of novels, *The Leopard's Spots: A Romance of the White Man's Burdens, 1865–1900* (1902), *The Clansman: An Historical Romance of the Ku Klux Klan* (1905), and *The Traitor* (1907). In *The Leopard's Spots*, Dixon argued that like the leopard who could not change its spots, blacks could not change their skin color, social habits, or lowly status. Dixon also preached that whites were justified in using force to contain the "bestial instincts of the Negro." *The Clansman* followed a similar line of thinking and presented African Americans as a menace to Southern womanhood and the Southern way of life during Reconstruction.[12] Moviemaker D.W. Griffith later adapted the racist ideas in *The Clansman* as the centerpiece for a major motion picture, *The Birth of a Nation* (1915). The racist film gained national acclaim when President Woodrow Wilson viewed the film in the White House and allegedly attested to its accuracy by stating that it was "like writing history with Lightning. And my only regret is that it is terribly true."[13]

Progressivism also influenced the U.S. educational system. Historian Lawrence Cremin argued that Progressive education emerged from the larger Progressive movement and described it as a "many sided effort to use the schools to improve the lives of individuals." According to Cremin, Progressive education extolled (a) a broad program that addressed issues related to "health, vocation, and the quality of family and community life"; (b) application in the classroom of pedagogical principles based on scientific research, psychology, and the social sciences; (c) differentiated curricula to fit the needs of children of various classes and backgrounds; and (d) democratic ideas that everyone could succeed.[14]

The characteristics that Cremin attributed to Progressive education were largely a response to the changing demographic of schools. In response to student population increases in city school systems—the result of immigration from Europe and internal migration from the farms to the cities—Progressives believed that schools should be prepared to meet the needs of all students who came through their doors.[15]

As a result of their concern about the varied needs of students, many Progressives advocated for a differentiated curriculum. Some Progressives, for instance, called for industrial and vocational education to meet the needs of those students who did not intend to go to college. Industrial and vocational education, Progressives argued, also made sense because they provided students with the skills necessary for living and working in an increasingly industrial and technological society.[16]

Such Progressive educational ideas, along with the growing ethnic diversity of the country, impacted black education during the late 1800s and early 1900s. Blacks continued to view education as a means to improve their social and economic plight where other initiatives had failed. Many black and white educators believed that the system of universal schooling that blacks helped to advance during Reconstruction would prepare blacks for the mammoth social, economic, industrial, and agricultural changes that occurred in the United States after the Civil War.

Northern industrialists and Southerners who were not necessarily Progressives recognized the necessity of a unified economic North and South to take advantage of industrialization. Moreover, many believed it was necessary to develop a reliable labor source for Northern industry and Southern agriculture. As a result, a number of Northern industrialists and Southerners advocated for industrial and agricultural education and schooling that would train blacks to become laborers and workers.[17]

The state of black public and private schooling during the late 1800s and early 1900s reflected both promise and problems. African Americans made significant strides in literacy, rising from a rate of 42 percent in 1890 to 81 percent in 1930. Historian Henry Bullock attributes this impressive increase in literacy to the many private schools opened after the Civil War. This explanation has been buttressed by historians Ronald Butchart and James Anderson, who have also documented the prevalence of black educational agency in the development of private black schools and Sabbath (church-sponsored) schools during the last decades of the nineteenth century. Similarly, between 1870 and 1900 black enrollment in colleges increased significantly. For instance, in 1876, 137 blacks graduated from black colleges and by 1900, 1,883 blacks had graduated from black colleges.[18]

Despite such gains, a number of issues hindered the overall progress of African American education. African Americans, for instance, typically had a shorter school term than whites, which contributed to lower levels of achievement among black youth.[19] In addition, black schools tended to receive less funding than white schools, which resulted in inadequate heating, poor lighting, holes in the floor, leaky roofs, and too few desks for the students. In addition, black teachers were paid substantially lower salaries than white teachers. Such institutional racism persisted throughout the first few decades of the twentieth century and resulted in high teacher–pupil ratios, overcrowded classes, irregular student attendance, and deplorable work conditions in many black schools.[20]

THOMAS JESSE JONES

One of the most influential educators of the Progressive era with regard to African American education was sociologist Thomas Jesse Jones. A student of Franklin Giddings, Jones applied "scientific" reasoning to determine what he believed was an optimal educational strategy for blacks. Educating African Americans in the basic principles of making a living, he concluded, was the best way to help blacks reach higher levels of civilization and become part of the American culture.[21]

In 1917, Jones laid out his concerns about and plans for black education in his controversial study, *Negro Education: A Study of the Private and Higher Schools for Colored People in the United States*. Jones argued that the misunderstanding and distrust many blacks exhibited about the value of industrial education for their race were major impediments to black progress. Jones argued that industrial education was "the adaptation of educational activities, whether industrial or literary, to the needs of the pupil and community."[22]

In his 1918 *Crisis* essay, "Negro Education," Du Bois responded harshly to Jones's study, calling it a "dangerous" and unfortunate publication. Du Bois was concerned with Jones's advocacy of industrial and manual education to the exclusion of classical and college education for blacks. Du Bois also addressed Jones's failure to recognize African American "taxation without representation," noting that African Americans had very little influence on the curricula of the public schools that were focusing on industrial and manual training.[23]

JOHN DEWEY

The most prominent philosopher of education during the Progressive Era was the Vermont-born John Dewey. A student of Charles Peirce while at Johns Hopkins and William James while at Harvard, Dewey translated pragmatism into social action in education. He integrated his views in psychology, philosophy, and social reform and advocated a practical philosophy of democratic and social reform. Early in his career, Dewey believed that contemporary education was disconnected from the everyday realities of life. Migration from agrarian communities into cities, Dewey believed, had taken young people away from their contact and experience with nature, causing them to be undisciplined, dislocated, and alienated. As a result, he advocated an education that would evolve and adjust to real-life events according to an individual's environment. He also believed schooling should help students to achieve individual growth while building a better society.[24]

Dewey believed that schools could play a vital role in redressing social problems by fostering real-world learning environments. To facilitate such environments, Dewey argued that a child's education should be infused with daily life and that teachers should facilitate learning that fosters continuous, reflective learning experiences. Contrary to popular interpretations, Dewey did not advocate a pedagogical approach that endorsed unguided learning, but instead called for teachers to guide student learning. It should also be noted that even early in his career as a philosopher, Dewey did not advocate a type of vulgar vocationalism. Instead, he believed in an education that infused work with the disciplines and argued that the purpose of education was "to make each one of our schools an embryonic community life, active with types of occupations that reflect the life of the larger society and permeated throughout with the spirit of art, history, and science."[25]

Dewey was able to develop some of his ideas beginning in 1896 when he set up his Laboratory School at the University of Chicago. In Dewey's school, students became members of a cooperative community and engaged in weaving, gardening, and wood and metal work. They studied subjects like physics, history, and chemistry, but in relationship to real-world experiences and occupations. They also studied manners, morale, and ethics. In essence, Dewey supported a broad curriculum that focused on educating the child as an authentic member of a moral community.[26]

Dewey also weighed in on the question of the appropriateness of industrial education in schools. In 1914, he forthrightly declared:

> No question at present under discussion in education is so fraught with consequences for the future of democracy as the question of industrial education. Its right development will do more to make public education truly democratic than any other one agency now under consideration. Its wrong treatment will as surely accentuate all undemocratic tendencies in our present situation, by fostering and strengthening class divisions in school and out.[27]

Dewey's major concern was that industrial education isolated from a general education that included the arts and sciences would stifle the overall development of children. Such education, Dewey believed, would become beholden to manufacturing and business interests that were rarely democratic in their relationships with workers. Dewey did not oppose industrial education, but he did oppose a utilitarian approach to vocational education that was disconnected from broader knowledge of the humanities.[28]

Dewey was a Progressive, but he did not share many Progressives' view about the inferiority of African-descended people. He believed that the United States should provide a democratic social environment in which African Americans could strive for and reach their highest potential. As a founding member of the interracial and progressive National Association for the Advancement of Colored People (NAACP), Dewey delivered a brief speech at the 1909 National Negro Conference (the predecessor of the NAACP) in which he refuted the idea of black racial inferiority and called for education to help equalize opportunities between races. He further argued that:

> All points of skill are represented in every race, from the inferior individual to the superior individual, and a society that does not furnish the environment and education and the opportunity of all kinds which will bring out and make effective the superior ability wherever it is born, is not merely doing an injustice to that particular race and to those particular individuals, but it is doing an injustice to itself for it is depriving itself of just that much of social capital.[29]

For Dewey, white racism was irrational not only because of the falsehood of the concept of racial inferiority, but also because it deprived the United States of a potentially valuable social and economic resource.[30]

Dewey and Du Bois were, in many ways, of like mind and spirit. They were involved in some of the same organizations, such as the short-lived League of Independent Political Action and the NAACP. Their training under James in pragmatic philosophy set them on a similar path toward questioning, rethinking, and revising not only their own ideas, but those of others. They both believed that education could help bring about a more democratic society and should continuously adjust to address and resolve social, economic, and political problems. For both Du Bois and Dewey, however, this did not mean that the disciplines and humanities had no place in education and schooling.

Du Bois and Dewey corresponded periodically, and on several occasions Du Bois asked Dewey to submit an essay on black education to *The Crisis*. One such request read:

> Would you be willing to furnish to this number of the *Crisis* a short statement concerning Negro education or perhaps I should call it a re-statement. It seems to me that the Booker T. Washington idea has broken down because of great economic changes, and that a re-statement of educational philosophy for the Negro is needed.[31]

Du Bois acknowledged a response from Dewey on January 22, 1932, stating, "I thank you very much for your kind words of January 20. If you could do something for us, even after April 1, I should appreciate it." While an essay by Dewey did not appear in *The Crisis*, it is clear that Du Bois and Dewey held similar views on many educational issues. As pragmatists, they allowed for flexibility in their thinking on education and their thought changed over time. Both believed that schools should help democratize society and that children should have both experiential education and education in the humanities. As such, they were kindred spirits.[32]

THE EDUCATOR AS SCIENTIST

After returning from Germany in 1894, Du Bois accepted a teaching position at Wilberforce University, an African Methodist Episcopal church-sponsored school in Ohio. In 1895 he completed his doctoral degree at Harvard and defended his dissertation, entitled *The Suppression of the African Slave Trade to the United States of America, 1638–1870*.[33]

Full of Germanic idealism that social science research could reform society, Du Bois had lofty ideas about the role of black universities in addressing the problems of black communities, and he hoped Wilberforce would provide him with an opportunity to help "build a great university." At Wilberforce, Du Bois taught Latin, Greek, and English. He believed it was a good place to begin his career but felt limited by the school's fervent religious culture and the administration's reluctance to allow him to teach sociology. Of the school's religious culture, Du Bois later noted that tensions arose between him and school administrators after he wandered into a meeting and someone announced that he would lead a prayer. Du Bois noted that he aptly responded by saying "No, he won't" and nearly lost his job over the incident. Du Bois was private about his spirituality and it was not his temperament to express it publicly.[34]

During his brief stint at Wilberforce, Du Bois met a lovely, light brown–complexioned Wilberforce student named Nina Gomer. Nina was from Iowa and the daughter of a German father and African American mother. Yolande Du Bois Williams, Gomer's granddaughter, notes that the young Du Bois constructed two lists of possible coeds who might make him a suitable wife and companion. One list was composed of young women who could cook; the other list was composed of the prettiest women on campus. The name Nina Gomer appeared on both lists. Feeling that it was time to find a wife and start a family, Du Bois courted Nina and they were married in 1896. Nina would prove to be a strong stabilizing force in Du Bois's life.[35]

While a professor at Wilberforce, Du Bois delivered a speech in which he expressed his views on the role universities should play in improving society. Titled "The True Meaning of a University," Du Bois traced the history of universities to ancient Rome and Europe and identified England,

France, Germany, and the United States as great university centers of his day. Du Bois noted that throughout history, universities were often established by churches, but that churches often stifled free thought and promoted religious dogma. The Renaissance, he argued, broke the shackles the church had placed on many universities and allowed universities to blossom into the "free spirit of Grecian scientific inquiry."[36] During the Renaissance, libraries and technological advancements blossomed alongside or within universities.

Since his days as a student, Du Bois had been developing a vision of the role of black colleges and universities. Fisk introduced him to the role that black colleges could play in improving black life, while Harvard and Berlin provided him with models of what black colleges could aspire to be. The speech was therefore also a cloaked critique of Wilberforce and a plan of action for black colleges, including Wilberforce. He stated: "We are not simply an institution of higher learning, but a university of the Afro-American people: as such, the material must be framed to their needs and our ideals must become their ideals. . . . In order to do this then we must never lose sight of the central duty of the university: the search for truth."[37]

Du Bois's speech was more than a history of the university. It was also an indictment of the influence of religious dogma on higher education. Du Bois envisioned black colleges and universities not only as places of intellectual activity and scientific research, but also as organic and engaged participants in black communities and African American life.

As a social scientist, Du Bois felt an obligation to critique some of the pseudo-scientific work that had been written about African Americans in the United States. For instance, in 1897 he published a review of Frederick L. Hoffman's *Race Traits and Tendencies of the American Negro* in the *Annals of the American Academy of Political and Social Science*. In his review, Du Bois used his training as a social scientist to attack Hoffman's argument that African Americans were on their way to becoming extinct. Du Bois harshly criticized Hoffman's simplistic and inadequate database and questioned Hoffman's extrapolations of black life based on the eleventh census, statistics of soldiers in the Civil War. Hoffman also based his conclusions on "recent vital statistics of large cities," and Du Bois countered that reputable scholars considered these data sets to be inaccurate and unreliable.[38]

Du Bois further noted that Hoffman failed to discuss structural and institutional disadvantages African Americans faced that contributed to higher black mortality in comparison to whites. Finally, Du Bois pointed out that black death rates were equal to those of Europeans in large cities such as Munich, Montreal, Naples, Budapest, Breslan, and Madrid. As a sociologist, Du Bois was very cognizant of the need to critique racial and social issues within their historical and social context. In examining the "Negro problem," Du Bois often refuted scholarship that attempted to draw generalizations about African Americans based on isolated variables. Du Bois concluded that Hoffman's interpretations should be dismissed.[39]

In the fall of 1896, Du Bois accepted a position as "assistant instructor" in sociology at the University of Pennsylvania to begin a study of the social conditions of black Philadelphians. The idea for the study was proposed by Susan Wharton, a member of the Executive Committee of the Philadelphia College Settlement.[40] Wharton was active in social reform activities among the poor in Philadelphia, and her family had endowed the Wharton School at the University of Pennsylvania. Wharton asked University of Pennsylvania provost Charles C. Harrison to undertake a study of social conditions among the black population in Philadelphia's Seventh Ward. Samuel McCune Lindsay, a professor of sociology at the University of Pennsylvania, secured the young black social scientist at Wilberforce to spearhead the project.[41]

Du Bois's close contact with African Americans in Nashville, his training in history and philosophy at Harvard, and his study in political economy in Berlin had all prepared him to study black life in Philadelphia. Finally, he would have the opportunity to use his education and training in the social sciences to provide a scientific and empirically-based analysis and interpretation of certain aspects of the "Negro problem." He would now be able to show that ignorance and misinformation were at the root of the "problem." "The world was thinking wrong about race, because it did not know. The ultimate evil was stupidity. The cure for it was knowledge based on scientific investigation."[42] Rather than merely theorizing about social conditions, Du Bois saw his work on *The Philadelphia Negro: A Social Study* as a meeting between philosophy and praxis.

Drawing upon the reform ideas he learned from Schmoller and his other German professors and his observation of the squalid poverty and racism in Nashville, Du Bois undertook to use scientific methodologies to address the "Negro problem":

> The main result of my schooling had been to emphasize science and scientific attitude. . . . I was going to study the facts, any and all facts, concerning the American Negro and his plight, and by measurement and comparison and research, work up to any valid generalization which I could. I entered this primarily with the utilitarian object of reform and uplift.[43]

Despite these lofty goals, Du Bois's historical and sociological analysis of education in *The Philadelphia Negro* has not received much attention among scholars since its publication in 1899. While Du Bois recognized disadvantages for black education and black teachers, as well as the history of black illiteracy in Philadelphia, he surprisingly did not identify poor schooling as a major contributor to the social, economic, and political plight of black residents in the Seventh Ward. Instead, he noted that illiteracy rates had declined over the previous decades and estimated that the black illiteracy rate in the Seventh Ward was about 18 percent.[44]

Du Bois also noted that while many black schools were inefficient, black teachers were pillars of the black community. Given his findings regarding the relative effectiveness of black schools in Philadelphia, Du Bois concluded that one must look beyond schooling to explain the social problems of the black community: "It must be acknowledged that there are other social problems connected with this people more pressing than that of education; that a fair degree of persistence in present methods will settle in time the question of ignorance, but other social questions are by no means so near solution."[45]

Throughout his life, however, Du Bois advocated educational strategies that were responsive to the social, economic, and political conditions of black people. Moreover, Du Bois's examination of black education in Philadelphia was one part of his overall study and illustrated his belief that to understand a social problem, one has to take into account its historical and political contexts. As a result, he would later argue that to be effective, black education must be grounded in African Americans' social and historical experiences.

While working on *The Philadelphia Negro*, Du Bois accepted a professorship at Atlanta University (AU) at the invitation of President Horace Bumstead in 1897. Atlanta was an ideal city in which to continue his scientific study of black social conditions. Like Philadelphia, Atlanta had a sizable black community at the turn of the twentieth century, and a number of black workers were entering the middle class. AU was situated in the heart of the black community, which was in close proximity to the outlying white communities that vigorously enforced Jim Crow segregation and the ways and mores of the New South.

The first years Du Bois and his wife, Nina, spent in Atlanta were not happy ones. In the spring of 1899 their two-year-old son Burghardt died of diphtheria. The Du Boises later believed that Burghardt might have lived had appropriate medical facilities and services been available for African Americans in Atlanta. Du Bois paid tribute to Burghardt in *The Souls of Black Folk* (1903) in a chapter entitled "Of the Passing of the First-Born." In this soliloquy to his son, Du Bois's emotional turmoil and his feelings about Georgia are expressed. "I held him in my arms, after we sped far away from our Southern home,—held him, and glanced at the hot red soil of Georgia and the breathless city of a hundred hills, and felt a vague unrest."[46]

In 1900, Du Bois and Nina's daughter Yolande was born. Yolande's birth helped soothe the pain of the loss of baby Burghardt. In Yolande, Du Bois would instill the ideals of the talented tenth and gain the experiences of fatherhood and a firsthand experience with public schooling.

In that same year a black man named Sam Hose was lynched in Newnan, Georgia, after he was accused of killing his landlord and raping the landlord's wife. On his walk to the *Atlanta Constitution* office to sub-mit a statement on the brutal lynching, Du Bois heard that Hose's knuck-les were on display in a local Atlanta store. Du Bois then turned around and headed back to AU. It was in the aftermath of this event that Du Bois questioned the use of scientific research as the primary method of working for equal rights. He recalled that "Two considerations thereafter broke in upon my work and eventually disrupted it: first, one could not be a calm, cool, and detached scientist while Negroes were lynched, murdered, and starved; and secondly, there was no such definite demand for scientific work of the sort I was doing."[47]

During the early 1900s, in addition to *The Souls of Black Folk*, Du Bois wrote a biography, *John Brown* (1909), and founded two literary magazines, *The Moon* (1905) and *Horizon* (1907). In 1906 Du Bois penned "A Litany of Atlanta" in response to what he saw and felt when he witnessed the At-lanta race riots of that year. Afterward he kept a shotgun in his home for protection against the white mobs.[48]

Despite Du Bois's hardships in Atlanta, his years at AU were produc-tive and he continued his scientific work. Du Bois's vision for his work in Atlanta was in many ways a continuation of the study of black social, eco-nomic, and political conditions that he had researched for his seminal *The Philadelphia Negro* published in 1899. Atlanta, however, was different. Du Bois was exposed to the harshness and rigidity of a segregated society far different from his experience at Fisk, where the university provided a haven for him and his classmates, or his experience in Philadelphia, where life in a Northern urban center offered less blatant forms of institutional-ized discrimination.

As director of the famous *Atlanta University Studies*, established by Atlanta University to systematically study black life in the United States, Du Bois envisioned a one-hundred-year longitudinal study of black life focusing on topics such as black businesses, education, crime, social and physical conditions, the church, and other areas. Du Bois planned to study a differ-ent topic each year. With the passing of each year and every decade, he pre-dicted, the research methods would become more refined and the studies increasingly comprehensive.[49]

Of the sixteen *AU Studies* he supervised, four dealt specifically with black education: *The College Bred Negro* (1900), *The Negro Common School* (1901), *The College Bred Negro American* (1910), and *The Common School and the Negro American* (1911). *The College Bred Negro* was the first sys-tematic study of African Americans in higher education. By soliciting re-sponses to a fifty-six-item questionnaire from black college graduates, Du Bois attempted to develop a profile of their status and occupations. He found that many black college graduates had obtained positions as teachers, clergy-men, physicians, lawyers, and businessmen. Such occupations, Du Bois argued, helped to improve black communities and positioned college graduates to become leaders of black public opinion. Du Bois noted that black women were also obtaining college training and assuming leadership within black communities.[50]

In *The Negro Common School*, Du Bois observed that public schools for black children throughout the South were "woefully inadequate." Continuing high black illiteracy in the former "slave states,"[51] Du Bois argued, was a result of African Americans being denied schooling during slavery and unfair allocation of funds to black and white schools after Emancipation. He acknowledged that some progress had been made in the schools established by the Freedmen's Bureau and those opened by African Americans themselves during Reconstruction.

To help reduce high illiteracy rates among African Americans, Du Bois believed that black public and private schools needed more teachers, better wages, longer school terms, better schoolhouses, more efficient supervision, and renewed interest in teacher training.[52] In *The Negro Common School*, he stressed that improving teacher training was one of the most important strategies for improving black schooling. In their current state, Du Bois noted, "the mass of so-called 'normal' schools for the Negro are doing simply elementary, common school work, or at most, high school work with a little instruction in methods." Du Bois further stated that the black colleges and postgraduate programs tended to provide better training for teachers than normal schools.[53]

Despite their struggles to obtain schooling, Du Bois praised African Americans' ambition and accomplishments in securing some type of education. He also noted blacks' sense of self-determination and the broader impact of their efforts in bringing about public education in the South. Du Bois observed:

> Although recent researches have shown in the South some germs of a public school system before the war, there can be no reasonable doubt, but what common school instruction in the South, in the modern sense of the term, was founded by the Freedman's Bureau and missionary societies, and that the State public school systems were formed mainly by Negro reconstruction governments.[54]

Between the publication of *The Negro Common School* and *The College Bred Negro American*, Du Bois engaged the social Darwinist discourse of the era and challenged biological explanations for poor academic achievement. In "Heredity and the Public Schools," a speech delivered in 1904 in Washington, D.C., Du Bois argued that there was no variation in "stature and muscular development" between black Americans and European whites. Black academic achievement was lower than that of whites, Du Bois believed, because of poorer social and home environments among blacks, not because of heredity or innate inferiority. He noted:

The larger part of the training of human beings must come from the social surroundings in which [blacks] live, and when [blacks] are found deficient, when the results of their training are not what we wish, we must seek not simply to improve the schools, but just as strenuously to improve the social surroundings, the social opportunities, and the social heritage of the unfortunate and untrained.[55]

If the larger American society focused on improving the social environment and conditions for the black population, Du Bois believed, academic achievement would improve. Such an argument would later be used by the NAACP to advocate public school integration. Although Du Bois did not use the terms *social* and *cultural capital* to define his belief that a positive social environment could improve the lives of blacks, his "Heredity and the Public Schools" speech delineated such a theory for blacks.

Du Bois extended the emphasis on environmental influences by arguing that the historical legacy of the African slave trade and the institution of slavery negatively affected the black family and inhibited black social advancement. He believed that the lowly social and economic conditions of blacks could not be studied outside of their historical context and would require systematic and deliberate strategies for amelioration. Systematic education and training, he believed, could help African Americans counter the traumatic conditions created by the actions of white supremacists. Du Bois eventually extended his thesis to argue that Europe continued to colonize and dominate Africans and rob them of their natural resources.[56]

The College Bred Negro American (1910) returned to the topic of black college graduates. The study was based on the reports of eight hundred black college graduates, college catalogues, and letters from college and university officials. The purpose of the study was to determine the number of black college graduates and their social status in society.[57]

The study concluded that by 1910 there were 3,856 black college graduates. Of those graduates, most worked professional jobs in the fields of teaching, the ministry, medicine, and law. The study also reported that most black college graduates belonged to learned societies and were involved in civic activities. Thus, black college graduates were leaders in their communities. The resolutions for the study included the following: 1) "There is an increased and pressing demand for college trained Negroes," 2) "The Negro college graduates are at present, with few exceptions, usefully and credibly employed," and 3) "There should be at least one college for Negro students in each state, liberally endowed." Clearly, while *The College Bred Negro American* was an empirical study, Du Bois's appreciation for liberal education as a means of training black leadership permeates it.[58]

The Common School and the Negro American (1911) revisited some of the issues that were originally addressed in the 1901 study. *The Common*

School and the Negro American relied on data from the annual reports of the U.S. Commissioner of Education, school reports from the Southern and a few Midwestern states, survey questionnaires sent out to school superintendents and teachers, and historical data. In this study, Du Bois found that the tightening of Jim Crow laws throughout the South exacerbated the problems of already abysmal black educational systems. On the whole, he noted that black public schools were underfunded and received dramatically fewer resources than white schools and that many state taxes paid by black residents were used to fund public education for whites.[59]

In his surveys of public school administrators, Du Bois also reported superintendents' statements that some black teachers lacked the necessary training and broad learning to teach effectively. While Du Bois agreed with the assessments of the superintendents, he argued that the ill-prepared teachers were hired by school systems because of the prejudices of white administrators against college- or liberally trained black teachers. Du Bois also noted that the heavy teaching load and numerous extracurricular responsibilities (i.e., fundraising, repairing the school, etc.) sometimes prevented black teachers from focusing on teaching reading, writing, and other basic subjects.[60]

Du Bois also concluded that external factors negatively impacted black public education. Because white voters usually elected unsympathetic white superintendents, black parents were often denied a voice in their children's education. As a result, with the exception of a few states (West Virginia, Kentucky, and Texas) and the District of Columbia, Du Bois argued, black public schools suffered from great neglect.[61] Perhaps the greatest impediments to black public education, however, were whites' use of literacy tests, property qualifications, and poll taxes to prevent blacks from voting, thereby denying them a voice in public schooling.[62]

The *AU Studies* on black education were by no means perfect. The data were lacking in some places and some interpretations were based on limited data. Nonetheless, given Du Bois's minimal resources, the newness of social science research methodologies, and his overly ambitious goals, the studies on education were a monumental achievement. Until the *AU Studies*, no such works existed on the education of black people. A century after the publication of the studies, they remain an invaluable source of data for scholars working in the field of African American education.

CONCLUSION

Du Bois's work as a social scientist reflected the Progressive and social ethos of the late 1800s and early 1900s and the pledge he made in Berlin to "make a name in science." During these years, however, he also reassessed his educational strategy as the dynamics of racism and white supremacy were exposed as more potent and enduring than he had previously thought. As a result, while his vision of an Enlightenment education for blacks held sway in his thinking, he also integrated the concept of an advanced form of industrial and vocational education into his educational thought. Du Bois's willingness to revise and synthesize his views reflected the need for educational strategies to meet the ever-changing needs of black people living in a rapidly changing environment.

Within the Progressive ethos and social reform environment of the 1890s and early 1900s, Du Bois also came to realize that liberal education and social science research alone could not alleviate the social problems of African Americans or solve the "Negro problem." Social activism, racial solidarity, and verbal persuasion would also be necessary to bring increased attention to and foster greater enthusiasm for addressing the "Negro problem" in concrete ways. The Niagara Movement, the predecessor to the NAACP, and the establishment of the NAACP were initial and critical steps in the direction of social activism. As a result of these steps, Du Bois would further revise and develop his educational ideas to reflect his growing emphasis on collective activism in the decades that followed.

CHAPTER 3

Black Educators and the Quest to Uplift and Develop the Race

Du Bois's educational thought during the 1890s and early 1900s did not develop in a vacuum. Other African American educators were also developing ideas about an optimal education for African Americans during this critical stage in the struggle for equality. Collectively, African American educational thought during this period was born primarily of the pain, oppression, and suffering experienced by African Americans; their ideas emerged organically from their daily interactions as educators with black children and adults. As a result, these educational ideas spoke directly to the social, economic, and political conditions of blacks. Examining the educational ideas of these African American educators is thus essential to understanding the intellectual context within which Du Bois's educational thought developed and evolved.

ALEXANDER CRUMMELL

One of the earliest scholars to address the plight of African Americans was the Cambridge-educated Episcopal priest Alexander Crummell. Like many Progressives, Crummell believed that African Americans lagged behind whites culturally, but had the potential to catch up. He observed in 1897: "We have no art; we have no science; we have no philosophy; we have no scholarship. . . . And until we attain the role of civilization, we cannot stand up and hold our place in the world of culture and enlightenment."[1] Therefore, Crummell rejected industrial or vocational education or a separate "Negro curriculum," as he called it, as a sole strategy for "elevating the race." Education, broadly defined, was needed to build a black civilization.

Crummell articulated his educational views in an early lecture, "The Necessities and Advantages of Education Considered in Relation to Colored Men," delivered on July 4, 1844. Crummell argued that the main purpose of advanced education should be to train black leaders to uplift the race. The curriculum, Crummell believed, should cultivate "higher knowledge" among blacks, while also educating them for the practicalities of life. He stated, "The Education of Colored Men sho[uld] be general and critical. The youth sho[uld] be introduced into the whole range of the Sciences, into Mathematics, both pure and mixed, into the treasures hoarded upon in the languages, and into the [requisite] avenues of Morals and Philosophy." Citing the education of other peoples, Crummell believed that African Americans should not limit their education solely to "industry and application," but that practical studies should have a place in "classical education."[2]

In 1897 Crummell helped found the American Negro Academy (ANA) for the purpose of raising "the civilization of the Negro race in the United States, by the scientific processes of literature, art, and philosophy."[3] Embracing concepts of racial uplift and progress through liberal education, the organization dedicated itself to black advancement. This organization, it might be argued, was the first organized manifestation of the talented tenth and an outgrowth of Crummell's philosophy of education.

Crummell had a great influence on the young Du Bois, as evidenced in Du Bois's "race uplift" allocution, "The Conservation of Races," delivered at the ANA meeting in 1897. Like Crummell, Du Bois believed that African peoples had not yet reached their full potential in contributing to modern civilization. Through the leadership of individuals like himself, Crummell, and the members of the ANA, black people would elevate themselves. "For the accomplishment of [social advancement] we need race organizations: Negro colleges, Negro newspapers, Negro business organizations, a Negro school for literature and art, and an intellectual clearing house, for all these products of the Negro mind, which we may call a Negro academy."[4]

Du Bois later expressed his admiration for the old sage and spiritual leader in *The Souls of Black Folk*. Crummell's view that educated African Americans were responsible for "uplifting the race" and his belief in their potential to forge a great civilization reinforced the ideas Du Bois began formulating during his years at Fisk. In addition, Crummell's belief that both classical and practical training were essential elements of the educational agenda for blacks would become a major component of Du Bois's educational thought.

BOOKER T. WASHINGTON

The best known among the vanguard of black educators in the Progressive Era was undoubtedly Booker Taliaferro Washington. Since his death in 1915, Booker T. Washington has been perhaps the most studied and written-about black educator in American history. Many historians have portrayed this larger-than-life figure as the archnemesis of Du Bois, and some have portrayed him as a black agent for white business interests in the South.[5]

Washington articulated his racial and educational philosophy to the country in his well-known speech at the Cotton States Exposition in Atlanta, Georgia, in 1895, and in his subsequent biographies *Up from Slavery*, *Working with the Hands*, and *My Larger Education*. Grounded in ideals of Christian morality, cleanliness, and the Protestant work ethic, Washington's philosophy of progress and "civilizationism" stressed black advancement through hard work rather than the pursuit of civil rights through political activism.

Following Washington's famous "Atlanta Compromise" speech in 1895, Du Bois praised Washington for the wisdom of his words, stating, "Let me heartily congratulate you upon your phenomenal success at Atlanta—it was a word fitly spoken."[6] A few years later, however, Du Bois began to publicly express skepticism about Washington's educational philosophy, arguing that Washington was not a popular leader among the black masses.[7]

Du Bois's analysis of Washington in *The Souls of Black Folk* was critical but balanced. Du Bois believed that Washington's rise was "easily the most striking thing in the history of the American Negro since 1876." However, in his historically significant chapter "Of Mr. Booker T. Washington and Others," Du Bois took issue with Washington's social and educational philosophy. According to Du Bois, Washington advocated that African Americans forgo political power, civil rights, and higher education and focus on the accumulation of wealth. Du Bois noted that Washington sometimes spoke out against lynchers and mob violence and at times used his influence to improve black conditions.[8] However, Du Bois also criticized Washington's educational philosophy as a program that "accepts the alleged inferiority of the Negro race" and argued that "Mr. Washington distinctly asks that black people give up, at least for the present, three things, First, political power, Second, insistence on civil rights, Third, higher education of Negro youth."[9]

Despite Du Bois's critique of Washington, the two men stayed in contact with each other even after the publication of Du Bois's essay in *The Souls of Black Folk*. Even during their debates over classical versus industrial education for African Americans, they remained cordial toward one another. In 1903 Washington wrote to Du Bois:

> My dear Dr. Du Bois:
>   When you are in New York again I hope you will make it a point to meet Hon. John E. Milholland, 52 Broadway. Mr. Milholland is a loyal friend of the race. He is inclined to take radical views but withal is a very [fine] able man, and he is very anxious to get into personal touch with you. I think you will like him. I am still at work on the matter of the New York meeting and it now looks as if sometime in June might be the season that would be most convenient to most of the people.
>   Yours truly, Booker T. Washington[10]

In another letter to Du Bois dated July 1903, Washington invited Du Bois to dinner. This correspondence between Washington and Du Bois reveals that in the early years of the twentieth century their relationship was more complicated than is typically presented.[11]

However, the relationship grew strained over the years. For example, in 1910, Washington expressed bewilderment over Du Bois's attitude in a letter to Daniel Merriman, a Boston minister. Washington complained, "I do not know why it is that Dr. Du Bois and Atlanta University take the attitude that they do. I never abuse Dr. Du Bois, never refer to him in public except in some complimentary manner."[12]

While both men admired each other's accomplishments, they also were suspicious of each other. For instance, while in 1894 Washington offered Du Bois a position at Tuskegee to teach mathematics, in 1900 he also may have prevented Du Bois from securing an assistant superintendency in Washington, D.C. Similarly, while Du Bois worked with Washington on several projects and publicly praised him, he also despised Washington's accommodationism and Washington's attacks on those who criticized him publicly. Du Bois was also incensed by Washington's influence with white philanthropists and his interference in stifling progressive agendas of race uplift.[13]

Leading up to and following Washington's death in 1915, however, Du Bois began to express sympathy toward Washington and seemed to understand the problems in Washington's personal life. In an interview with educator and longtime editor of the *Journal of Negro Education* Charles H. Thompson, Du Bois noted an alleged incident in New York City in which Washington was assaulted when he stumbled into a neighborhood seeking out prostitutes. Regarding the alleged incident, Thompson noted that Du Bois believed that "there was something to it" and attributed Washington's indiscretion to the fact that Washington "'teed' himself off just before a speech." Washington's alcohol binge, Du Bois reasoned, caused Washington to "go off on this hunt by himself." In addition to the alcohol, Thompson noted that Du Bois rationalized Washington's mishap by stating that "Most great men have had an occasional moral lapse. Thus, the only surprising thing is that B.T. had only one to come to surface."[14]

In his later years, while Du Bois continued to highlight the weaknesses in aspects of Washington's educational beliefs and practices, Du Bois's views began to appear more similar to some of Washington's. For instance, Du Bois would later adopt a form of voluntary segregation as an economic strategy for black advancement. This idea was so similar to Washington's accommodation to segregation that some members of the NAACP accused Du Bois of adopting Washington's views.

Washington's social and educational philosophy resonated with African Americans decades after his death. For instance, in a recent book, *The Education of Booker T. Washington: American Democracy and the Idea of Race Relations*, historian Michael West offers a unique and insightful analysis of Washington's social and educational ideas and their enduring influence on American race relations. However, West also argues that Washington's social and educational philosophy of self-help and practicality, and his ideas about progress through meritocracy, constrained some of the potentially revolutionary social reform that the civil rights movement might have brought about. At the same time, West presents Washington as an introspective thinker who wanted to help black people.[15] While West's thesis provides new insights, it also extends the work of Louis Harlan and others who argue for a more complicated understanding of Washington.

Nearly a century after his death, Washington's educational ideas and his relationship with Du Bois are an ongoing topic of debate among scholars and laypeople alike. His educational views are often presented as accommodationist, pragmatic, and Machiavellian. He is also portrayed as a realist who, like other African American educators, was concerned with the uplift of black people. Each of these descriptions accurately depicts aspects of Washington's personality and educational ideas and together reflect the complexity of the man and his thought. As historian Pero Dagbovie observes, "As it is the case with all historical phenomena, Washington must be viewed holistically from many different, often seemingly contradictory, vantage points."[16] This view equally applies to Washington's educational thought. Washington's ideas and his relationship with Du Bois must be considered holistically in the historical and ideological contexts of the period. Only then will we be able to move beyond the clichéd representations of the Washington versus Du Bois debate and vocational versus classical education dichotomy too often used to describe Washington's educational philosophy.

ANNA JULIA COOPER

Anna Julia Cooper, a protégé of Alexander Crummell and contemporary of Du Bois, was another prominent African American educator of the Progressive Era. Cooper was born in Raleigh, North Carolina, in August 1858 and received her B.A. and M.A. degrees from Oberlin in Ohio in 1884 and 1887 respectively. In 1925, Cooper received her Ph.D. in French history from the Sorbonne in Paris, France. Like her mentor, Cooper was driven by the notion of racial progress and uplift and embraced a Christian and mythical vision of herself and other educated blacks as "saviors of the race." Introducing Cooper to the challenges of leading the race, Crummell wrote her a rather cryptic message in 1886, stating: "It is an awful, but also a majestic truth that even while we are in the flesh, and moving about amid earthly relations, we are already in the invisible world."[17] Crummell's message reflected the messianic and spiritual duty he believed race leaders like himself and Cooper should assume. For Crummell, race leaders navigated a higher level of spiritual consciousness of which they might not even be aware. Such cryptic messages and notions of messianic race leadership were reflected in Cooper's own writings and other work throughout her life.

Echoing Crummell, Cooper's educational ideas incorporated a philosophy of black progress, and she embraced Christianity as a civilizing force. In making her case for black women to be educated, she criticized the repressive way in which Asian and Islamic societies denied formal schooling to women. The result, she argued, was that women were relegated to a "life of ignorance and stagnation," which inevitably led those societies to a state of barbarism. Like Du Bois a decade later, she called for a "talented tenth" among black women to obtain higher education. In doing so, she believed they would become "strong," "brave," "active," "energetic," "well-equipped," and "thoughtful," with the ability to use their "womanly" instincts to "teach [the world] to be pitiful, to love mercy, to succor the weak and care for the lowly."[18] Cooper later became the only female member of the ANA.

Cooper anticipated the classical/vocational education debate between Du Bois and Washington by at least three years and emphasized the role of black women in black advancement. Her treatise on black women and education, *A Voice from the South*, called for the establishment of a black intelligentsia with black women playing an integral role in racial progress. Grounded in Victorian ideals of "genteel womanhood" and the idea that unrestrained masculinity must be moderated by "womanly instincts," Cooper argued forcefully for the education of black women:

> Now I claim that it is the prevalence of the Higher Education among women, the making it a common and everyday affair for women to reason and think and express their thought, the training and stimulus which enable and encourage women to administer to the world the bread it needs as well as the sugar it cries for; in short it is the transmitting the potential forces of her soul into dynamic factors that has given symmetry and completeness to the world's agencies.[19]

While advocating an educational philosophy that praised classical education and supporting a leadership model for black women, Cooper also believed that the education of the masses was critical for black progress. For example, the year before Washington delivered his "Atlanta Compromise" speech, Cooper attended a meeting of educators and leaders at the Second Hampton Negro Conference on May 25, 1894, at which Washington presided. Cooper's view expressed at the conference demonstrated her receptiveness to industrial and vocational education as part of her educational vision:

> I believe in industrial education with all my heart. We can't all be professional people. We must have a back bone to the race . . . The people of this country will inevitably look around for a stable working class. When the time comes for the need to be appreciated and satisfied, the Negro must be ready to satisfy it. There will be no prejudice against the colored man as a worker.[20]

Throughout her life, Cooper often stated that she supported both classical and vocational education. The overarching theme of her educational philosophy, however, was that liberal arts should be a core component of all advanced curricula and training. At M Street High School in Washington, D.C., where Cooper was the principal, she developed a curriculum that reflected both classical and vocational education. However, her success in strengthening the classical component of the curriculum and in sending some of her students to prestigious liberal arts colleges alarmed some white Americans and supporters of Washington. As a result, in 1906 Cooper was dismissed from her position as principal.[21]

Although Cooper and Du Bois never had a sustained relationship, they attended some of the same conferences, including the Pan African Congress in 1900; both were members of the ANA; and the two corresponded, albeit infrequently. Du Bois, however, failed to cite Cooper in his famous essay "The Damnation of Women," in which he quoted Cooper's words, "Only the black woman can say 'when and where I enter, in the quiet, undisputed dignity of my womanhood, without violence and without suing or special patronage, then and there the whole Negro race enters with me.'" Du Bois attributed Cooper's words only to "one of our women."[22] While the essay enthusiastically supported the equality of black women, Du Bois's failure to cite Cooper may have reflected a continuing insensitivity to the role of black women as leaders. Despite this oversight, Du Bois and Cooper's relationship continued. In fact, Cooper later encouraged Du Bois to write a response to Claude Bower's racist book *The Tragic Era* (1929), and Cooper published several essays in *The Crisis* during Du Bois's editorship.[23]

Just as Du Bois influenced Cooper and other women writers, he was equally impressed and influenced by their accomplishments. Cooper and other black women intellectuals offered a woman's perspective on the "Negro problem" that complemented the views of Du Bois, Crummell, and other male leaders.[24]

KELLY MILLER

Howard University professor Kelly Miller was another African American intellectual and educator of the Progressive era, born in Winnsboro, S.C., in 1863. Miller's educational ideas often reflected Victorian and civilizationist views regarding black education. As a member of the American Negro Academy, he believed that African Americans had much to contribute to American society and civilization, but that appropriate education was necessary. At the same time, Miller periodically embraced Washington's ideas of industrial education.

Initially, Miller opposed Washington's advocacy of industrial education, believing that it was not sufficient to elevate the race. Later, he developed educational views that reflected his belief that both industrial and liberal arts education were necessary to address the practical realities of making a living while improving blacks' social status. Black education, he believed, should serve two purposes: (1) "to develop and perfect the human qualities of the individual as a personality," and (2) "to render the African American a willing and competent participant, as an instrumentality in the federation of the world's work."[25]

Miller's position was similar to others who advocated both strategies in their educational agendas. However, Miller sometimes favored Washington's positions to such a degree that Du Bois expressed concern about Miller's ambiguous stance. With regard to a meeting to take place with Washington, Du Bois cautioned Miller: "Want to warn you to be careful and not let Wash[ington] conference degenerate into a 'B.T.W. ratification meeting.'"[26]

Like many males of his era, Kelly Miller believed that women's place was primarily in the home. In his essay, "Surplus Negro Women," Kelly advocated the establishment of domestic schools for blacks that could satisfy whites' demand for domestic help and help the large number of unemployed black women find work. Miller's viewpoint about women sheds light on his view about women and education. He was a product of the early twentieth century and, like Du Bois and even some black women educators, he was pragmatic in encouraging women to become proficient workers, but his views were problematic in terms of his delivery.[27]

Kelly Miller drew on and criticized the social and educational philosophies of both Washington and Du Bois. He was the consummate iconoclast who at various points advocated and disavowed vocational and classical education. In this way, he represented the difficulty that many educators of his time had in adopting an either/or educational philosophy regarding the education of blacks.[28]

NANNIE HELEN BURROUGHS

Nannie Helen Burroughs was another African American educator who proposed educational ideas for black people during the early twentieth century. Born in Orange County, Virginia, in 1879, Burroughs received her education in Washington, D.C. Early in life, she committed herself to teaching and developing an educational agenda that would meet the most immediate needs of a people still suffering from the social, psychological, and economic remnants of slavery.

During the early 1900s, Burroughs advocated a separate education for women, but also proposed education that would prepare black women to lead the race alongside men. Burroughs believed black women needed education to help them become self-sufficient so they could take care of themselves and declare their independence from men. In this way, as with Cooper, Burroughs's ideas might be considered a precursor to black feminism.

In 1900, Burroughs delivered a speech titled "Hindered from Helping" at the National Baptist Convention, in which she extolled her educational philosophy. Burroughs made a strong case that black women could contribute to the race uplift movement through Christian uplift. Her address resulted in the establishment of the Women's Convention Auxiliary of the National Baptist Convention. The Women's Convention (WC) later became a separate organization.[29]

In 1909, the WC opened the National Training School for Women and Girls (NTS). This single-sex school offered practical daily living skills as well as courses in the liberal arts. The NTS motto of "Culture, Character, and Christian Education" advocated strong Christian values and cleanliness. A major purpose of the NTS was to professionalize domestic work and to prepare black women for that work. Like Anna Julia Cooper, Burroughs realized that educated and refined black domestic workers were excellent representatives of the race and believed their intimate contact with whites might help the black race uplift movement.[30]

Burroughs supported aspects of both industrial and classical education. Her emphases on self-determination, cleanliness, and learning practical daily life skills earned her the title of the "female Booker T. Washington." At the same time, she agreed with many of Du Bois's views and supported his campaign against lynching. Like Du Bois, Burroughs also offered scathing critiques of the elite blacks who accommodated white supremacy.[31]

Burroughs's similarities to Du Bois and Washington are reflected in her essay "12 Things the Negro Must Do for Himself," which outlines what African Americans must accomplish to become self-sufficient. Examples include:

1. The Negro Must Learn To Put First Things First. The First Things Are: Education; Development of Character Traits; A Trade and Home Ownership.
2. The Negro Must Stop Expecting God and White Folk To Do For Him What He Can Do For Himself.
3. The Negro Must Keep Himself, His Children And His Home Clean And Make The Surroundings In Which He Lives Comfortable and Attractive.
4. The Negro Must Stop Charging His Failures Up To His "Color" And To White People's Attitude.

Burroughs's educational ideas reflected both practical learning and learning for life. Her "12 Things the Negro Must Do for Himself" and her activities with a diversity of organizations reflect her dual educational agenda.[32]

Nannie Helen Burroughs was a race woman who espoused both vocational and classical education as viable educational strategies for her people. She encouraged black people to develop skills in order to make a living. At the same time, she understood that education in the humanities and vocations helped the race fight for equality.

CONCLUSION

Du Bois and other African American educators of the late nineteenth and early twentieth centuries constructed educational ideas within the social and ideological context of prevailing views of black inferiority, oppressive social conditions, and institutionalized racism that sought to prevent blacks from achieving their full human potential. As a result, their educational ideas focused on black racial uplift, black self-determination, and the struggle to gain equal rights. In espousing their educational ideas, Du Bois and other black educators of his day adopted and adapted the prevailing language and ideology of the times to construct agendas that would elevate black people.

Du Bois and other African American educators, however, did not always agree on an optimal educational plan for blacks. While Booker T. Washington was the most adamant in advocating industrial education as the primary strategy for African American educators, Crummell, Du Bois, Cooper, Miller, and Burroughs all saw value in both types of education, understanding that both liberal and industrial education were necessary and that the emphasis on one or the other must be guided by the circumstances and individuals. Despite their differences, African American educators of the early twentieth century, including Washington, believed that education was a powerful tool that could be used to ameliorate the problems of black people. By the time of Washington's death in 1915, African American educators' ideas tended to coalesce around education that provided blacks with a comprehensive educational curriculum.

Education for Black Advancement

During the early years of the twentieth century, Du Bois focused much of his energy on developing black leadership that would help advance the race. His educational thought of this period was steeped in the views and rhetoric of the time. Influenced by the ideas of the Enlightenment, Du Bois envisioned a racial vanguard, refined and cultured, that would pull the black masses up the ladder of civilization and progress. To accomplish this goal, African Americans would have among themselves "men and [women] of careful training and broad culture, as teachers and teachers of teachers."[1]

LEADERSHIP AND LIBERAL EDUCATION

In his 1903 essay "The Talented Tenth," Du Bois eloquently presented his ideas about the role educated African Americans should play in elevating African-descended peoples. At that time, Du Bois believed:

> The Negro race, like all races, is going to be saved by its exceptional men. The problem of education, then, among Negroes must first of all deal with the Talented Tenth; it is the problem of developing the Best of this race that they may guide the Mass away from the contamination and death of the Worst, in their own and other races.[2]

The talented tenth were educated men and women who, according to Du Bois, were obligated to work for the uplift of the black masses.[3] Women were central figures in Du Bois's notion of the talented tenth, and he pointed to women such as Colonial-era poet Phillis Wheatley as an example. He also saw promise in young women whom he believed would become members of this leadership cadre. In a letter, Du Bois encouraged a young African American girl to prepare herself for leadership of the race:

> I wonder if you will let a stranger say a word to you about yourself? I have heard that you are a young woman of some ability but that you are neglecting your schoolwork because you have become hopeless of trying to do anything in the world. I am very sorry for this. . . . There are in the United States today tens of thousands of colored girls who would be happy beyond measure to have the chance of educating themselves that you are neglecting. If you train yourself as you easily can, there are wonderful chances of usefulness before you: You can join the ranks of 15,000 Negro women teachers, of hundreds of nurses and physicians, of the growing number of clerks and stenographers, and above

all the host of homemakers. Ignorance is a cure for nothing. Get the very best training possible & the doors of opportunity will fly open before you as they are flying before thousands of your fellows.[4]

In a 1902 article addressed to the women of Spelman College, Du Bois praised the contributions of black women but noted that they should take up their responsibilities as childbearers for the race. "I wish, therefore, to impress upon these young women of Spelman, both graduate and under-graduates, the duty of motherhood—the hard work of bringing forth and rearing children, the physical burden of peopling the future earth, as the first and greatest function of their lives."[5] Educated black women, he posited, were the ideal mothers and were best suited to transmit vital knowledge and culture to subsequent generations.[6]

Du Bois, like his white male counterparts and fellow "race men," could not escape the patriarchal mind-set of male-dominated leadership in the uplift movement. Du Bois often left his wife, Nina, for long periods to attend meetings and conferences or to lecture and travel. Throughout their marriage, Nina longed for Du Bois's companionship for herself and their daughter, Yolande. Nina's letters to Du Bois reveal the excruciating loneliness she and Yolande felt. In 1902 Nina wrote, "Yolande comes in your room and looks about, but she seems to know you're gone for when I ask her where you are she looks as indignant as though she thought well I know he's gone away and it's useless to look for him."[7]

Du Bois's relationship with Nina was complicated and reflected his ideas about the education of women. On the one hand, he admired educated and refined women such as Nina. At the same time, as he told the women of Spelman in 1902, he saw it as black women's duty to take care of the home and raise children. Part of the black woman's role was to educate her children in the ways of the world, black and white. Thus, Nina bore the main responsibility of educating Yolande. Because Du Bois's support for black women often was framed within a Victorian and male-centered perspective, philosopher Joy James has described him as profeminist rather than feminist.[8]

In June 1905 Du Bois further operationalized the idea of leadership through the talented tenth and called for a meeting of black men to organize a movement to deal with the pressing issues facing African Americans. Un-like members of the talented tenth involved in the ANA, the Niagara Move-ment was a militant but nonviolent organization of black men whose purpose was to organize for freedom of speech, better education, the abolition of Jim Crow laws, and universal manhood suffrage. In its platform, the group in-cluded education as one of its central concerns and opposed the efforts of Booker T. Washington and others to limit schooling for black children to industrial education.[9]

Similar in many ways to Du Bois's "An Open Letter to the Southern People" (1887) and "Harvard and the South: A Commencement Pact, 1891," the Niagara Movement's "Address to the Country" warned the U.S. government that "Either the United States will destroy ignorance or ignorance will destroy the United States." Members of the group called for schooling that stimulated the mind and developed intelligent leadership. They also vowed to oppose any "proposal to educate black boys and girls simply as servants and underlings, or simply for the use of other people."[10]

Du Bois understood that there were advocates for two approaches to formal schooling for African Americans. One group called for schooling that provided the skills required to make a living. The other group advocated schooling to provide a broader understanding of life, civilization, and culture. However, these need not be competing approaches, Du Bois concluded, because a "synthesis of these two types of education has ever been the dream of teachers and philosophers, but the dream has seldom if ever been wholly realized in actual life."[11]

Du Bois realized, however, that for the black masses to make significant strides, the talented tenth must lead the way and the nation must provide these future leaders with the collegiate-level liberal arts education they would need. He asked, "Can the nation afford, while it is giving the masses of the blacks common-school and industrial training, to train an aristocracy of talent and character to be the apostles of liberal culture among those masses? Without doubt we must answer this question affirmatively."[12] This message harkened back to the messianic vision of race leadership to which he dedicated himself at Fisk, Harvard, and Berlin universities. Clearly, Du Bois's vision of the talented tenth was that of an elite vanguard that he did not hesitate to refer to as an "aristocracy."

During the first two decades of the twentieth century, Du Bois joined other organizations that embodied his idea of the talented tenth. In 1909, he became a member of the Alpha Phi Alpha fraternity through its Epsilon chapter at the University of Michigan. Founded in 1906, Alpha Phi Alpha was founded on the principles of racial uplift and thus complemented the work that Du Bois was already doing. In 1912, Du Bois became a member of the Sigma Pi Phi fraternity (also known as the Boulé) through its Zeta Boulé in New York. Founded in 1904 in Philadelphia, Sigma Pi Phi was also a race uplift organization committed to elevating black life through strong leadership.[13]

While the talented tenth organizations that Du Bois belonged to were male organizations, with the exception of the ANA, he continued to see women as members of the talented tenth. For instance, through his relationship with his daughter, Yolande, we gain further insight into his ideas about education and its role in preparing African American women for leadership. In 1914, Du Bois enrolled Yolande in the Bedales School, a coeducational experimental school in Hampshire, England. Bedales was considered an elite institution even by European standards.

In a letter to Yolande, one can sense the importance Du Bois placed on a liberal education for the talented tenth and the role that she, as a young African American girl, could one day play in the race uplift movement:

> Above all remember, dear, that you have a great opportunity. You are in one of the world's best schools, in one of the world's greatest empires. . . . Read some good, heavy, serious books just for discipline: Take yourself in hand and master yourself. Make yourself do unpleasant things, so as to gain the upper hand of your soul.[14]

Du Bois's vision for Yolande was clear. She was a daughter of the talented tenth and by birth was of the talented tenth. She would be expected to make sacrifices and endure hardships in the race uplift movement. A liberal education in Europe and immersion in European culture would do for Yolande what it did for him—provide her with the intellectual tools to engage in the race uplift movement of her people in the United States.

Du Bois, nonetheless, recognized that not all African Americans would receive a college education and that some would be "needed for providing the world's physical wants." Hampton and Tuskegee Institutes and the Slater Foundation, he noted, had popularized technical and vocation study (i.e., housekeeping, farming, building, and manufacturing). Du Bois believed that vocational education should "have a large and important place in Negro education"; however, black students should also have a broad liberal arts education as part of their curriculum. A broad education would prepare the race for the challenges they faced within the larger society and for the technological changes brought about by the industrial and modern age.[15]

As Du Bois had encouraged African Americans in Boston to embrace liberal education, he encouraged black students to move beyond the narrow "Negro industrial education" designed only for making a living toward an education that developed the whole person:

> If we are to be trained grudgingly and suspiciously; trained not with reference to what we can be, but with sole reference to what somebody wants us to be; if instead of following the methods pointed out by the accumulated wisdom of the world for the development of full human power, we simply are trying to follow the line of least resistance and teach black men only such things and by such methods as are momentarily popular, then my fellow teachers, we are going to fail and fail ignominiously in our attempt to raise the black race to its full humanity and with that failure falls the fairest and fullest dream of a great united humanity.[16]

Contrary to many scholars' binary presentations of Du Bois supporting either classical or vocational education during the early twentieth century, it is important to reiterate that Du Bois saw value in both. Liberal education, he believed, should be a critical component of all curricula. He realized, however, that liberal education would not be the sole form of education for the black masses. Moreover, he believed that liberally educated college students should also receive some training in the vocations.

While Du Bois recognized the necessity of educating the black masses for making a living, he adamantly opposed technical or practical education that was separated from liberal education. According to Du Bois, liberal education provided workers with a sense of culture and an understanding of themselves. During the subsequent decades, Du Bois would become even more precise in presenting an optimal curriculum for blacks.

EDUCATION AND IDENTITY

As early as his student days at Fisk, Du Bois was concerned about the impact that slavery, Jim Crow, and prevailing views of "Negro inferiority" might have on African Americans in general and the talented tenth in particular. Du Bois formally addressed the issue in his essay "Strivings of the Negro People," first published in the *American Monthly* in 1897 and included in a revised version in *The Souls of Black Folk* in 1903. In the essay, he outlined this dilemma in one of the most famous passages in this classic work:

> After the Egyptian and Indian, the Greek and Roman, the Teuton and Mongolian, the Negro is a sort of seventh son, born with a veil, and gifted with second-sight in this American world,—a world which yields him no self-consciousness, but only lets him see himself through the revelation of the other world. It is a peculiar sensation, this double-consciousness, this sense of always looking at one's self through the eyes of others, of measuring one's soul by the tape of a world that looks on in amused contempt and pity. One ever feels his two-ness—an American, a Negro; two souls, two thoughts, two unreconciled strivings; two warring ideals in one dark body, whose dogged strength alone keeps it from being torn asunder.[17]

In the past several decades, scholars have examined and debated the Du Boisian meaning of double-consciousness and provided a variety of interpretations.[18] Although I believe that his concept of double-consciousness has much relevance for other racial groups and ethnicities, I would argue that when Du Bois articulated his idea of double-consciousness in 1897 and 1903, he was responding first and foremost to the social and psychological dilemma of African-descended people living in oppressive majority-white societies such as the United States. As Du Bois saw it, African people could transcend this "twoness" through a "merge[r] of his double self into a better and truer self" by grounding themselves in African and black culture and history.[19]

For Du Bois, education in African and African American history and culture provided African-descended peoples with a vantage point from which to neutralize the notions of black inferiority, hopelessness, and ignorance that were promulgated by white supremacists. Without an African or black frame of reference, Du Bois believed that African Americans would suffer a type of psychic disequilibrium.[20]

Du Bois engaged the idea of double-consciousness well beyond his initial public articulations of the concept in 1897 and 1903. In fact, after 1903 Du Bois further developed this idea and operationalized the reconciliation of double-consciousness in his novels. In *The Quest of the Silver Fleece* (1911), Du Bois engaged the dilemma of double-consciousness and its transcendence in his characters Blessed Alwyn and Zora Cresswell. Bles struggles with double-consciousness as the result of his socialization by whites on the plantation and his subsequent commitment to the formal education provided by white cultural institutions after emancipation. While Bles benefits from his education and obtains the skills to get a government job in Washington, D.C., his alienation from his Southern black roots and culture makes it difficult for him to navigate the white majority life in D.C. He eventually realizes that the only way he can liberate himself from the psychic tensions of his environment is by immersing himself in the black culture of the South.

Throughout most of his novels, Du Bois engaged the concept of double-consciousness and psychic duality to develop ideas for black survival in white-dominated societies. Du Bois believed that the psychic tensions among African Americans were an inevitable result of being black in white America and that these tensions could only be reconciled through immersion in black culture. In his analysis of double-consciousness in Du Bois's novels, James B. Stewart concludes, "General knowledge of the larger society alone, however, is not sufficient to allow an effective accommodation to the pressures of psychic duality. This must be combined with a positive perception of the Black Experience. Du Bois appears to adopt the position that balance in the 'double-consciousness' is more sustainable if an Afro-centric appreciation of racial differences occurs early rather than later in an individual's life."[21]

Du Bois further illuminated his educational views regarding double-consciousness in his children's magazine, the *Brownies' Book*, published from 1920 to 1922 under the auspices of *The Crisis*. In his essay "The True Brownies," published in the October 1919 issue of *The Crisis*, Du Bois laid out the reasons that Black children needed such a magazine:

> . . . in the problem of our children we black folk are surely puzzled. For example, a little girl writes us—we remember her as red-bronze and black-curled, with dancing eyes—"I want to learn more about my race, so I want to be early. . . . I hate the white man just as much as he hates me and probably more!"[22]

Reflecting on the comments of the little girl and the necessity for the *Brownies' Book*, Du Bois asserted, "To educate [children] in human hatred is more disastrous to them than to be hated; to seek to raise them in ignorance of their racial identity and peculiar situation is inadvisable—impossible."[23]

The "peculiar situation" that Du Bois referred to was the dilemma of double-consciousness that black children would confront early in life. For Du Bois, the strategy of the *Brownies' Book* was clear. It would help black children "realize that being 'colored' is a normal and beautiful thing," while also teaching them "delicately a code of honor and action in their relations with white children."[24] Clearly, Du Bois was educating blacks to be proud of themselves while also learning to navigate successfully the white community.[25]

While Du Bois did not articulate the concept of double-consciousness as an educational curriculum or model for blacks, he educated blacks about the existence of double-consciousness and suggested ways to transcend and reconcile it. In the subsequent decades of his life, Du Bois would revisit the concept of psychic duality in his academic writings, popular essays, and novels to suggest that blacks address in education and curricula the dialectical tension of being of African descent and living in America.

CONCLUSION

From 1895 to 1920, Du Bois established himself as the foremost African American intellectual of his day. The main focus of his educational thought during the period was that African Americans were capable of achieving high levels of progress and civilization through appropriate leadership and education. African Americans, Du Bois believed, should be educated to provide leadership to the race. While he supported industrial education as part of a larger curriculum, he believed that liberal education should be the primary education for the most talented blacks and should be a part of the curriculum for the masses. Education should also provide blacks with an intellectual grounding in black history and culture to strengthen black individual and collective identity and to guard against the ravishes that white supremacy could have on the black psyche.

In the decades to come, however, the challenges of African Americans would extend beyond the need for black leadership and positive black identity. On the horizon, intensification of the "Negro problem" would demand a clearer and more concise educational agenda. To respond to the changing needs of his race, Du Bois would have to articulate a more comprehensive plan for African American education.

PART III

Educating the Black Masses in the Age of the "New Negro," 1920–1940

From 1920 to 1940, Du Bois modified his educational thought to offer more pragmatic solutions to the problems facing African Americans, especially racism and discrimination. During this period he presented his educational ideas in a wide variety of publications and forums—including novels, newspapers, conferences and symposiums, and popular magazines—to educate and inform a wide range of people around the world about the contributions and accomplishments of African and African-descended people and the challenges they faced.

Du Bois's educational ideas in the period were developed within the context of the world wars, the New Negro Movement, the Harlem Renaissance, the Great Depression, his greater understanding of Marxism, and the vibrant social and intellectual environment of the Popular Front. In his ideas about education, Du Bois would respond to many of the issues that would move to center stage in the black mass movement of the 1950s and 1960s.

The "New Negro," Economic Cooperation, and the Question of Voluntary Separate Schooling

The interwar years were extremely challenging for all Americans on both the global and domestic fronts. The United States emerged from World War I as a world power and set in motion military and cultural expansion that paved the way for the "American century," a period in which the United States gained military and economic global dominance. Du Bois's life, as historian David Levering Lewis has noted, was at the epicenter of the American century. During the period between 1920 and 1940 a "New Negro" consciousness emerged, leading many African Americans to demand equal rights.

WAR AND BLACKS

The Spanish-American War of 1898 helped to position the United States as a dominant power in the Western hemisphere. Despite Americans' newfound sense of confidence, most wanted to steer clear of European conflicts and adopted an isolationist posture regarding European affairs. On June 28, 1914, however, the world and U.S. foreign affairs would change dramatically when a Bosnian-Serb gunman assassinated Austro-Hungarian Archduke Franz Ferdinand and his wife in Sarajevo, Austria-Hungary. Following the assassinations, Austria-Hungary demanded concessions from the Serbian government. After Serbia refused, Austria-Hungary declared war on Serbia. Serbia's longstanding alliance with Russia and Germany's alliance with Austria-Hungary soon catapulted Europe into war in August 1914. The Central Powers, which consisted primarily of Austria-Hungary and Germany, clashed with the Allied Powers, including Serbia, Russia, Great Britain, and France.[1]

While the United States pledged to remain neutral, its resolve was challenged on May 7, 1915, when a German submarine sank the British ocean liner *Lusitania* near the Irish coast. Over 1,200 passengers perished; 128 of these were Americans. Almost a year later, in March 1916, the Germans sank the French passenger ship *Sussex*. The resulting pressure from the United States forced Germany to agree to the Sussex Pledge, which was a declaration to refrain from sinking passenger ships.[2] Despite the signing of the Sussex Pledge, however, many Americans had begun to fear the inevitability of U.S. involvement in the war. The sinking of the *Lusitania* and *Sussex* galvanized

71

Americans, and public opinion shifted toward U.S. involvement. Americans' consciousness was further raised in 1917 when the Germans reneged on the Sussex Pledge and vowed to sink any ships in the war zone. On April 4, 1917, the United States declared war on Germany.[3]

African Americans would find themselves in a precarious position with the American involvement in the war. Many African Americans questioned whether they should fight for freedom and democracy abroad while they had few democratic rights at home. Nonetheless, believing that their participation in the war might bring about greater democracy and freedom in the United States, most African Americans rallied behind the war effort. After some initial reluctance, Du Bois helped to lead this movement by calling for African Americans to "close ranks" with other Americans and forgo, temporarily, their struggle against racial discrimination in the United States. Support for the war, Du Bois believed, would bring about greater acceptance and hopefully equal treatment in the United States.[4]

By the end of the war in November 1918, approximately 370,000 black men had served in the armed forces and 2.3 million had registered for the draft. Despite making up less than 10 percent of the U.S. population, African Americans comprised almost 13 percent of the draftees. While black soldiers served valiantly in the war, however, white Americans were not ready to provide blacks with equal rights at home.[5]

While the war did not bring about equal rights for African Americans, it did result in their greater determination to improve their social conditions in the country. For instance, black soldiers' exposure to democratic practices in Europe, and the absence of Jim Crow in the European countries in which they were stationed, provided them with an alternate view of what life could be like for black people in America. In addition, the booming war industry in the North provided greater job opportunities for black workers and fueled black migration from rural areas to industrial Southern and Northern cities. In large cities like Detroit, Cleveland, Pittsburgh, and Milwaukee, "the percentage of black men employed in industrial jobs increased from 10 to 20 percent of the black labor force in 1910 to 60 to 70 percent in 1920 and 1930." As a result, increased job opportunities improved the quality of life for many blacks.[6]

THE "NEW NEGRO" CONSCIOUSNESS

New York City's Harlem became the focal point for the larger New Negro literary movement of the 1920s that spread across the United States, the Caribbean, Brazil, and Paris in the Negritude movement. The "Harlem Renaissance," as it was called, was nourished and sustained by artists and intellectuals such as Langston Hughes, Aaron Douglass, Zora Neale Hurston,

Claude McKay, Paul Laurence Dunbar, Charles S. Johnson, Alain Locke, Carter G. Woodson, Marcus Garvey, Du Bois, and many others. This new sense of consciousness ushered in the age of what those involved in the movement called the "New Negro." Alain Locke described the emergence of the New Negro:

> For the younger generation is vibrant with a new psychology; the new spirit is awake in the masses, and under the very eyes of the professional observers is transforming what has been a perennial problem into the progressive phases of contemporary Negro life. . . . the Negro to-day wishes to be known for what he is, even in his faults and shortcomings, and scorns a craven and precarious survival at the price of seeming to be what he is not. He resents being spoken of as a social ward or minor, even by his own, and to being regarded a chronic patient for the sociological clinic, the sick man of American Democracy.[7]

Du Bois was a significant figure in the New Negro literary movement and the Harlem Renaissance and used his renown to promote art and education that portrayed blacks in a positive light. In addition to using *The Crisis* as an outlet to showcase black writing of the period, he started a theatrical ensemble called the Krigwa Players whose purpose was to provide black playwrights an opportunity to feature their work and to present positive images of blacks through theater. Du Bois also tried to influence Hollywood directors to feature blacks in positive roles in film. For instance, in 1926 he wrote famous Hollywood director Cecil B. DeMille requesting that DeMille cast black actors in his films. Clearly, Du Bois understood that the new medium of film was a powerful educational tool.[8]

During the period of New Negro consciousness blacks also developed community resistance strategies to improve their conditions. For instance, they formed all-black labor unions, black churches provided a variety of programs to help newcomers to urban centers, black women formed clubs and organizations to promote the social welfare of blacks, black newspapers actively brought black news to black communities and illuminated the problems of blacks, and black businesses provided financial resources to black communities.[9]

During World War I and in the midst of the New Negro artistic consciousness, a sense of cultural and political nationalism evolved. In 1914, the charismatic Marcus Mosiah Garvey started the Universal Negro Improvement Association (UNIA) in his home country of Jamaica. In 1916, he moved his organization to New York. Often speaking in depressed black urban centers in the North, Garvey preached a message of black racial pride, economic solidarity, and self-determination. He also emphasized the important contribution of blacks to world history and encouraged blacks to be proud of their dark complexion. Garvey's organization and message appealed particularly to African Americans of lower socioeconomic status, and by 1919 he had established over thirty branches of the UNIA.[10]

The rise of Garvey in the 1920s is important for several reasons. With perhaps the exception of Frederick Douglass, never before had a leader had as much mass appeal among blacks. While Du Bois and others espoused messages similar to those of Garvey on issues such as the need to study black history, black self-determination, and racial pride, Garvey's ideas were born and bred within the social and economic contexts of the black proletariat. As such, his message resonated for many blacks in a way that Du Bois's did not. Even Du Bois acknowledged Garvey's brilliance and charisma.

Garvey also placed great value on education as a means of helping to liberate African peoples. As early as his days in Jamaica, he had admired Booker T. Washington and his philosophy of industrial education and had a high regard for Washington's work at Tuskegee. On several occasions, he wrote Washington and the two men established a cordial correspondence. Garvey, however, would not have an opportunity to meet his hero because Washington died a year before Garvey moved the UNIA to the United States.[11]

Garvey and Du Bois also had the similar goals of improving black life and building confidence in black people through education. Moreover, Garvey attempted to establish a relationship with Du Bois in 1916. Like Du Bois, Garvey was disturbed by the apolitical nature of some of the art and literature of the Harlem Renaissance and the images of black sexuality and "fast life" promoted and supported by bohemian whites. Garvey also preached African history to the masses and pointed to the pyramids and the Sphinx as examples of great African accomplishments.[12]

Over the years, however, Garvey and Du Bois would come into verbal conflict as a result of their differing approaches to black racial advancement. Whereas Du Bois advocated a leftist agenda in which the races would work together to improve black life, Garvey advocated a purely black-based agenda free of white influence. Moreover, Garvey's move to the political right and his animus toward socialism placed another wedge between him and Du Bois. The men also differed in their views about the future of Africa and a Pan-African movement. Garvey advocated a black nationalist Pan-Africanism that called for black rule of Africa and the political mobilization of African people throughout the world. Du Bois advocated a pluralistic Pan-Africanism that united African peoples through socialism and the support of other colonized peoples.[13]

Du Bois and Garvey also engaged in a rather embarrassing discourse on skin complexion. Garvey periodically pointed to Du Bois's light complexion as an impediment to Du Bois's ability to help the black race. Du Bois, in turn, called Garvey a "little, fat, black man; ugly, but with intelligent eyes and a big head."[14] While the racial discourse between Du Bois and Garvey was juvenile, it reflected the intraracial schism of the period between blacks of various hues. Such personal attacks were unfortunate because both men had dedicated their lives to the common goal of instilling racial pride in blacks. Du Bois subsequently regretted his race-baiting of Garvey and after Garvey's death established a cordial relationship with Garvey's second wife, Amy Jacques Garvey. In numerous letters between Du Bois and Amy Garvey, she encouraged Du Bois to refrain from using the term "Negro" and to use "African" instead when referring to black people.[15]

After World War I, Du Bois and other African American educators revived their efforts to promote liberal education as the primary education for blacks. At the same time, white industrial philanthropists made a last-ditch effort to reestablish industrial education as the primary form of schooling for blacks by launching endowment campaigns to support industrial programs at liberal institutions such as Fisk. Despite such efforts, the Hampton-Tuskegee model of education was waning. Moreover, education at many industrial schools was poor and in many cases was not at the academic level of many high schools. The generation of students and parents awakened to the New Negro consciousness was not amenable to industrial education, which they viewed as training for subservience to whites.[16]

THE ECONOMIC CONDITIONS OF AFRICAN AMERICANS

African Americans' increasing consciousness and commitment to activism was sorely tested following the stock market crash in October 1929, marking the onset of the Great Depression. Between January 1930 and March 1933, the number of unemployed workers in the United States increased from 3,216,000 to 13,689,000. By November 1934, however, the number had decreased to 10,500,000. While the number of unemployed workers remained high throughout the decade, federal relief programs helped to decrease the number of unemployed Americans even further by the late 1930s.[17]

Yet black workers realized less of that general relief during the Depression. Most were employed in the areas that were hardest hit by the economic downturn—agriculture and domestic service. Black economic conditions were also abysmal because blacks were already unemployed in high numbers before the Depression. By 1929, three out of four black farmers, compared to two out of five white farmers, received 40 percent of their gross income from the production of cotton; as a result, black farmers were more adversely affected by the downturn in the cotton industry in the 1930s.[18] Historian Raymond Wolters points out that in 1930, 56 percent of the black population lived in rural areas and approximately 40 percent of black wage earners worked in agriculture. Of these black farmers, 97 percent resided in the South, and fewer than 20 percent owned their land. Approximately 70 percent were sharecroppers, wage hands, or share tenants; 10 percent held low-level cash tenant jobs.[19]

Black urban industrial workers were not much better off than farm owners and workers. In fact, the downturn in agriculture exacerbated unemployment in urban industrial areas because purchases of farm products were down. The number of black workers in manufacturing, mechanical, and mining work fell from 1,100,100 in 1930 to 738,000 in 1940. Moreover, during the Great Depression the number of unemployed blacks in American cities was 30 to 60 percent higher than that of whites. High unemployment among black industrial workers was the result of several factors. Scarce jobs tended to go to whites and technological advancements in industry often replaced black workers. To make matters worse, employed black workers were often paid less than white workers.[20]

Lack of black business ownership also helped solidify abysmal economic conditions in urban areas. Moreover, many African Americans who owned businesses lost them during the Depression. For instance, during the early 1920s there were more than thirty black-owned banks. From 1899 to 1926 the assets held by black-owned banks increased and reached a peak of $13 million. However, by 1927 resources began to decline, with losses accelerating after the stock market crash in 1929. In 1931, the total resources of black banks had declined to a meager $7 million.[21]

African Americans also suffered in the savings and loan industry. In 1929 there were over eighty African American building, loan, and savings associations, but the number had declined to forty-eight by 1938. According to the U.S. Department of Commerce, between 1929 and 1939 the number of African Americans who owned general stores decreased from 761 to 149. The number of general merchandise groups owned by African Americans decreased from 128 to 83; lumber, building, and hardware groups owned by African Americans decreased from 147 to 41; and black-owned drugstores decreased from 712 to 548.[22]

In every sector of the economy, African Americans bore a substantial and disproportionate amount of the economic hardship of the Great Depression. It became very clear to the NAACP and Du Bois during the early 1930s that blacks would not be able to depend on Roosevelt's New Deal programs or other government subsidies to provide major economic relief. It became clear, therefore, that African Americans needed an economic plan of their own.

BLACK ECONOMIC COOPERATION

Understanding Du Bois's ideas on black economic and social cooperation is essential to fully comprehending the evolution of his views on black education and schooling. Black communities, Du Bois argued, contained viable black working and middle classes that had the potential to amass considerable economic and political strength. In the late 1890s and early 1900s, Du Bois began formulating his ideas about black "economic cooperatives" in which African Americans would unite within "closed economic circles" to develop economic, political, and cultural power within their communities.

Black economic cooperation, Du Bois argued, had cultural roots in Africa and had been established in many parts of the New World. For example, he noted that the Maroons in Jamaica had set up economic and political cooperatives that had lasted many decades. Enslaved Jamaican workers also tilled their fields and shared produce with other members of the black community. In the United States, Du Bois believed, the black church was the foundation of the black cooperative movement. From the black church sprang black banks, organizations, schools, and other churches. The church and other black institutions were already practicing the type of economic cooperation and communalism that benefited African Americans politically and socially.[23]

Working as a researcher for the U.S. Department of Labor, in 1898 Du Bois identified Farmville, Virginia, as a city with a successful black communal system and cooperative economy. Du Bois noted the establishment of black cooperative-type endeavors in Farmville, where African Americans comprised three-fifths of the population. In Farmville, a black businessman owned and controlled the entire brick-making business; there were at least seven black-owned grocery stores; all the barbershops were black-owned; and the only steam laundry business in the county was owned by two black men. These businesses worked collectively to provide social and economic services and resources to the entire black community. In addition, Du Bois noted that black churches were a critical cooperative entity in Farmville that provided not only spiritual sustenance but also social, intellectual, and economic stability for the black community and funeral and other benefits for their congregants.[24]

Black businesses and churches worked in tandem to serve the black community and to raise the social and economic status of the entire black community. As a result, blacks created a self-sufficient community within Farmville. Such interdependence was a key element in Du Bois's developing views on black communal enterprises and cooperatives.[25]

A major reason for the success of black businesses in Farmville was that African Americans had established a communal economic infrastructure in which each person or family in the community contributed to the collective. Farmville, therefore, was not an individualistic enclave in which people prospered without the community prospering. Instead, it established a collective consciousness that facilitated a community-based economy in which the masses of blacks benefited. Du Bois applauded African Americans in Farmville for building a collective economy that supported the entire community. In a statement that reflected the black economic strategy voiced by Booker T. Washington, Du Bois noted, "Instead of the complete economic dependence of blacks upon whites, we see growing a nicely adjusted economic interdependence of the two races, which promises in the way of mutual forbearance and understanding."[26]

Durham, North Carolina, was another city Du Bois identified as representing a successful black economic cooperative and communal economy. Durham in many respects was not that different from other black communities in the South, and most black workers there were employed as laborers, domestics, and janitors. However, a number of African Americans also worked in the building trades industries, while many black women worked as spinners in local mills. Living together within the confines of a segregated community, African Americans in Durham established an insurance company, a bank, fifteen grocery stores, eight barbershops, two drug stores, funeral businesses, and other enterprises.[27]

As oppressive as segregation was, Du Bois believed that African Americans in other communities should emulate African Americans in Durham by taking advantage of the insular and self-sustaining communities created by Jim Crow and use that reality to build a "group economy" and to expand the social and economic opportunities and political leverage of the black Durham community. Du Bois applauded other black communities in places such as Tuscaloosa, Alabama, for developing "nations within nations" as a method of building up their communities and expanding black collective power to circumvent the inequities created by legal segregation. Merging his newfound understanding of capitalism with the realities of a society entrenched in racial and class stratification, Du Bois also envisioned black churches, burial societies, fraternities, and sororities as the elements of a separate black economy of producers and consumers.[28]

In the 1930s, Du Bois had become more adamant than he was in the early 1900s about the need for blacks to establish cooperative endeavors as a means to address their economic plight. Writing in the *Pittsburgh Courier* in 1937, he argued that blacks should organize and pool their resources and become producers and wholesalers, instead of merely consumers. He pointed to the Rochdale Pioneers in England as a model that blacks might emulate. Between 1894 and 1934, the Rochdale Cooperative generated $150,000,000 in business and significantly improved the economic conditions of its participants. Such cooperatives were successful, Du Bois argued, because they provided their members with a critical education in economics. In order for black economic cooperation to work, Du Bois believed black schools would have to provide a sound curriculum in economics, capitalism, and economic cooperation.[29]

During the interwar years, Du Bois also reassessed the utility of industrial education. In 1935, he received a fellowship from the Oberlaender Trust to compare Germany's and Austria's industrial educational programs with industrial education as espoused by Booker T. Washington in the United States. In a letter to Wilbur K. Thomas, secretary-treasurer of the Oberlaender Trust, Du Bois proposed to study why Booker T. Washington's philosophy of industrial education had failed in the American South. He also proposed to bring lessons from Germany to help improve industrial education in the United States.[30]

Upon his initial observations, Du Bois was impressed with Germany's rapid industrialization and industrial efficiency after several years of deindustrialization and economic depression. He was also impressed with the relationship between industry and education in Germany, noting, for instance, that Siemans, a German electronics company, educated its students in industrial processes rather than merely in the mechanical aspects of industry. As a result, Du Bois proclaimed that "What Germany has is not Industrial Education, but Educational Industry."[31]

While Du Bois recognized that big business controlled industrial education, a situation Du Bois had criticized in the past, he attempted to justify Siemans's and other companies' control of education by pointing out that the German state retained control of industry. Du Bois's basic assessment of industrial education in Germany and Austria was that industrial education should educate individuals in advanced processes of industry and not merely train workers to complete specific tasks. German industrial education, he observed, was a broad-based and intellectually stimulating approach to industrial education that was far more effective and efficient than the model advocated by Booker T. Washington and promoted in industrial schools in the United States.[32]

Du Bois's praise of German industrialization and industrial education was based on his advocacy of a country having the ability to survive on its own brawn and natural resources. Germany's anti-Semitism and Hitler's demagoguery, however, stifled Du Bois's support of German industrial education as a model for African Americans. Germany's treatment of the Jews, Du Bois noted, was horrific and too similar to America's historic treatment of blacks.[33]

VOLUNTARY SEPARATE SCHOOLING

Du Bois's advocacy of black economic cooperation was intertwined with his belief that African Americans must control their own schooling. While arguing that the right to vote was a primary objective, he believed that African Americans desired the ballot primarily to protect their property rights and to help them gain control of their schooling. For too long, Du Bois argued, whites had controlled black public schooling, resulting in lower educational standards and inadequate resources. In a speech to the NAACP in 1919, Du Bois argued that discriminatory practices in school funding and white control of black public schools contributed immensely to the inadequate training and preparation of black students. An important objective, therefore, was for African Americans to gain control of their public education and have a voice in choosing the curriculum.[34]

Black control over black schooling was a recurrent theme in Du Bois's writing during the 1920s and 1930s. However, he was initially reluctant to embrace voluntary separate schooling in the way that he embraced black economic cooperatives. For instance, in a 1923 letter to Rev. J. A. Waldron, Du Bois wrote:

> I may say that I believe that a "Jim Crow" school system is the greatest possible menace to democracy and the greatest single hindrance to our advance in the United States. At the same time, we have separate schools in the South and in some cases in the North and these schools have done and are doing excellent work. The teachers in them in most cases have been capable, self-sacrificing persons. I believe in these schools in the sense that without them we could not have gotten our present education. I should be sorry and alarmed to see their number increased and I look forward to the time when all separate institutions based simply upon race will disappear.[35]

In the same year, Du Bois further proclaimed the ability of determined black teachers: "I believe in Negro schoolteachers. I would to God white children as well as colored could have more of them. With proper training they are the finest teachers in the world because they have suffered and endured and nothing human is beneath their sympathy."[36]

During the late 1920s Du Bois continued to respond to the issue of the segregation of black and white citizens. On a Sunday evening in Chicago on March 17, 1929, he debated historian and white supremacist Lothrop Stoddard over the question, "Shall the Negro Be Encouraged to Seek Cultural Equality?" Author of racist tracts such as *The Rising Tide of Color Against White Supremacy* (1920) and *The Revolt Against Civilization* (1922), Stoddard was known for his theories of white supremacy and his xenophobic response to the immigration of people of color to the United States. In responding to questions put forth by the moderator, Du Bois attacked Stoddard's theory of Nordic supremacy as false and inaccurate.[37]

Du Bois, however, most passionately attacked Stoddard's concept of biracialism, which proposed separate societies of blacks and whites. Du Bois saw biracialism as anathema to black equality. For Stoddard, biracialism meant separation of the races from one another in public schools and other contexts because of innate differences. Stoddard noted that there was nothing immoral about biracialism because all schools and accommodations would be of good quality. Du Bois viewed Stoddard's concept of biracialism as merely a tool to preclude black equality, stating:

> You can certainly make the colored school just as good as the white school. But as a matter of fact, everybody knows that this does not happen because the community cannot bear the cost of two good school systems. . . . The Nation ought to be ashamed of this flat failure of "Bi-racialism." It is ashamed of

it. You cannot furnish two separate systems of public schools and have them both decent. Consequently, the Negroes get the worst schools.[38]

Du Bois continued to address the issue in his writings. In his essay "Pechstein and Pecksniff," published in *The Crisis* in 1929, Du Bois critiqued Dr. L. A. Pechstein's "Report at the National Society of College Teachers" given in Cleveland, Ohio, in 1928. Du Bois blasted Pechstein for reporting that black students benefited more from segregated schools than from racially mixed ones.[39] While acknowledging that various groups had successfully educated themselves in ethnically segregated schools, Du Bois argued that the most democratic educational environment would foster the "increase of direct knowledge and sympathetic human relationship among men" and would "multiply understanding, sympathy, and human acquaintanceship." According to Du Bois, Pechstein's plan would create greater segregation in American society and cause black students to "grow up as a Negro and not as an American."[40]

After the publication of his "Pechstein and Pecksniff" essay, however, Du Bois began to openly support separate black schooling as long as the segregation was voluntary and not mandated by law. In the January 1934 issue of *The Crisis*, he openly espoused the advantages of voluntary separate schools:

> [T]here is no objection to schools attended by colored pupils and taught by colored teachers. On the contrary, colored pupils can by our own contention be as fine human beings as any other sort of children, and we certainly know that there are no teachers better than trained colored teachers. But if the existence of such a school is made reason and cause for giving worse housing, poorer facilities, poorer equipment, and poorer teachers, then we do object, and objection is not against the color of pupils' or teachers' skins, but against the discrimination.[41]

Ideally, Du Bois argued, black children should attend integrated schools, but he believed they could also receive a good education in separate black schools that were adequately funded and employed trained and competent teachers. As a result, he objected to fighting for integrated schools that might have insensitive white teachers and inferior resources.

Du Bois's position eventually led to a showdown with the NAACP leadership, especially Executive Secretary Walter White. In April 1934, the NAACP issued one of several statements calling any form of "segregation" an evil that should be "combated to the greatest extent possible." In a July 11, 1934, letter to the NAACP, Du Bois resigned as editor of *The Crisis* and as a member of the NAACP Board of Directors, citing the differences in their views. He stated, "I automatically cease to have any connection whatsoever in any shape or form with the National Association for the Advancement of Colored People."[42]

After resigning from the NAACP, Du Bois again joined the faculty at Atlanta University, where he taught from 1934 to 1944. Within a year of resigning from the NAACP, he more forthrightly expressed his views on separate schooling. In his 1935 essay, "Does the Negro Need Separate Schools?" Du Bois stated that "the Negro needs neither segregated schools nor mixed schools. What he needs is Education."[43] Du Bois acknowledged that racially mixed schools provided "wider contacts" and "greater self-confidence," and that attending such schools "suppresses the inferiority complex" that black children might acquire from being forced to attend segregated schools. However, he reasoned that racially mixed schools seldom addressed the social or academic needs of black children. In such cases, he argued, separate schools were better for black children. The other major points of the essay included:

1. Blacks could not receive a proper education in white schools because of institutionalized white racism.
2. Black children in segregated schools in cities such as Washington, D.C. tended to receive a better education than those who were in integrated schools in the North.
3. Dedicated and competent black teachers in segregated schools were better suited to understanding and teaching black children than racist white teachers in integrated schools.
4. Black schools were better suited to teaching black children about their culture, history, and the realities of being black in a white-dominated society than integrated schools.
5. Adequately funded and equipped black schools were a more pressing and immediate necessity for black children than studying with white children.[44]

"Does the Negro Need Separate Schools?" was a critical essay in Du Bois's evolving educational thought for several reasons. It clearly articulated Du Bois's position on the subject of segregated schooling and reflected a clear congruency between Du Bois's ideas about the strengths of separate black schools and his advocacy of black economic cooperatives. The essay also reflected his belief that entrenched racism and the failure of black and white workers to unite justified separate schools that would educate black children to build strong social, economic, and political institutions for black empowerment.[45]

After the publication of "Does the Negro Need Separate Schools?" Du Bois was compelled to further explain how he could support separate black schools and other institutions while calling for the eventual dismantling of segregation in the larger society. In his 1936 unpublished essay, "Race Segregation with Special Reference to Education," he used Hegelian dialectical arguments to explain his position:

> The Hegelian dialectic . . . has been long discredited as a complete method of explaining the universe, but it [s]till has its practical and intriguing value in clearing up human paradox; and there is a certain higher variety in the fact that one great universally admitted truth continually gives rise to an absolutely contradictory fact; and that after years, the two become reconciled and under-standable in a vast illuminating synthesis.[46]

The "universally admitted truth" that Du Bois referred to was the NAACP's and others' belief that integrated schools were best for all children. The "absolutely contradictory fact" that Du Bois referred to was the reality that most integrated schools in the North had "unsympathetic" white teachers and curricula that were not grounded in the black experience. As a pragmatist and Hegelian idealist, Du Bois believed the solution to this problem might be found in establishing integrated schools with adequate funding, black and white teachers, and high-quality education.

Du Bois expressed the dialectical tensions that African American educators themselves felt regarding their decision to teach in segregated or integrated schools. In his unpublished and incomplete novel *The Wharton School*, Du Bois told the story of a black community grappling with the desegregation of schools in their town. In the novel, William Johnson, a black schoolteacher, struggles with his desire to remain in the black school rather than transfer to the racially mixed school. Johnson's dilemma is further complicated by his love for Emma Lancaster and by the strong views of her father, who despises separate schools and believes they should be eradicated at any cost.[47]

In the end, William Johnson ponders the quality of education and treatment black children might receive from white teachers in racially mixed schools. Such thoughts compel him to feel an even greater obligation to continue his work in separate black schools. Johnson eventually accepts the position of principal in the segregated black school, thereby ruining any future he might have had with Emma.[48] *The Wharton School* reflects Du Bois's views about the difficult decisions African American educators would have to make when public schools became integrated. After integration, he realized, many schools would remain segregated along racial lines. He pondered how African American educators and administrators would respond. Should African American educators fully embrace integrated schooling by taking positions in integrated schools, or should they stay in segregated black schools and try to improve them? *The Wharton School* engages this dialectical educational issue for African American educators and foreshadows questions that would confront African American educators and integrated schooling for decades to come.

While Du Bois supported voluntary separate schools for blacks as an alternative to inadequate mixed schools, it is important to note that he also supported intercultural education, the predecessor to multicultural education. The main proponent of this movement was a white New Jersey high school teacher named Rachel Davis Du Bois, no relation to Du Bois. Rachel Du Bois had had little association with blacks and other nonwhites, but was enlightened by Du Bois's essay "The Dilemma of the Negro," published in the *American Mercury* in October 1924. She would later establish a relationship with Du Bois in her efforts to develop multicultural curricula for American students. In a 1938 letter from Du Bois to U.S. Commissioner of Education J. W. Studebaker, Du Bois willingly accepted Studebaker's invitation to work on a multicultural radio broadcast project with Rachel Du Bois, noting "I shall be glad to act as consultant in the planning of your series of broadcasts 'Immigrants All.' I am glad that you have the cooperation of Mrs. Rachel Davis Du Bois. I think she is one of the best authorities in the United States."[49]

In 1941, Rachel Du Bois founded the Intercultural Education Workshop to assist schools in developing curricular and extracurricular activities that would facilitate understanding of various racial and ethnic groups. By exposing racial groups to one another, Rachel Du Bois believed, racial stereotypes would be challenged and friendships would emerge among people in different racial groups. Du Bois strongly believed in the concepts promoted by Rachel Du Bois and the Intercultural Education Workshop.[50]

Du Bois's educational beliefs and practices during the Atlanta years are also reflected in his philosophy of teaching. While teaching at Atlanta University between 1934 and 1944, Du Bois inspired his students and encouraged them to take up the mantle of leadership necessary to address the problems facing African Americans. Though some students noted his aloofness, most appreciated his intellectual abilities and many praised his academically rigorous courses. Du Bois was known, for instance, to call students by their last name or not to greet them at all. His stylish dress and punctuality also contributed to students' perception that Du Bois was very formal.[51]

Some students also noted that as a teacher Du Bois was a "hard taskmaster" and at times antisocial. Most students, nonetheless, had tremendous admiration and respect for him and the role he was playing in "uplifting the race." In reflecting on his role as a teacher at Atlanta University, Du Bois noted, "I stimulated inquiry and accuracy. I met every question honestly and never dodged an earnest doubt. I read my examination papers carefully and marked them with sedulous care. But I did not know my students as human beings; they were to me apt to be intellects and not souls."[52] Du Bois, therefore, was the consummate teacher who believed his primary responsibility was to help provide students with the heuristic tools necessary for the battle against racism, discrimination, and inequality. As such, with the exception of a very few students, he rarely engaged with his students on a personal level.

CONCLUSION

By the 1920s, Du Bois realized that blacks needed an economic plan to ameliorate their dire economic conditions and to provide a strong economic base to leverage for their civil rights. Black economic cooperation, he believed, was a pragmatic and viable option given the solidification of white racism and the difficult economic times brought on by the Great Depression. To facilitate black economic cooperatives, blacks needed to provide future generations with a sound economic education. Black schools, Du Bois believed, were best situated to provide such education, given their insularity as a result of Jim Crow and his belief that black teachers would be most likely to teach about black economic cooperation.

CHAPTER 6

African American Educators, Emancipatory Education, and Social Reconstruction

In the midst of the New Negro consciousness and the debates regarding the economic plight of African Americans during the Great Depression, black educators spoke directly to the unique problems affecting black people. The educators of this generation vigorously promoted education aimed at building strong and cohesive social, economic, and political institutions. During this period black educators sometimes supported the views put forward by Du Bois, while at other times they clashed with Du Bois publicly and privately. The dialogue between Du Bois and other black educators of the period is important because it reveals serious intellectual debate among black educators and illuminates the further crystallization of educational ideas for black empowerment that would help lay the intellectual foundation for the civil rights movement.

ALAIN LOCKE

One of the most learned intellectuals of the 1920s and 1930s was educator and philosopher Alain Leroy Locke. Born in Philadelphia on September 13, 1886, into a family of educators, Locke would become one of the most respected black intellectuals of the twentieth century. Locke's father and mother were teachers and he excelled in elementary and secondary school, graduating from Central High School in Philadelphia in 1902 and the Philadelphia School of Pedagogy in 1904. In 1907, he received a bachelor's degree in philosophy from Harvard, where he studied with philosopher Josiah Royce and was a classmate of Horace Kallen, who later achieved some renown for his views on cultural pluralism. Locke was the first African American Rhodes Scholar and, like Du Bois, studied at the University of Berlin from 1910 to 1911. He received his Ph.D. in philosophy from Harvard in 1918.[1]

Like Du Bois and other progressives of the day, Locke believed that education could help prepare certain individuals to change society and that the most talented should lead these efforts. Reminiscent of Du Bois, Locke stated, "There is only one kind of aristocracy which is safe in the world at present time—and it is the aristocracy of talent. . . . what was to have been booty for the Superman is now the dower of the 'talented tenth.'"[2] The most educated in society, Locke argued, must assume the superhuman task of bringing about greater democracy and higher levels of morality. The talented tenth, he argued, should also be educated in the "study of . . . the needs of society" and it must be their role to equip society with moral values. Like his fellow progressive educators, Locke accepted the rapid social and technological changes in society and believed that the talented tenth would "deliberately and speedily have to assume the task" of meeting the needs of an ever-evolving society.[3]

Locke's ideas about the dynamic role of education and its connections to the larger society were perhaps best reflected in his work in the field of adult education, which he began to develop as early as 1912. In 1924, Carnegie Foundation president F. P. Keppel appointed Locke as a delegate to the American Adult Education Movement conference, which was sponsored by the Foundation.

Locke's vision of education for children also reflected his belief in the importance of connecting the school and the community. He believed that while the school could help mold children, parents and schools would have to share responsibility for children's education. Schools should expose children to cultural diversity through the new visual media of the day and encourage interaction between various groups.[4]

Locke and Du Bois had a precarious relationship. Both men spoke and thought highly of each other, but they also seemed cautious of each other. During the 1920s, for instance, they respectfully disagreed about the purposes of black art. Du Bois believed that black art should be propagandistic and call attention to the plight of black people, educate blacks about themselves and the world, and serve the black struggle for advancement. Locke believed that such criteria stymied the creativity of New Negro artists and poets and that they should not be limited to producing propagandistic art. Instead, they should be given free reign to express their creativity outside the narrow confines of racial uplift. Despite their differences, the two men collaborated in 1924 to write an essay for *The Crisis* entitled "The Younger Literary Movement," in which both men praised the work of the New Negro artists and writers.[5]

Locke's and Du Bois's relationship experienced additional tensions during the 1930s. The Depression's devastating effects on the black community led Du Bois to advocate separatist economic and educational development. Locke was a cultural pluralist who believed that while ethnic groups such as African Americans should retain their cultural traditions and uniqueness, they should integrate and assimilate into the larger American society. As a result of this position, Locke could not support Du Bois's advocacy of voluntary separation.

Locke's ideas on race and cultural pluralism are espoused in a series of lectures he delivered at Howard University in 1916. Later published as *Race Contacts and Interracial Relations: Lectures on the Theory and Practice of Race*, the essays in the volume attempted to settle the question of "race" by arguing that race was not biologically based, but that differences among groups were a result of social adaptations to environment.[6]

The clash of ideas between Locke and Du Bois began again in 1935 when Locke solicited contributions for a series of educational booklets called the *Bronze Booklets*, sponsored by the Carnegie Corporation. Du Bois accepted Locke's invitation to publish a pamphlet in the series, which Du Bois titled "The Negro and Social Reconstruction." In the essay, Du Bois called for a socialization of the U.S. economy that would allow African Americans to capitalize on an already segregated economy within black communities. In addition, in a section of the essay titled "The Basic American Creed," Du Bois called for racial pride, public equalization of wealth, and the application of socialistic principles to the U.S. economy. After much delay, Locke informed Du Bois that he would not publish Du Bois's essay. It is likely that the Carnegie Corporation viewed the essay as too controversial and adversarial to the New Deal. In addition, the essay was not consistent with Locke's views on education and segregation. Eventually, "The Basic American Creed" appeared in the concluding chapter of Du Bois's second autobiographical work, *Dusk of Dawn*, published in 1940.[7]

While the episode of the *Bronze Booklets* created some tension between Du Bois and Locke, it appears that the two men continued to hold each other in high esteem. In his eulogy for Locke in 1954, Du Bois hailed Locke as a scholar, intellectual, and moral leader. Locke's commitment to his people and to truth, Du Bois argued, was noble and courageous. Du Bois also noted: "His severe logic, his penetrating analysis, his wide reading gave him a world within, sparsely peopled to be sure, but finely furnished and unforgettable in breadth and depth."[8] In Locke, Du Bois perhaps saw his intellectual equal, and his eulogy of Locke reflects the commitment that race men and women must have and the loneliness that often accompanies such commitment.

CARTER G. WOODSON

While Alain Locke was the leading black philosopher and intellectual in the first half of the twentieth century, Carter G. Woodson was the most respected black historian of the period. Woodson was born in New Canton, Virginia, in 1875 to former slaves. Early in his life he developed a love of reading. Woodson would eventually become the second African American to earn a Ph.D. in history at Harvard University, completing his doctoral work in 1912. Woodson taught at the prestigious M Street High School in Washington, D.C. Taking part in the training of the talented tenth, he instructed pupils in history, English, French, and Spanish.

Woodson produced a number of works and engaged in a variety of activities aimed at correcting misinformation about Africans in world history and providing African Americans with an accurate view of their rich histori- cal past. In 1919, he wrote *The Education of the Negro Prior to 1861: A History of the Education of the Colored People of the United States from the Beginning of Slavery to the Civil War*, which chronicled slaves' and free blacks' quest for education and schooling during the antebellum period. Woodson's study constituted a significant contribution to African American educational history.

In 1915, Woodson along with five others founded the Association for the Study of Negro History and Life as a means of organizing historians, teachers, and educators to promote systematically the study of black history. To facilitate the organization's agenda, Woodson established the *Journal of Negro History* (*JNH*) in 1916. The purpose of the *JNH* was to provide a venue for scholars to publish their work in the fields of African and African American history. To increase awareness of the rich history of African peoples, Woodson established Negro History Week in 1926. To reach teachers and nonacademics, he began publishing *The Negro History Bulletin* in 1937. *The Negro History Bulletin* was comprised of articles and curriculum ideas for schoolteachers.

While Du Bois first sought to publish an encyclopedia on African peoples, their history, and their cultures, Woodson also dreamed of publishing such an encyclopedia.[9] Such a work, he believed, would go a long way in estab- lishing black history as a serious field of study and would provide students and teachers with easy access to scholarly information on black history. Woodson proposed:

> The work is projected to treat in at least a general way Negroes and Negroid peoples throughout the world, especially [those] in Africa, Europe, the West Indies, Latin America and the United States. Such peoples dispersed in the Far East and on the distant islands of the seas will also be embraced in this treatment.[10]

However, some tensions developed between Woodson and Du Bois over the encyclopedia. In 1931 the Phelps-Stokes Fund proposed an "Encyclope- dia of the Negro." The Phelps-Stokes Fund did not invite Woodson or Du Bois to participate in the initial meeting. After protests by Tuskegee Univer- sity president Robert Russa Moton and Atlanta University president John Hope, Du Bois and Woodson were invited to join the project. Du Bois de- cided to join the efforts of the Phelps-Stokes Fund, but Woodson demurred. Realizing the importance of having Woodson as a member of such a project, Du Bois appealed to Woodson in 1932: "I do not doubt but what you have made up your mind on this matter and that nothing I can say will change it. . . . A place on that Board was left for you. If you do not accept it, that will leave us so much weaker. I hope you will see your way open to join us."[11]

Despite Du Bois's plea, Woodson did not accept his invitation to work on the *Encyclopedia*. Although a preliminary overview of the encyclopedia was produced by Du Bois and renowned anthropologist Guy B. Johnson, in the end it was not published because the General Education Board (GEB), a philanthropic organization, failed to provide additional funding for the project. During the episode, Woodson also became estranged from his young protégé, historian Rayford Logan, who had previously worked for the Association for the Study of Negro Life and History (ASNLH) but decided to join Du Bois's efforts with the encyclopedia.[12]

Despite their differences, Du Bois had an abiding respect for Woodson and his work. After Woodson's death in 1950, Du Bois discussed Woodson's contributions to African American education and history. He noted that Woodson was an unrelenting and selfless advocate for black history education:

> He did not usually attend meetings of scientists in history; he was not often asked to read papers on such occasions; for the most part so far as the professors in history of this country were concerned he was forgotten and passed over; and yet few men have made so deep an imprint as Carter Woodson on thousands of scholars in historical study and research.[13]

Woodson's advocacy of teaching and researching African American history was implicit in his educational philosophy. His most explicit articulation of his educational philosophy was his seminal work *The Mis-Education of the Negro*, published in 1933. Woodson's treatise laid out what he saw as the major problems and challenges in the education of black people. Among those problems was the failure to embrace historical and social scientific research that addressed their social realities. Too often, Woodson argued, black college curricula relegated the study of black history to the sidelines. As a result, he believed, black students often were not prepared to deal with the racial realities that confronted them.[14]

Woodson argued that African Americans must educate themselves about their own history and equip themselves to make a living. He did not advocate industrial education alone. Instead, he believed that African Americans should move into higher levels of industry and commerce. He noted, for instance, that many black college graduates had failed to embrace the occupations of their parents and to build on that knowledge:

> The Negro boy sent to college by a mechanic seldom dreams of learning mechanical engineering to build upon the foundation his father has laid . . . The Negro girl who goes to college hardly wants to return to her mother if she is a washerwoman, but this girl should come back with sufficient knowledge of physics and chemistry and business administration to use her mother's work as a nucleus for a modern steam laundry.[15]

Woodson, like Du Bois, believed that African Americans needed higher education to prepare them for the complexities of black life in the United States:

> When a Negro has finished his education in our schools, then, he has been equipped to begin the life of an Americanized or Europeanized white man, but before he steps from the threshold of his alma mater he is told by his teachers that he must go back to his own people from whom he has been estranged by a vision of ideals which in his disillusionment he will realize that he cannot attain. . . . While he is a part of the body politic, he is in addition to this a member of a particular race to which he must restrict himself in all matters social. While serving his country he must serve within a special group. While being a good American, he must above all things be a "good Negro"; and to perform this definite function he must learn to stay in a "Negro's place."[16]

Both Du Bois and Woodson criticized not only the curricula at the black colleges, but also the activities and interests of black college students in the 1930s. In their view, black colleges and universities should play a greater role in socializing African American students for the realities of living in a white society.

MARY MCLEOD BETHUNE

Mary McLeod Bethune is one of the most widely known African American educators of the twentieth century. Her social and economic independence, her tenacity as a black woman and race leader during the Jim Crow era, and her activism in education and politics endeared her to many as a great African American educator and a progenitor to the womanist and black feminist movements of subsequent generations. Born in Mayesville, South Carolina, in 1875, Bethune grew up in the heart of the Jim Crow South and experienced firsthand the struggles of her people. At age 10 she attended Trinity Presbyterian Mission School, and at age 12 enrolled in Scotia Seminary in Concord, North Carolina. Recognizing her intellectual gifts, Bethune's family felt they were blessed with an exceptional child.[17]

Bethune began her career in education in 1896 in Augusta, Georgia. As a teacher at Haines Institute, founded by renowned African American educator Lucy Craft Laney, Bethune was soon influenced by Laney's Victorian views of womanhood, her emphasis on hard work, and her commitment to holistic education.[18]

In 1904, Bethune opened her own school, Daytona Educational and Industrial School for Negro Girls in Daytona, Florida. Initially, the school focused on helping its students gain the necessary skills to become economically

self-sufficient. Bethune's goal in establishing the school was to professionalize domestic work to make it an attractive employment option for black
women. During the early 1900s, Bethune was influenced by the educational
views of Booker T. Washington and solicited his help for some of her educational outreach projects.[19] However, Bethune also saw value in teaching the
humanities and eventually included mathematics, science, English, and foreign language in her school's curriculum. In 1923 the school changed its name
to Bethune Cookman College after a merger with Cookman Institute in Jack-
sonville, Florida. The school also became primarily a liberal arts college.[20]

Bethune's social and political activism were major elements in her work
as an educator. In 1924, she was elected president of the National Association of Colored Women (NACW) and served two terms in this position. In
1935, she founded the National Council of Negro Women (NCNW) and from
1934 to 1943, during the presidency of Franklin Roosevelt, she served as
director of the Division of Negro Affairs' National Youth Administration.
In all her social and political activities, Bethune lobbied for policies and programs that benefited blacks and the disadvantaged.[21]

Bethune expressed her educational philosophy through both her educational and organizational work. She often argued that black women as
mothers and teachers played a critical role in nurturing and stabilizing black
families. At the same time, she encouraged scholarship that would counter
negative and inaccurate views of black people. Her strong belief in such
scholarship led her to work closely with the Association for the Study of
Negro Life and History (ASNLH) and to serve as its president from 1936
to 1951.

Addressing the ASNLH membership in 1936, Bethune laid out what she
perceived as her generation's central mission. She stated that men and women
of her generation should secure "knowledge and information that is characterized by its clarity—information that is objective and precise, information
that is relevant in the field of Negro life and history."[22] Bethune understood
the importance of gathering historical facts, but she also emphasized that
blacks must produce philosophers and critics of history and science who
would offer interpretations to counter those propagated by racist scholars.
Encouraging the dissemination of accurate information was a critical facet
of her educational thought.[23]

Bethune also interacted and corresponded with W.E.B. Du Bois. For
instance, they served together as consultants to the NAACP to prepare for
the founding meeting of the United Nations in San Francisco in 1945. While
such a gathering of black intellectuals must have been spectacular, according to Du Bois, he and Bethune accomplished very little and had virtually no
impact on the proceedings at the United Nations meeting. Regarding Bethune,
in a letter to Arthur Spingarn, Du Bois stated rather casually, "Mrs. Bethune
was rather a nuisance, but a harmless one."[24] Du Bois's meaning here is not

entirely clear, but his comment seems to reflect his periodic lack of confidence in women's work in the movement, which nevertheless alternated with his expressions of great confidence in the abilities of black women. Despite his periodic lapses in supporting women's contributions, Du Bois seemed to have had a friendly relationship with Bethune, and the two corresponded occasionally on issues regarding the education of black people.

Mary McLeod Bethune was an African American educator of tremendous social and political influence. As a teacher and intellectual who easily traversed the world of the black masses, academia, and politics, she achieved great influence in a variety of arenas of black life. In this way, Bethune may be considered one of the most influential black educators of the twentieth century, comparable in status to Washington and Du Bois. An African American educator to be reckoned with, Bethune and her work are deserving of much further research to explicate her educational thought.

CHARLES H. THOMPSON

Charles H. Thompson, founder and longtime editor of the *Journal of Negro Education* (*JNE*), and compatriot of Du Bois's in improving black education, has been largely overlooked by scholars of African American history and education. Born in 1896, Thompson was the son of professors who taught at Jackson State College in Mississippi. Thompson served in the military during World War I and graduated from Virginia Union University in 1917. Soon after receiving his master's and doctorate degrees from the University of Chicago, Thompson embarked on a career to improve the educational conditions of African Americans.

One of Thompson's first essays was "The Educational Achievements of Negro Children," published in *The Annals of the American Academy of Political and Social Science* in 1928. Thompson challenged educational research that attributed blacks' lower performance on achievement tests to differences in innate abilities. Such conclusions, Thompson believed, were the result of the faulty premise of black inferiority.[25]

Instead of having inherent impediments, Thompson argued, black students scored lower on academic achievement tests because of the more adverse environments in which they lived. He further argued that:

1. white children from the "same general locality" as blacks were superior in their academic achievements;
2. white children selected from localities inferior to those of blacks often were inferior in their academic achievements;
3. the greatest disparity in academic achievement between white and black children occurred in separate or segregated school systems, with

the greatest disparity in academic achievement between black and white schools;

4. there were more significant differences in academic achievement between children of diverse environmental (socioeconomic) status, regardless of race, than there were between white children and black children.[26]

Thompson concluded that the "inherent mental inferiority" of black students was a myth; that intellectual and scholastic achievement among blacks and whites was a direct function of environment; and that previous interpretations based on the faulty framework of black mental inferiority yielded faulty results and interpretations.[27] Thompson's belief in the relationship between environment and academic achievement would guide most research on mental testing in the decades that followed.

As editor of *JNE*, Thompson used the journal as a means to solicit and present research to counter views of black mental inferiority in academic achievement and to challenge segregated schooling. Perhaps the most significant issue of *JNE* under Thompson's editorship was his 1935 special issue entitled "The Courts and the Negro Separate Schools." In this issue, Du Bois published one of his most important and controversial essays on education. However, it was almost not published. On November 1, 1934, Thompson formally invited Du Bois to contribute an essay to a symposium that would discuss the question: "Should the Negro resort to the courts as a means of remedying any or all of the inequalities of educational opportunity incident to the separate school?"[28] Du Bois responded a few days later, stating that the question of whether African Americans should resort to the courts was moot and that there should be no question as to whether African Americans should use the courts on the matter. However, Du Bois stated that he would be interested in writing an essay discussing "whether given equal educational opportunity separate schools should in any cases be advocated and maintained."[29]

In a letter dated February 11, 1935, Thompson sent Du Bois an outline of the table of contents for the special issue. On February 14, 1935, Du Bois withdrew his contribution from the journal, noting the placement of his proposed essay in a section entitled "Should Negroes Resort to the Courts?" Du Bois believed that such a title was moot given the fact that all essays in the section would reply in the affirmative. He declared:

No matter whether a man believes in segregated schools or not, or believes in segregation in some places and not in others, he must approach the courts to settle the fundamental question as to what the law is. I see, therefore, no room for any contribution that I could make, and I am unwilling to discuss the subject, except, as I have said, by saying "Certainly the Negro should resort to the courts."[30]

Thompson masterfully reengaged the issue with Du Bois in a subsequent letter, asking:

> I wonder whether you will consider making a slightly different type of contribution for this issue? I remember that in a previous letter you pointed out that a real contribution could be made on the question: "Whether given equal educational opportunity separate schools should in any case be advocated and maintained." Specifically, will you consider contributing a chapter under Part I, of the outline which I sent you, on the above question as a part of the definition of the problem of the Negro separate school?[31]

Part I of the revised outline within which Thompson proposed to publish Du Bois's essay was entitled "The Problem of the Negro Separate School." On February 28, 1935, after considering Thompson's new invitation for a submission to the *JNE* special issue, Du Bois agreed to submit his essay "Does the Negro Need Separate Schools?"

Du Bois and Thompson appear to have sustained a cordial relationship for at least twenty years. However, while Thompson greatly admired Du Bois, he also admired Booker T. Washington. Over a period of years, Thompson collected an impressive number of primary source materials on Washington and even began to write a manuscript about him. Thompson's work as an administrator and editor for *JNE*, however, kept him from completing the manuscript.

Given his work as editor for *JNE* for three decades and his research in the field of black education, Thompson has not adequately been recognized as a major African American educator. During his lifetime, however, educators such as Du Bois considered Thompson one of the major players in the field of education and it was in the context of the study of black education that he and Du Bois developed an enduring relationship.

HORACE MANN BOND

One of the youngest of the educators and intellectuals writing in this period was Horace Mann Bond. Born in Nashville, Tennessee, on November 8, 1904, Bond grew up in a middle-class family. His father was a minister and his mother a schoolteacher; both attended Oberlin College. The Bonds had a rich family history of civil rights activism that dated back to the abolitionist era.[32]

While growing up, Bond attended schools in Alabama and Georgia and graduated from Lincoln University in Pennsylvania in 1923. Bond took courses in education at Penn State in 1923 and received his master's degree in educational psychology from the University of Chicago in 1926, studying with renowned psychologist Charles H. Judd. Bond also studied sociology at Chicago under the tutelage of the famous sociologist Robert E. Park. Bond would later earn his Ph.D. in education, specializing in the history of education, from the University of Chicago. His degree program allowed for interdisciplinary work, enabling Bond to integrate his study of psychology and sociology with his primary focus on the history of education.

Soon after completing his Ph.D., Bond put his historical and psychological training to work to challenge educational psychologists who propagated unscientific, race-based views regarding the intellectual abilities of black children. Bond challenged psychologists' and educators' use of IQ tests to support the claim that African Americans were mentally inferior to whites in order to promote segregated schooling. Rather than measuring innate intelligence or ability, Bond argued, the tests had "ceased to be scientific attempts to gain accurate information and have denigrated into funds of propaganda and encouragements of prejudice."[33] Bond found that black students in the North scored higher on IQ tests than both black and white pupils in the South. Bond attributed this result to disparities in the quality of school and home environments. He noted that as a result of their higher socioeconomic status, black students in the North typically had better schools and home situations than many blacks and whites in the South. Bond also attributed higher scores among black students in the North to higher per pupil expenditure in Northern black schools than in Southern white schools.[34]

Bond, like Woodson and Du Bois, stressed the need for curricula that provided black students with the facts about their history. Knowledge of black history, Bond believed, helped instill pride and a sense of accomplishment. Bond noted: "Negro children will be taught to know the history of their people; they will be taught to respect the great men of the race; and they will be taught that the future road to racial greatness lies in constructing a society stratified by economic class, in which the great men will be manufacturers, merchants, industrialists, business men and bankers." However, Bond was also concerned that curricula that focused primarily on black history were too nationalistic. He also cautioned that the curriculum advocated by Woodson was devoid of international events and history.[35]

While Bond developed his educational ideas in the midst of the Progressive education movement, he had less faith than most Progressives in the notion that schools could reform society. He noted:

> Of one thing, at least, we can be sure: that is the unsoundness of relying upon the school as a cure-all for our ills. Far more than in the past, we need to correlate, in our thinking and in our practice, the massed agencies and factors working upon individuals and groups, with a proper recognition of the limitations and possibilities of the school. In the restricted sense of pupil-teacher relations within the classroom, no "school" can be expected to solve the problems of Negro health, economic dependence, or family disorganiza-

tion. . . . the school has never built a new social order; it has been the product and interpreter of the existing system, sustaining and being sustained by
the social complex.[36]

Bond had admired and corresponded with Du Bois since his days as a
graduate student. The two men also had shared interests and were similar in
many ways. Like Du Bois, Bond was a distinguished man who was very serious about his scholarship. Both were members of the Sigma Pi Phi fraternity (also known as the Boule) and along with sociologist E. Franklin Frazier
were part of a scholarly group called the Estate of the Scholar.[37] Bond and
Du Bois were both historians of the African American experience, had similar temperaments, and understood the relationship between scholarship and
activism. For instance, Julian Bond, the son of Horace Mann Bond, noted
that although his father was not actively engaged on the ground with civil
rights activists, he counseled groups such as the Student Nonviolent Coordi-
nating Committee (SNCC) and spoke at their events. In an interview, Julian
Bond noted: "These two men, while different in age and different in experience, for a part of their lives they lived the same life, and found themselves
in the same place at the same time."[38] Bond and Du Bois were kindred spirits who believed that education alone could not reform society. However,
they strongly believed that education could play a pivotal role in improving
the social, economic, and political conditions of black people.

THE SOCIAL RECONSTRUCTIONISTS

Throughout the 1920s, the upheaval of the Depression, and World War II,
American educators became increasingly concerned with the role of education in society. In addition to African American scholars and teachers, men
such as George Counts, Harold Rugg, R. Freeman Butts, and William Heard
Kilpatrick were among the many notable educators who believed that schools
should play a more active role in responding to the social and economic realities of American life. Social reconstructionists, as these Progressive educators were called, believed that American public education was largely
disconnected from the real-world experiences of the people, yet at the same
time reinforced social and class inequities in the larger society. One way to
address the issue was to foster cooperative and collective social and economic
models that would bring about a new social order. While a full-blown examination of social reconstructionist thought is beyond the scope of this study,
a summary of the views of one of its chief proponents helps inform the larger
ideological context within which Du Bois's ideas emerged.
　　One of the most radical of the social reconstructionists was George S.
Counts. After receiving his Ph.D. in education and sociology from the

University of Chicago, Counts emerged on the educational scene with his study *The Selective Character of American Secondary Education* (1922), in which he argued that high schools perpetuated racial, class, and ethnic inequalities. According to Counts, schools needed to be restructured to eliminate such inequalities.[39] This was followed by *The Social Composition* (1927), *School and Society* (1928), and *Secondary Education and Industrialism* (1929), all of which extended his argument that schools reinforced existing social and class hierarchies. Counts's most famous articulation of his educational views and the need for a social reconstruction of education was delivered in a speech before the Progressive Education Association at its twelfth annual meeting in Baltimore, Maryland, in 1929. In "Dare Progressive Education Be Progressive?" Counts criticized the Progressive Education movement and the "liberal-minded upper middle class" for their detachment from the social and economic realities of children. Schools, he believed, should be active and organic entities that engaged the real lives of students and steered them toward democratic participation.[40]

In addition to Counts's belief that schools should address the racial and class realities of the real world, even if that meant allowing room for "indoctrination" of certain principles, he also believed that educators should offer concrete solutions to social and economic problems. He therefore called for a reformulation of American economic policies to facilitate a more carefully coordinated, "planned economy." Such an economy would focus on the needs of communities and groups rather than individuals. Clearly influenced by Marxism and socialist thought, Counts believed that the schools should help pursue his vision of a "coordinated, planned, and socialized economy."[41]

While Counts and Du Bois shared similar ideas regarding the importance of education in improving the lives of children, Du Bois seemed less convinced than Counts of schools' transformative abilities. In 1935, for instance, Du Bois noted: "If we are to expect the school will change the basis of our economic life, rationalize our religion, balance our psychological impulses and in general guide our society, we are wrong. The school is an institution for educating the young."[42] Both men, however, believed that schools and education should become less individualistic and more communalistic and cooperative in an effort to empower the working class. At the same time Counts was advocating an education that facilitated economic cooperation, Du Bois was advocating a similar agenda for African American communities.

While personal contact between Counts and Du Bois was limited, it appears that they supported the same causes. In a letter from well-respected adult educator Soren A. Mathiasen dated January 6, 1931, Mathiasen praised Du Bois's support of a People's College for which Counts and John Dewey served on the board. The People's College concept was modeled after Danish folk schools that focused on adult education. People's Colleges were typically open to all students regardless of prior educational attainment.[43] The classroom setting was usually informal and allowed students to take an active role in deciding what they would learn. Counts's and Du Bois's shared interests are also apparent in a letter from Counts to Du Bois in which Counts requested Du Bois's support for the Progressive Collegiate Association. Progressive and liberal theologian Reinhold Niebuhr was also listed on the letter.[44]

The social reconstructionists' belief that schools should play a more active role in transforming society and bringing about greater democracy resonates with the educational perspectives of Du Bois. Social reconstructionists' advocacy of communal and community education were also consistent with Du Bois's ideas. Nonetheless, ever the dialectician, Du Bois was also cautious about the ability of schools to bring about full democracy, arguing that a transformation of economic and political institutions was equally necessary to change the social order. He was also critical of schooling that did not teach the disciplines, as he believed that a core curriculum in history, mathematics, and literature was essential for providing blacks with an understanding of the world in which they lived.

Du Bois also corresponded with Progressive historians of the era. For instance, in 1932, Merle Curti, a leader in the field of intellectual history who accepted many of the social reconstructionists' views, wrote to Du Bois requesting information to be used in what would become perhaps Curti's most important and best-known book, *The Social Ideas of American Educators*.[45] In his letter to Du Bois in 1932, Curti solicited Du Bois's insights about whether Northern philanthropies such as the Peabody and Slater Funds had denied funding to black schools that emphasized classical education or "cultural values," as Curti referred to them. Curti believed there was a "positive correlation between the migration of northern capital to the South for industrial development and the movement for industrial education."[46]

Curti further noted that the Northern industrialists had sided with the "dominant Southern white class" as a result of their mutual economic interests. Given the economic collusion between the dominant Northern and Southern industrialists over black education, Curti believed there was a "justification of the Marxian claim that education is responsive to the interests of the owning [capitalist] class."[47] Du Bois responded by stating that "the Peabody and the Slater Funds have both given most of their income to institutions which did not emphasize cultural values." Du Bois noted, however, that in recent years funding agencies had reversed their trend and supported liberal higher education for blacks.[48]

Du Bois's interactions with Progressive scholars of the period reveal the level of respect that Du Bois enjoyed within larger American intellectual circles. While his interactions with Dewey, Counts, Curti, and other Progressives were not extensive, their personal correspondence reveals significant agreement on issues of race, class, world affairs, and education.

CONCLUSION

During the Great Depression, WWII, and the postwar years, Du Bois and other African American educators and the social reconstructionists espoused ideals of democracy, equality, and economic cooperation to address the problems of racial and economic inequality. In addition to Locke, Woodson, and Bond, African American educators such as Mary McLeod Bethune, Charles Hamilton Houston, Charles S. Johnson, Benjamin E. Mays, and others helped lay the ideological foundation for the civil rights activism of the 1950s and 1960s.

These educators also believed schools should play a role in reforming the social order. With the exception of Alain Locke, African American educators emphasized the need for the social reconstruction of society. In addressing Charles H. Thompson's concerns about the positive and negative aspects of segregated schooling, Du Bois viewed separate black schools as part of the communal and cooperative social institutions needed for black survival during the Great Depression. While Du Bois and Bond shared white social reconstructionists' views about the need for socialistic approaches to economic development, they questioned the belief that schools alone could transform economic and political structures in the larger society.

Collectively, African American educators of the 1930s and 1940s had moved far beyond the dichotomy of industrial versus vocational education that dominated the previous decades. Their educational ideas reflected broader concerns regarding the economic conditions of blacks and a growing emphasis on education as a major tool for reforming society. The belief that education could play a key role in promoting greater equity and democracy in society helped lay the ideological foundation for the civil rights activism of the 1950s and 1960s.

CHAPTER 7

Education for Social and Economic Cooperation

Drawing from the social and ideological contexts of World Wars I and II, the New Negro movement, and the Great Depression, Du Bois strengthened, developed, and revised his ideas regarding an optimal educational strategy for African Americans. By the second decade of the twentieth century, he understood that white supremacist views were much more deeply ingrained in the fabric of American society than he had previously imagined. Incorporating Marxist economic determinism into his research and analysis, he also realized that white workers and labor unions would not align themselves with black workers, mainly because they were paid public and psychological wages for being white. Poor whites, Du Bois surmised, used whiteness as a psychological mechanism to compensate for and rationalize their relatively close position in the social and economic order to enslaved African Americans and the freedpeople following Emancipation. While these exploited proletarians may have been poor, they could console themselves that at least they were white.[1]

By the late 1920s it had become evident to Du Bois that African Americans needed their own economic plan. Economic self-sufficiency, he reasoned, would provide a power base to obtain the leverage needed to advance their social and political rights. Du Bois therefore encouraged African Americans to take advantage of their segregated communities and use their collective economic strength to improve their social and political situation. "It must be remembered that in the last quarter of a century," Du Bois concluded in 1934, "the advance of the colored people has been mainly in the lines where they themselves working by and for themselves, have accomplished the greatest advance."[2]

COMMUNAL AND COMMUNITY-BASED EDUCATION

During the 1930s, Du Bois believed that separate black schools would facilitate communal and community-based education and that black colleges and universities could lead the way in providing black communities with the educational programs they needed. Black colleges and universities should not ignore the education and experiences of the poor as many white universities had, but should function as part of the black community and address African Americans' real-life experiences. Pointing to the African village as a model, Du Bois argued that black colleges and universities should provide a communal

environment that served as a center of knowledge in which all members of
the community could learn:

> There under the Yorubas and other Sudanese and Bantu tribes, the education
> of the child began almost before it could walk. It went about with mother and
> father in their daily tasks; it learned the art of sowing and reaping and hunt-
> ing; it absorbed the wisdom and folklore of the tribe; it knew the lay of the
> land and river.[3]

Moreover, the communal and community-based education he envisioned
for black colleges and universities could be used to address and solve everyday issues and problems as well as to contemplate larger questions about
the meaning of black life: "The American Negro problem is and must be the
center of the Negro university. . . . It has got to be. You are teaching American Negroes in 1933, and they are the subjects of a caste system in the Republic of the United States of America and their life problem is primarily this
problem of caste."[4]

Segregated black schooling, Du Bois believed, provided black teachers
with an environment in which they could focus on the problems of the black
community. Such an educational environment provided a practical means
of educating African Americans to build strong social, economic, and political institutions.[5] Du Bois asserted that the purpose of black education should
be "action toward economic salvation."[6]

Many problems beset the black community, only some of which could
be addressed by Du Bois's vision of a communal and community-based educational model. According to Du Bois, one significant problem faced by black
children was the lack of parental care. Most black children, he believed, were
not being raised in well-maintained homes and did not receive appropriate
parental care due largely to their parents' low wages. In addition, low wages
prevented most black workers from being able to provide their children with
funds needed to buy their children school materials. Public schools alone could
not deal with these problems. A more communal and community-based
approach to schooling, Du Bois believed, would help to address these issues.[7]

Du Bois's belief that black colleges and universities should become integrated with black communities while providing the masses with access to
education was manifested in the People's College at Atlanta University. Established in 1942 under the direction of AU sociologist Ira De A. Reid, the
People's College was similar to adult education programs offered by the social
settlements of the early twentieth century. AU's People's College offered
adults courses in English expression, art, vocational preparation, and daily
living. There was no cost to attend the People's College, no transcript was
required for entrance, and students received no credit for courses taken. In-
structors were hired from AU and the community.[8]

Du Bois participated in the People's College by serving on its board, teaching courses, and sharing his vast knowledge of black history with citizens of Atlanta. In 1943, for instance, he gave a radio interview, as part of the People's College outreach activities, that presented a lesson on black history. Titled "Africa and World Freedom," the program extolled the importance of Africa and African history. Du Bois pointed out the great accomplishments of African civilizations such as Egypt and Ethiopia and documented Africans' historic quest for freedom. Such lessons reached a larger audience than Du Bois could reach in a classroom or auditorium. Through the radio address and his teaching at the People's College, Du Bois reached the everyday people.[9]

TOWARD A BROADER EDUCATIONAL VISION

Since the early 1900s, Du Bois had advocated a broad educational agenda for blacks that promoted liberal arts education as its core. However, by the 1920s, economic changes caused him to reassess his educational plan. By this time he understood that neither he nor Washington had been completely right or completely wrong in their earlier views of an optimal educational strategy for African Americans. Classical or vocational education alone, he noted, would be too one-dimensional to meet the demands of the cultural, economic, and technological changes occurring during and after WWI. Capital aggregations, expanding capital, worldwide credit cartels, and chain stores were taking hold around the globe. Industrial education had not provided the breadth or depth necessary for educating African Americans about these developments. Classical education, on the other hand, missed the mark by concentrating too heavily in areas that were not reflective of the changing times. What blacks needed, Du Bois maintained, was a broader educational curriculum he had proposed during the early 1900s—education that embraced both classical and vocational education.[10]

Black children, he believed, should receive a solid education that prepared them for "living a life and making a living." Whether their training be classical or vocational, all curricula, Du Bois argued, should encourage students to challenge the status quo:

> Children must be trained in a knowledge of what the world is and what it knows and how it does its daily work. These things cannot be separated; we cannot teach pure knowledge apart from actual facts, or separate truth from the human mind. Above all we must not forget that the object of all education is the child itself and not what it does or makes.[11]

While Du Bois was receptive to integrating advanced forms of vocational and industrial education into his educational philosophy by the 1920s, he remained concerned about schools becoming the "hand-maiden" of big business and industry, emphasizing training solely to increase worker productivity and efficiency. This type of technical education, Du Bois believed, would deprive Negroes of the leadership necessary to address the larger problems of blacks.[12]

While Du Bois contemplated the influence of industry and big business on education, George Streator, a Fisk University student, notified him that the Fisk administration was repressing students' ideas and free speech and compromising Fisk's mission by adopting a philosophy of industrial education that catered to business interests. After investigating the situation, Du Bois discovered Streator's observations to be true and addressed the issue as the commencement speaker at Fisk in 1923. As he had at Wilberforce decades earlier, Du Bois cautioned Fisk against the repression of ideas and free speech. Such a practice, he argued, was antithetical to the purpose of a university whose mission was to possess "Freedom of Spirit," "Self-Knowledge," and "Truth." Fisk University, he told his audience, had stifled free speech and thinking to appease Southern white politicians and businessmen. Fisk had also compromised its curriculum to appease the industrial educational interests of whites.[13]

Speaking seven years later at Howard University in 1930, Du Bois began to lay out his broad-based educational vision for students enrolled in black colleges and for those attending vocational institutions. In a speech titled "Education and Work," Du Bois proposed that only a broad education could meet the varied needs of blacks. While he opposed practical or vocational education as the sole form of education for all blacks, Du Bois believed that some blacks would benefit more from a vocational educational and others would benefit more from a liberal education that prepared them for work in the learned professions.

Du Bois increasingly infused vocational and industrial education into his larger educational philosophy for black people, believing that a broad education for the "mind and hand" was the most suitable for race development and uplift of the black community. It is important to note, however, that the type of vocational and industrial education Du Bois advocated moved beyond merely encouraging students to become "industrious" workers. Du Bois called on an advanced form of vocational and industrial education that included some knowledge of the humanities and prepared students to become highly skilled technicians in industry. Du Bois believed that such an education was essential for a segment of the black population during a period of rapid technological growth.

Further embracing Marxism, Du Bois encouraged students to gain an understanding of how industry works and to inquire into the human and humane meaning of unalienated labor and the history of work under industrial capitalism. With liberal arts education as a component of vocational education, Du Bois believed workers would gain a greater sense of how education and work contributed to class formation.

The broad curriculum that Du Bois called for in the 1920s and 1930s emphasized the learning of basic educational skills. Du Bois believed that a major problem among blacks in higher education was their failure to receive an education in the fundamentals of arithmetic, algebra, and geometry. He also stressed the need for students to learn basic ideas in Western thought. Such knowledge, he believed, was essential for succeeding academically in college. He stated, "Not even the dumbest college professor can spoil the education of the man who as a child has learned to read, write, and cipher."[14]

Du Bois more thoroughly explicated his view of a broad but basic curriculum in his unpublished essay, "Curriculum Revision." In the essay, Du Bois laid out a concise curriculum and pedagogical approach for broadly educating students. According to Du Bois, public schools had "divided the curriculum up into separate, unrelated parts." What children needed, he argued, was a broad and balanced curriculum that would teach the particulars of reading, writing, and arithmetic. Du Bois also criticized the Progressive grade school his daughter attended for failing to properly teach mathematics. He stated, "The learning of the multiplication table cannot be done by inspiration or exhortation. It is a matter of *blunt, hard, exercise of memory, done so repeatedly and for so many years, that it becomes second nature, so that it cannot be forgotten* [emphasis Du Bois's]." While Du Bois supported the Progressive educators' advocacy of democratic education and creativity in the curriculum, his essay reveals that he also supported traditional pedagogical methods of repetition and memorization.[15]

In 1939, Du Bois reiterated the importance of learning the basic elements of mathematics in a letter to his granddaughter, Yolande Du Bois Williams, whom he called "Du Bois." He stated:

> Dear Du Bois:
> This will reach you on or about your birthday and I want to be among the first to congratulate you upon attaining the age of seven full years. You are no longer a baby now and must be feeling quite grown. I hope you will do very careful and earnest work in school. Above all I want you to give great attention and careful thought to your arithmetic. Learn the multiplication tables perfectly and be sure to understand all of the processes of addition, subtraction, multiplication and division. I have lots of men and women in my classes here who cannot do their work well because they do not know arithmetic.[16]

Du Bois (Yolande) remembered that as a young child she often persuaded her grandfather to concede to some of her whimsical desires, such as taking her to children's cafeterias—places he could never imagine dining in. However, she remembers that he was uncompromising when it came to what he expected of her as a learner. She recalled:

As I talked about education with him, I don't ever remember him using words like education or pedagogy. He spoke to me in almost all of these areas in action terms, action verbs . . . learning. I was to figure out. I was to solve. I was to understand, you know, words like this. He would send me to look up a word and never told me how anything was spelled.[17]

Du Bois embraced Progressive educational views about interactive learning, creativity, and the espousal of democratic ideas in the curriculum, but also advocated traditional curricula that promoted canonical knowledge and rote memorization of certain principles. Such a position is not surprising given Du Bois's embrace of dualism and his belief that a broad education incorporating a variety of curricular and pedagogical methods was the most effective way to address the wide range of issues blacks faced during the 1920s and 1930s.

BLACK HISTORY EDUCATION AND COLLECTIVE RACIAL CONSCIOUSNESS

Between 1920 and 1940 Du Bois also maintained his focus on enhancing black racial consciousness and self-identity. Throughout this period, his scholarly work and social activism provided African Americans with greater knowledge about themselves, their culture, and their history. He sought to instill racial pride and to help African Americans reconcile the double-consciousness many experienced in white-dominated society. Du Bois had explored black historical and cultural immersion as a means of addressing double-consciousness from his student days at Fisk. His primary tools for disseminating black history to the masses during the 1920s and 1930s were his published volumes on black history and his articles and editorials in *The Crisis* magazine.

Throughout Du Bois's tenure at *The Crisis*, he also provided his readers with images and stories of blacks' contributions to civilization. He attempted to instill race and cultural pride in blacks by highlighting their contributions to civilization through stories and pictures of black kings, queens, and other royalty on the covers and within the pages of the magazine. A notable example appeared in the March 1911 issue of *The Crisis*, when the magazine portrayed "Black Egyptian Ra-Maat-Neb" on its cover. Other covers included Touissant L'Ouverture, Paul Robeson, and other distinguished black people. Through such stories and pictorials, Du Bois sought to endow blacks with a sense of pride in the race and to provide an accurate view of Black history. Du Bois believed that such positive images were important in building a strong collective black identity.[18]

The magazine carefully presented the variety of complexions and hues among blacks that could be found throughout the diaspora. Such a strategy suggests that Du Bois realized the need to show color and other physical differentiations within the race in an effort to address the interracial tensions of skin color that often led to conflict within black communities. In his "Children's Number," an article and pictorial for children that appeared annually in *The Crisis*, Du Bois presented pictures of black babies and children across the color spectrum.

While using black history to instill racial pride in blacks, however, aspects of double-consciousness nevertheless still played out in the pages and advertisements of *The Crisis* during Du Bois's editorship, revealing color tensions among African Americans. For instance, in the April 1913 issue one ad read, "Don't Strive for Another Complexion: Beautify the One You Have." The advertisement also provides a testimonial from a reader that states, "I have a very dark brown complexion, and the white face powder I use gives me an ashy appearance. Your brown powder is just the thing. I like it." The ad ends by stating, "Whether the complexion is cream, olive, or brown, we have the tint to match it."[19] These types of advertisements were common in *The Crisis* particularly after 1915, and by 1917 the magazine was carrying advertisements for wigs, electric (straightening) combs, face powders, and hair growers. Such advertisements undoubtedly reflected African Americans' struggle with their identity, particularly during a time when the standard of beauty was white. Juxtaposed with the positive images of African Americans' contributions to society, the advertisements in *The Crisis* reflected blacks' struggle to transcend double-consciousness.

Du Bois also attempted to reach the masses by writing several historical works that would appeal to lay audiences. The purpose of these works was to teach African Americans about their own history while countering negative historical perspectives that promoted the idea of African inferiority. In *The Negro* (1915), for instance, the history of African kingdoms such as Ghana, Mali, and Songhay was presented along with descriptions of the various peoples who inhabited sub-Saharan Africa.[20]

Du Bois further developed his Afrocentric approach to education when he published *The Gift of Black Folk* (1924). In this book, he argued that "the Negro is the central thread of American history," and that it was black workers who provided the foundation on which America was built. His later volumes, including *Africa—Its Place in Modern History* (1930), *Black Folk Then and Now* (1939), and *The World and Africa* (1947), all placed African people at the center of U.S. and global history. These are only a few of the works Du Bois wrote during the period that employed an implicit Afrocentric approach to educating the masses, a method he would later define and elucidate.[21]

African American colleges and universities, Du Bois believed, should embody the culmination of efforts to provide communal and community-based, broadly focused, Afrocentric education. He stated that the black university:

seeks from a beginning of the history of the Negro in America and in Africa to interpret all history; from a beginning of social development among Negro slaves and freedmen in America and Negro tribes and kingdoms in Africa, to interpret and understand the social development of all mankind in all ages. It seeks to reach modern science of matter and life from the surroundings and habits and aptitudes of American Negroes and thus lead up to understanding of life and matter in the universe.[22]

Ultimately, Du Bois believed that black colleges and universities should be centers for the study of black people and the black experience and the promoters of an Afrocentric historical vision. His advocacy for an Afrocentric historical agenda for black colleges and universities helped lay the foundation for the emergence of Black Studies during the 1960s.

CONCLUSION

The 1920s and 1930s represent the most complex period in Du Bois's educational thought. During this time, he offered some of his most controversial and innovative ideas on the education of black people and more vigorously focused on the goal of building social, economic, and political power through the black masses as a platform for demanding equal rights. While liberal arts education, the development of race leaders, and the solidification of a healthy racial identity remained at the core of his educational thought, between 1920 and 1940 he also sought to build greater community cohesion between blacks and develop a stronger sense of collective racial consciousness, which he believed would provide great leverage in their quest for equal rights. Such an agenda laid a solid foundation for the modern civil rights revolution that would emerge in the decades to come.

PART IV

The Freedom to Learn: Liberation and Education for the World Community, 1940–1963

The period from the United States' entrance into World War II in 1940 through 1963 brought the United States to the status of a superpower on the world stage. The Cold War tensions between the United States and the Soviet Union, the only other superpower, ushered in a new era of geopolitical conflict that would dictate American foreign policy and influence domestic policy for almost half a century. On the home front, racial tensions further escalated during this period, and many African Americans believed that direct-action tactics and increased social activism would be necessary to obtain first-class citizenship rights.

CHAPTER 8

The Cold War and the Civil Rights Movement

The Cold War and the civil rights movement were perhaps the most defining periods in U.S. history in the twentieth century. Together, they would shape the African American struggle for equality for decades to come. It was also during this period that African Americans would more broadly cast their struggle as part of the larger global struggle against oppression.

THE COMING OF THE COLD WAR

During the reign of Czar Nicholas II (1894–1917), Russia entered World War I. Severe food shortages and breakdowns in transportation, industrial, and agricultural infrastructures contributed to the rise to power of Vladimir I. Lenin's Bolshevik party, Nicholas's abdication of the throne, and the execution of Nicholas and his family in 1917. That year the Bolsheviks signed a separate peace treaty with Germany and the Axis nations and withdrew from the war. Nicholas was replaced with a provisional government, whose failure to deliver on its promises to stabilize the country eventually led to its ouster. The vacuum of power left by the provisional government and the instability of the country provided fertile ground for the charismatic and idealistic Vladimir Lenin to return from exile and unite the proletariat class to undertake a socialist and class revolution known as the Bolshevik Revolution.[1]

Alarmed by events in Russia and by Lenin's rise to power, and fearing the spread of communism to new territories, President Woodrow Wilson dispatched troops to Russia to help the anti-communist Bolshevik resistance. The U.S. government refused to recognize the new Soviet government as a legal entity until 1933.[2]

Between World Wars I and II, tensions between the ideals of American democracy and Soviet communism escalated. In the United States, many politicians and individuals feared that communists were forging a revolution within the United States. This era, called the Red Scare, led to a number of activities and acts to stop the "red menace" of communism in the United States. Another menace, however, was emerging in Europe that would threaten both America and the Soviet Union.[3]

With the outbreak of war in Europe in 1939, the Nazi government's attack on the Soviet Union in 1941, and the U.S. entrance into the war, a fragile alliance between the United States and its allies and the Soviets was forged. The alliance held together through the war, and at a meeting of the

Allied leaders in February 1945 at Yalta, in the Soviet Union, they agreed to divide Germany into occupation zones controlled by the Americans, British, French, and Soviets. They also agreed to the establishment of the United Nations.

Cold War tensions escalated on the domestic front as well. In 1938, Congress established the House Un-American Activities Committee (HUAC) to pursue citizens whom it believed might be disloyal to the United States. After the war, HUAC shifted its pursuit to individuals whom it believed were communists or communist sympathizers. HUAC created an environment of fear and paranoia in which numerous prominent Americans, including actors, producers, and others in the film industry, were charged with being communists or communist sympathizers. In the Cold War hysteria of the postwar years, actor and activist Paul Robeson and Du Bois were two prominent blacks who were targeted by HUAC investigations. During HUAC's reign of terror, many careers were ruined and many activists were blacklisted and prevented from securing employment in their professions. Paul Robeson suffered tremendously from the onslaught by HUAC, as did Du Bois.[4]

THE DECLINE OF PROGRESSIVE EDUCATION
AND THE RISE OF THE COLD WAR

During and after World War II and in the midst of Cold War hysteria, the Progressive education movement struggled to maintain its popularity as Americans focused on using education as a means of addressing "communist infiltration" into American society. Many prominent Americans called for a return to a traditional curriculum that emphasized basic skills and traditional subjects such as history, English, science, reading, and mathematics. Nonetheless, Progressive education reemerged during the postwar years in various forms. A number of vocational educators, for instance, argued that a specialized curriculum was needed to help prepare children for life in the real world. "Life adjustment education," as it was called, emphasized teaching youth skills that would help them function in society.[5]

The Cold War era witnessed intense discussions about the purpose and function of education. Moreover, educational policies and ideas were tempered by U.S. efforts to gain a strategic military and economic advantage over its communist enemies. Du Bois's educational thought was tremendously influenced by the anticommunist environment in the United States. Because he saw the Cold War atmosphere stifling learning and critical thought, Du Bois would press for education that analyzed systems of imperialism, criticized American and European capitalism and imperialism, and demanded solutions to racial and class inequities.[6]

DU BOIS AND THE COMING OF THE MODERN
CIVIL RIGHTS MOVEMENT

While decolonization and independence movements were taking place in Asia, Africa, and South America, African Americans in the United States were engaging in a mass social movement to liberate themselves from nearly a century of institutionalized discrimination. While it is difficult to pinpoint a single event that ignited black social protest activities during the postwar period, African American educators and activists had laid the intellectual foundation for the movement decades earlier. The drumbeat for equality in the civil rights movement became louder during the 1950s, and the hypocrisy of fighting a war abroad for democracy during the 1940s, while African Americans were denied civil rights at home, became a major concern for U.S. government officials.[7]

During the 1940s and 1950s, Du Bois more adamantly preached that black youth needed to aggressively attack Jim Crow segregation in the United States and reconceptualize American racism in a broader international context. On October 20, 1946, he delivered an address before the Southern Youth Legislature, a conference for black youth, which was held in Columbia, South Carolina and sponsored by the Southern Negro Youth Congress (SNYC). The SNYC was an organization dedicated to improving the lives of impoverished blacks and whites in the South. In his speech, Du Bois urged black youth to obtain an education and to fight a "great crusade" for equality in the South. The South, Du Bois maintained, was ripe for a mass social movement that would address racism and poverty among all peoples. "This is the firing line not simply for the emancipation of the American Negro, but for the emancipation of the colored races; and for the emancipation of the white slaves of the modern capitalist monopoly."[8]

Du Bois also suggested a plan of action. Recognizing the influence and power of the media, Du Bois encouraged youth to expose the racial and class oppression in the South through the press and use it to publicize their activities. "You have got to make the people of the United States and of the world know what is going on in the South. You have got to use every field of publicity to force the truth into their ears, and before their eyes."[9]

Prophetic in pointing out the challenges such protests would create, Du Bois warned of the massive resistance the student activists would face by launching an aggressive attack on Jim Crow: "You may be condemned for flamboyant methods; for waving your grievances under the noses and in the faces of men, that makes no difference; it is your duty to do more of this sort of thing than you have done in the past. As a result of this you are going to be called upon for sacrifice."[10]

Du Bois saw in these young activists a new generation of leadership. He believed they would have to make greater sacrifices than previous generations and would have to intensify their commitment to exposing and eradicating white racism.

Among the youth who were present at the conference was a young man from Lane College in Jackson, Tennessee, named Donald L. Hollowell. Hollowell remembered the dynamic enthusiasm and progressive activism at the conference and recalled that the presence of Du Bois, singer and civil rights activist Paul Robeson, famed educator and president of Morehouse Benjamin E. Mays, and leftist novelist and famous author of *Spartacus* Howard Fast had a significant impact on him:

> I changed my direction and instead of being a dentist that I was going to be, I decided that I was going to be a lawyer. Because what I had heard there, what I talked with students about as we would sit around in bull sessions, would be the kinds of statements that were made by Dr. Du Bois and Robeson and Fast, and others who were there.[11]

Hollowell would later become a prominent civil rights attorney representing Martin Luther King Jr., Julian Bond, Hamilton Holmes, Charlayne Hunter, and many others as they challenged Southern Jim Crow practices. Hollowell represented the new generation of leadership and embodied the type of scholar-activist whom Du Bois had envisioned taking the reins of the civil rights movement. Du Bois's influence on youth such as Hollowell and many others of his generation cannot be overstated. Historian Gerald Horne concluded that Du Bois's ideas would form the foundation for the civil rights advocacy of the postwar generation.[12]

In the midst of the emerging youth revolution, tragedy struck Du Bois: in 1950 his beloved wife, Nina, died. After fifty-five years of marriage, Du Bois had lost a companion who supported him unconditionally. However, Du Bois later confessed, "I was not, on the whole, what one would describe as a good husband." Du Bois understood that his work had always come before his family obligations, and acknowledged the loneliness that his wife must have felt while he was away from her. While Du Bois was an avid supporter of women's rights and education, his personal relationship with Nina has brought his support for black women under question.[13]

In 1951, at age eighty-three, Du Bois married fifty-four-year-old writer and activist Shirley Graham. Highly educated and cosmopolitan, Shirley Graham was in many ways the opposite of Nina in style and temperament. A known mover and shaker in black political circles, Graham traveled with Du Bois around the world and was intimately engaged in his academic and political activities. Her sympathies toward and connections to the Communist Party also likely further encouraged Du Bois's radicalization during the final decades of his life.[14]

As the witch hunt for communists and radical progressives escalated during the post–World War II era, Du Bois became increasingly radical in his calls for the overthrow of imperialism and his denunciation of American foreign policy. He joined several international organizations that reflected his views, such as the Council on African Affairs and the Peace Information Center. While both organizations were committed to addressing issues of colonialism and peace, they were placed on the U.S. attorney general's list of "subversive" organizations.[15]

Du Bois's membership and positions in these organizations and others led to ongoing surveillance by the Federal Bureau of Investigation (FBI) and the U.S. Justice Department. The government was especially incensed by Du Bois's participation in the Peace Information Center and its efforts to have U.S. and other citizens sign the Stockholm Peace Appeal, which called for the abolition of the atomic bomb and for nuclear disarmament. The U.S. government viewed the appeal as propaganda connected to and sponsored by the Soviet Union.[16]

Du Bois, however, denied any direct influence from the Kremlin on the Center and ignored all attempts by the U.S. government to make him register as a "foreign agent." As a result, he was indicted and tried for being a foreign agent, but was eventually acquitted. The incident made him bitter toward the United States, especially toward the talented tenth, who failed to come to his aid and even distanced themselves from him. Although he was acquitted, Du Bois found himself alienated from many in the emerging civil rights movement in the late 1950s, a movement for which he had paved the way.[17]

FROM *BROWN V. BOARD* AND KING TO GHANA

The years 1954–1955 were pivotal in the civil rights movement. The 1954 Supreme Court decision declaring segregation in public education unconstitutional and the Montgomery bus boycott of 1955–1956 established the civil rights movement as a prescient entity in the consciousness of most Americans. Du Bois had helped lay the foundation for the movement, anticipated its arrival, and urged blacks and progressives to launch a mass social movement.

However, when the Supreme Court delivered its *Brown* decision and the Montgomery boycott activism began, Du Bois was only cautiously optimistic. Two weeks after the *Brown* decision, he observed, "We American Negroes therefore are freer, but we are not yet free. Many will say complete freedom and equality between black and white Americans is impossible. Perhaps; but I have seen the impossible happen. It did happen on May 17, 1954."[18] Du Bois later questioned the vagueness of the phrase "all deliberate speed," which was the Court's stated guideline for desegregating public schools, and lamented the reluctance of the Eisenhower administration to participate in school desegregation campaigns. Time and time again, he argued, the government acquiesced to "gentlemen's agreements" that disenfranchised black voters. The vagueness of "all deliberate speed," he cautioned, might be yet another failed promise to black Southerners.[19]

One month after the *Brown* decision, Du Bois expressed further concerns about *Brown's* impact on black children. Du Bois had long espoused the idea that knowledge of black history was essential to the healthy formation of black individual and collective identity. Du Bois had pondered whether black children would receive education in their history and culture under integration. While acknowledging that integrated schooling was ideal for all children, he pointed out that Jews and African Americans had a unique history and culture grounded in their legacy of struggle. As such, Jewish people and African Americans were justified in contextualizing their education within their history so that subsequent generations would never forget their struggle. As an African American educator, he argued that black history might not be taught in mixed schools. In such cases, Du Bois argued that African American parents and community organizations should teach black history to black children.[20]

Du Bois also questioned, as he had in the 1930s, the impact of desegregated schooling on black children and communities. While he fully supported the dismantling of legal segregation, he pondered the future of black children that would place them outside their cultural frames of reference. In a speech before a group of teachers at Johnson C. Smith University in Charlotte, North Carolina, in 1960, Du Bois discussed the dilemma:

> If and when they are admitted to these schools certain things will inevitably follow. Negro teachers will become rarer and in many cases will disappear. Negro children will be instructed in the public schools and taught under unpleasant if not discouraging circumstances. Even more largely than today they will fall out of school, cease to enter high school, and fewer and fewer will go to college.[21]

If school desegregation occurred without appropriate planning, Du Bois believed that the education of black children would deteriorate. Without black teachers, Du Bois believed, black history would be diminished or eliminated in the curriculum.

Du Bois was also aware of the developments in Montgomery in 1955 and the momentum that was developing around the young minister and philosopher Martin Luther King Jr. Shortly after the boycott, Du Bois wrote King a letter commending him on his work. King responded by thanking Du Bois.[22] Du Bois, however, would make his views on King known in an article in the *National Guardian* in 1957. In his brief essay "Will the Great Gandhi Live Again?," Du Bois questioned the feasibility of using nonviolence and advocating peace among white racists who were violent and irrational.[23]

Using Hegelian logic, Du Bois expressed skepticism about whether the tensions created by nonviolent activism could ever reach reconciliation and synthesis with unrestrained violence. However, he did not rule out this possibility. Education, he argued, might help provide some reconciliation. He argued that the "remedy for this abnormal situation would be education for all children, and education of all together, so as to let them grow up knowing each other as human."[24] If such education was given to all children, then Dr. King's Gandhian revolution might work. Writing a few months later in the *Gandhi Marg* (Bombay), Du Bois seemed more optimistic about King's tactics, noting that the enforcement of recent Supreme Court cases might only come through the "leadership of another Gandhi."[25]

With the exception of a few form letters from King to Du Bois soliciting support for his civil rights efforts, there is scant correspondence between the two men and no evidence of a relationship between them. Du Bois's references to King, however, reveal that Du Bois may have admired King, particularly the young minister's pragmatism in putting philosophical ideas to work. Perhaps Du Bois saw King as his own successor in the struggle for peace and democracy, or as a manifestation of his original conceptions of the talented tenth.

One can only speculate what these two men might have planned in a discussion about how to relieve the plight of black America. Du Bois, in any event, seemed to admire King's intellectualism and activism:

Here is a young colored man of good family and careful upbringing under the tutelage of a successful Negro minister. He receives his training at a Southern Negro college, in a New Jersey Theological School, and Boston University. . . . he broadens his theological training by wide contact with human beings black and white, and evolves a personal philosophy, which gradually follows the ideals of Gandhi, non-violence.[26]

During his last years Du Bois had serious doubts about Americans' moral fiber and remained cautious about the practicality of nonviolence. He also feared that violence might silence the voice of Dr. King. "It is possible any day that their leader will be killed by hoodlums perfectly well known to the white police and city administration, egged on by white councils of war, while most white people of the city say nothing and do nothing."[27] Du Bois's words were prophetic.

While Du Bois promoted and supported civil rights activism during the 1950s and early 1960s, he was also cautious about the objectives of the civil rights movement. During dinner conversations with his friend psychologist Edmund Gordon, Du Bois expressed his concerns about the civil rights movement. Gordon recalls that "As much as [Du Bois] supported the civil rights movement, he was fearful that . . . the growing economic disparities of the society were being neglected and we were almost being encouraged to focus on the race issue as a decoy."[28] Du Bois had long seen the economic plight of the poor as the most pressing issue for African Americans and believed that class would be the problem of the twenty-first century. While Du Bois was pleased that the civil rights movement was occurring, he had moved to the intellectual left by the late 1950s and was focused more on global economic oppression and colonialism than on racism within the United States.

Despite Du Bois's concerns about the movement, he had contact with various civil rights activists and youth movements in the 1960s. In April 1960, Howard Zinn, a white professor who served as chair of the Department of History and Social Science at Spelman and an advisor to SNCC, asked Du Bois to come to Spelman and the Atlanta University Center to speak. Considered a radical progressive himself, Zinn recognized the symbolic significance of Du Bois speaking before SNCC and AU students and the influence he might have on them. In a letter to Du Bois, Zinn wrote, "For everyone in the University System here it would be a historic experience. People seem to be beginning to sense that the times call for bold thinking, so this is a particularly good time for you to speak to us."[29]

The speech, however, would not come to fruition. Zinn notes that Du Bois likely felt hesitant because of Du Bois's negative experiences at AU under the presidency of Rufus Clement. Du Bois, Zinn notes, may also have been concerned about how his age limited his mobility. Whatever the reason, one can only speculate as to the influence a speech by Du Bois would have had on the youth of AU and SNCC members who would go on to launch a sit-in movement in Atlanta in August of that same year.[30]

Du Bois also commended the students involved in the civil rights movement for resisting Jim Crow. In an interview with folk music enthusiast and Folkways Record founder Moses Asch, Du Bois noted that he had feared youth would give up the struggle for equality as a result of Wisconsin senator Joseph McCarthy's harassment of individuals and groups that questioned American domestic or foreign policy. Du Bois noted, however, that students had become fed up with the "Negro problem" and the courts' failure to adequately address racial discrimination. In his day, black leaders had fought to stop the lynchings of black citizens. The new youth movement, he pointed out, was not only dismantling Jim Crow, they were taking part in a global movement for democracy and equality for all peoples. Speaking of the new social movement and youth activism, he noted "that [civil rights activism] gives me real satisfaction. Evidently, the older people like myself are not needed just now, there are younger people who are going on and doing their own thinking and I congratulate them upon it. They don't need any advice from me. Perhaps I need some from them."[31]

The Cold War environment was harsh on Du Bois. As evidenced by the FBI's unrelenting surveillance on Du Bois, he was obviously considered a security threat to the United States. Du Bois even elicited the detestation of some American citizens who thought his speeches and activities were anti-American. In a letter to FBI chief J. Edgar Hoover, one person referenced a speech Du Bois gave in Harlem in 1950 that was covered by the *New York Times*. The letter writer noted that the speech seemed to be "subversive to a degree that makes my blood boil. . . . how I wish we could squelch some of the people talking like this Du Bois."[32] The Bureau's surveillance of Du Bois was relentless and helped lay the foundation for its COINTELPRO (Counter Intelligence Programs) against black activities in the late 1960s, which—among other goals—sought to eliminate the rise of a "messiah" who could galvanize the black masses.

Through the final years of his life, Du Bois also engaged the issue of black education within the context of civil rights activities. In a 1957 petition to the U.S. Supreme Court, Du Bois encouraged the courts to reaffirm the principles in the Declaration of Independence, the Constitution, and the Bill of Rights by upholding *Brown*. He also encouraged the courts to refuse public funds for private schools. Four years later, he wrote a petition to President John F. Kennedy encouraging Kennedy to use his executive order to suspend funds to colleges and universities that segregated and discriminated based on race, creed, or culture.[33]

By 1961, Du Bois had lost confidence that the United States would ever grant full citizenship rights to African Americans. As a result, he accepted Kwame Nkrumah's invitation to move to Ghana to begin work on his life-long dream of publishing an *Encyclopedia Africana*. In a letter to his friend Grace Goens, he expressed his sentiments: "I just cannot take any more of this country's treatment. We leave for Ghana October 5th and I set no date for return. . . . Chin up, and fight on, but realize that American Negroes can't win."[34]

SEPTIMA CLARK: ECHOES OF A DU BOISIAN PEDAGOGY

Despite Du Bois's skepticism about the goals of the civil rights movement and America's ability to reform itself, his educational thought influenced educators of the civil rights movement and helped to provide civil rights activists with a framework within which to promote and teach blacks about democratic principles and strategies for gaining their freedom.[35]

No educator better represented the civil rights legacy of Du Bois's educational thought than his former student Septima Poinsette Clark. Born in Charleston, South Carolina, in 1898, Clark believed in the power of education and early in life knew she would become an educator. She noted, "From my early childhood I wanted to be a schoolteacher. That desire grew and strengthened through the years. And I believe it was born and nourished out of my heredity and my environment."[36]

Clark received her teacher training at Avery Normal Institute in Charleston. With its fine library and its variety of coursework, Avery provided an exciting intellectual environment for Clark. She received further training at Benedict College and Hampton University and studied under Du Bois at Atlanta University in 1937.

Clark's educational philosophy, however, first emerged while teaching on John's Island in South Carolina in 1916. John's Island was an impoverished community that seemed frozen in the time of the antebellum South. Most of its residents were illiterate and poor. John's Island was a laboratory of sorts for Clark, providing her with an opportunity to use education as a means to liberate the minds of people cut off from the modern world. She taught on John's Island for years, bringing literacy and basic skills to its people.[37]

Clark took a course on interpersonal relationships taught by Du Bois at Atlanta University in 1937. While in the course, she was exposed to Du Bois's educational ideas as well as his analyses of racism and classism in the United States. In an interview with Eliot Wigginton, Clark reflected on a conversation she had with Du Bois about a fellow student in Du Bois's class who was denied a seat on the front seat of a trolley car because she and her son were black. Clark stated that Du Bois instructed the woman, "Young lady, you tell your boy that he is as good as anybody sitting on that front seat and that when he grows up, he must register to vote so that he can get to sit on that front seat."[38] Du Bois's message to the young woman influenced Clark and reinforced her mission to provide blacks and the poor with emancipatory education to help them liberate themselves.

Clark would have an opportunity to further develop her emancipatory educational philosophy when she joined the staff of Highlander Folk School in Monteagle, Tennessee, in 1955. Established by white Tennessee native Myles Horton, Highlander was committed to educating poor and oppressed people by providing basic educational skills. The teachers also attempted to educate their students about the social conditions in which they lived and to help find ways to change them. Well versed in the ideas of John Dewey, Horton envisioned and instituted a pragmatic approach to education that did not separate goals from methods. Horton believed that education should be useful, but that it should also enlighten students and prompt them to question canonical views and practices in society by teaching students the tests of "critical thinking."[39]

In 1955 and 1956, Clark directed educational workshops on poverty, racism, and democracy at Highlander. Horton was so impressed with Clark that he appointed her director of education at Highlander in 1957. As director, Clark played an essential role in establishing the "citizenship schools" that focused on educating adults. The main purpose of the citizenship school program was to eradicate illiteracy among the poor and to provide students with information that would help them realize their full citizenship rights. The curriculum in citizenship schools was pragmatic rather than abstract and addressed the social problems of the community.[40]

Clark's work in freedom and citizenship schools reflected Du Bois's notions of communal, community-based, and democratic education not only for children, but for adults as well. In addition, the freedom and citizenship schools' focus on providing literacy and leadership training for adults reflected Du Bois's vision of the People's College, which Clark was likely exposed to as Du Bois's student at AU.

Like Du Bois, Clark believed that students should acquire liberal knowledge about democracy and basic skills necessary to navigate society. She believed in a curriculum that encouraged students to raise questions that challenged racial and class discrimination, to engage and debate the racial and class problems of the day, and to develop and implement solutions to those problems.

CONCLUSION

The Cold War and civil rights era was a complex period for Du Bois. He was embraced as a world citizen in many countries, but shunned by his government and by members of the civil rights establishment in the United States. His political activities on the international stage, his participation in peace conferences, and his critiques of U.S. colonialism and capitalism drew charges of subversion from U.S. officials who sought to limit the influence of Du Bois and his ideas on youth. Moreover, the emergence of the United States as a superpower after World War II provided the background for attacks on American apartheid as U.S. officials sought to influence leaders of newly independent "colored" nations.

The launching of civil rights protests was greeted with skepticism by Du Bois, who adopted a wait-and-see posture. His frustration with the gradual pace of change in the United States led him to accept Nkrumah's offer to return to the motherland to continue his scholarly work, which seemed little appreciated in the land of his birth. However, Du Bois would live to see the day when the foundations of Jim Crow America began to crumble and his longstanding dream of black liberation would begin to become a reality.

CHAPTER 9

Education for Liberation

The Cold War and civil rights movement tremendously influenced Du Bois's call for education to liberate the minds of all peoples. The Cold War forced him to contemplate the government's attempt to censor education and withhold important information that students needed to make sound decisions. As a result, during the final two decades of his life, Du Bois advocated education and schooling that challenged American imperialism, capitalism, and what he saw as propaganda that promoted the economic interests of the bourgeois elite.[1]

FREEDOM TO LEARN, CRITICAL THINKING, AND BASIC SKILLS

Du Bois's educational ideas regarding curricula and the role of education in the last two decades of his life were consistent with many of his earlier views. During this period he explicitly discussed the role of education in liberating all people and argued that education should encourage individuals to critically examine social and political systems and institutions. He also held steadfastly to his belief that schools needed to provide a solid academic foundation in reading, writing, and mathematics to provide students with basic skills for thinking critically and living successfully in society.

During these years, Du Bois continued to promote the acquisition of basic skills as an essential component of his educational thought. He believed that schooling in the United States had deteriorated since his days as a student in the public schools of Massachusetts and that the current quality of schooling was abysmal. Much of the problem, he argued, stemmed from inadequate preparation in the basic skills such as writing, reading, and arithmetic. According to Du Bois, elementary and secondary schools did not have adequate resources or enough trained teachers to teach basic skills. Many teachers, for instance, had not been trained in disciplines and subject areas, but rather in methods of teaching. He argued that the lack of quality teachers was further exacerbated by low teacher salaries, which prevented many talented individuals from entering the profession.[2] According to Du Bois, most colleges and universities also failed to offer a rigorous academic curriculum. Academic subjects such as philosophy, history, sociology, economics, and psychology were either dropped from the curriculum entirely or were taught uncritically and filled with so much misinformation that they were almost useless to students.[3]

Du Bois also noted that after his daughter Yolande became a teacher, he had another opportunity to observe the public school system through her experiences teaching at Dunbar High School. Du Bois observed:

> My daughter today daily has five classes of poorly trained high school students, many of whom cannot read or write, and others who are untrained in the elementary decencies of conduct; she is expected to fill reams of paper weekly on the progress of this education in the Dunbar High School of Baltimore. It is at times a sickening task.[4]

Du Bois observed that teachers in the public schools often had to deal with the social problems of their students and were burdened with spending valuable academic time on instruction in hygiene, good conduct, and other issues that should have been the responsibility of parents. Instead of instructing students in areas that were better left to parents, Du Bois argued, public elementary schools should focus on teaching the basic skills of reading and writing. Du Bois believed that students should not be promoted to higher grade levels until they mastered basic skills. In addition, he believed that secondary schools should broaden students' vision of the world through the teaching of literature, science, world history, and geography.

In his unpublished essay "The Problems of the High School and the Junior College," written in 1947, Du Bois argued that the high school curriculum had become too flexible and complicated. As a result, students and their parents had difficulty making appropriate curricular choices. Instead of a confusing curriculum disconnected from reality, Du Bois envisioned a high school curriculum in which students had to demonstrate their mastery of reading, writing, and mathematics, the foundational knowledge for critical thinking.[5] At the same time, Du Bois cautioned that schools could not completely fuse liberal and vocational education. "It is a mistake, however, to think that there can be a complete merger of these two lines of study which have different objects. If you are going to [study] science and literature, you cannot learn at the same time to be a carpenter; if you are going to learn how to cook, you will not have time to learn enough physics to understand the Atomic Bomb."[6]

While Du Bois strongly supported the teaching of basic skills, he also continued to advocate the critical examination of historical sources and encouraged black students to find alternative ways of looking at the world. For instance, in his seminal *Black Reconstruction in America* (1935), Du Bois challenged the popular view that the Civil War was fought merely over sectional differences between the North and South, rather than as a result of Southern whites' determination to preserve slavery in the South.

In *Black Reconstruction*, Du Bois openly adopted Marxism as a philosophical lens by which to examine racism, race relations, economic conditions, and education. In particular, Du Bois questioned why the black and white working classes had not united. He concluded that elites had stifled such unification through the alienation of the white and black poor.

Perhaps the greatest contribution of *Black Reconstruction* to the field of black education was the chapter entitled "Founding the Public School." Slaves and freed people, Du Bois argued, saw education as power. However, while blacks supported free public education, they could not wait until the government supplied it. As a result, Du Bois documented that the freed people started a significant number of private schools for themselves.

The momentum of blacks' struggle for education, Du Bois believed, led to public education in the South. Du Bois noted, "The first mass movement for public education at the expense of the state, in the South, came from Negroes. . . . Public education for all at public expense was in the South a Negro idea."[7] Over half a century after the publication of *Black Reconstruction*, a number of historians have documented the freed people's efforts to attain good education and expanded Du Bois's thesis regarding their struggle for public education.

Du Bois's book also offered a critique of U.S. history textbooks. In the final chapter, entitled "The Propaganda of History," he argued for an education that was factual and critical, no matter how painful such an education might be to American students. Most textbooks omitted facts that presented the United States or its leaders negatively, or glossed over certain events to avoid controversy. An education that concealed atrocities in American history and avoided factual but controversial topics was not education at all; it was merely propaganda. In order for Americans to learn from their mistakes and flourish as democratic citizens, Du Bois believed, school curricula must be both factual and critical.[8]

Du Bois was so concerned about how black history was taught in schools that he pondered the question, "Should Negro History Be Taught As a Separate Subject?" In this essay he noted how he was further inspired to promote the teaching of black history in schools after hearing a lecture by the anthropologist Franz Boas, a pioneer in the study of African contributions to world civilizations. American schools, Du Bois believed, could not be trusted to present black history accurately. Citing a veteran New York City teacher named Mary Quinn who publicly denounced "tolerance" and referred to Italian Americans as "greasy foreigners," Du Bois feared that African Americans would receive similar treatment from racist teachers like Quinn. "But there is still so much race feeling against Negroes in the United States, that we cannot hope to have Negro history integrated in general history by the average school board or especially by Mary Quinn."[9]

To ensure that black history was taught correctly, Du Bois concluded that it should be taught as a separate subject. Eventually, he believed, black history should be integrated into the curriculum. In the 1960s, students across the country would also call for separate courses on black history in colleges and universities and some public schools. Their Du Boisian–inspired call led to the development of Black Studies.

Du Bois's concerns about the suppression of information were further exacerbated in the Cold War environment of the 1940s and 1950s, when anyone who promoted education that was critical of the United States risked being labeled unpatriotic, a traitor, a liar, or a communist. In response to restrictions on free speech demanded by anticommunist crusaders, Du Bois noted that the hostile environment had suppressed individuals' "freedom to learn" by preventing teachers and schools from teaching critical thinking that raised questions about American democracy. More than ever, American citizens needed "The right to think, the right to express one's thought, the right to act in accordance with one's conclusions."[10] He believed that "especially we should insist upon the right to learn, upon the right to have our children learn, and upon keeping our schools, uncoerced by the dominant forces of the present world, free to exercise the right to join with the great Goethe in a worldwide cry for 'light, more light.'"[11]

The type of education that Du Bois advocated during the early Cold War years encouraged all citizens to challenge the social, economic, and political status quo that privileged a few and relegated many to poverty. He also encouraged Americans to see the connections between the "idea of democracy" and the "practice of democracy": "Do we still believe in democracy? And do we believe in it for all men? Or are we determined still to hug to our breasts the once popular idea that democracy is excellent for white Europe and North America but unworkable for Asia, Africa, and probably South America?"[12]

Another focus of Du Bois's critical educational ideas during this period was his belief that African Americans needed training in the area of economics. American dogma and fears of communism, Du Bois believed, had prevented schools from teaching students about alternatives to capitalism. Given the power of industrialists in the United States and their influence on markets around the world, he argued that African Americans and the poor in general had accepted the economic theories and ideas handed down from the dominant capitalist classes. Lack of education in economics in the public schools as well as in colleges and universities only exacerbated the problem, leaving many groups reluctant to join labor unions and unknowingly complicit in their own oppression.[13]

In a speech delivered before the California Labor School in San Francisco in 1948, Du Bois decisively explicated the relationship between education and economics. He argued that the leisure classes were in a constant struggle to gain greater wealth and social status. Education, he believed, was used by the leisure classes to maintain their status by teaching their children to be the developers and managers of industry, while the lower classes were taught to be workers. This problem could only be solved if everyone were provided with an education that taught the economic underpinnings of modern societies.[14]

Du Bois envisioned a critical curriculum in economics that would incorporate the following objectives:

1. To study the history and philosophy of human work.
2. To study what work is necessary and socially uplifting and what work is needless and hurtful.
3. To study the real meaning of income, the amount necessary for civilized existence and the amount which each family is now getting.
4. To study skills and technique and inquire which can best be used and taught.
5. To explore the possibilities of cooperative buying and selling.
6. To plan new and needed forms of work.
7. To explore the educational needs of the whole community old and young.
8. To inquire into planned recreation.
9. To study housing, food, and living conditions.
10. To study health and crime.
11. To reveal the actual work and possibilities of churches and fraternities. To explore, count, study and interpret a hundred other matters of social significance necessary for knowledge.
12. To coordinate the gathering of this scientific data by professors and students in these Negro colleges; facts upon which the community organizing itself and cooperating with all its elements could use to explore the effort of creating socially needed work, and especially of organizing cooperative expenditure. Bits of investigation like this have been done and are being done throughout the South. They need wider intensification, completion, integration; they need scientific guidance and wide knowledge of the newer technique of the social sciences.[15]

Clearly influenced by Marxist economic theory, Du Bois's educational thought during the post–World War II era emphasized the need for black colleges and universities to consider economics as a central element of the curriculum and to teach thoroughly the importance of labor and the power of economic cooperation.[16]

Reflecting on his own lack of economics education growing up in Great Barrington, Du Bois blamed his schools for not teaching basic economic principles. In his unpublished essay "Elementary Education and War," Du Bois painted a rather unflattering portrait of the Great Barrington of his youth, noting that capitalism and lack of funds contributed to open sewers and the absence of theaters, playgrounds, art, and music in the community. Had he and his fellow students received an education in economics, Du Bois argued, they would have been conscious of their situation. Central to Du Bois's advocacy of economic education in the schools was his belief that schools should prompt students to critique capitalism and to evaluate and address the economic problems of the poor and oppressed.[17]

Du Bois's support of critical education along with his emphasis on basic skills and traditional subject matter reveals that he supported aspects of both Progressive and traditional education. His perspective was Progressive in that he believed that education should have relevance to the everyday lives of individuals. At the same time, Du Bois promoted the idea of a core curriculum grounded in the traditional disciplines of history, philosophy, literature, and mathematics and believed that the acquisition of basic skills was essential for all individuals. With this in mind, it would be difficult to place Du Bois in any one educational philosophical camp. Instead, he was a synthesizer and dialectician who reconciled and integrated prevailing ideas of his time with his own ideas in formulating his educational vision.

Du Bois also took the opportunity to contrast American and Soviet education and schooling during the 1950s. Du Bois had visited the Soviet Union as early as 1926. However, by the 1950s, Du Bois noted, the Soviets had made significant progress in technology and modernization, improved the lives of farmers, attempted to eliminate poverty, and increased its emphasis on planned industry. The Soviet Union, Du Bois believed, had the potential to build the type of "people's democracy" that he had once envisioned for the United States. In terms of education, Du Bois observed that Soviet youth received technical and professional training and education in literature, arts, and culture as adults. While he acknowledged the "narrowness and pedantry" of Soviet education in some fields, Du Bois nevertheless noted, "as compared with the anarchy and license of America and the ignorance of Asia, Russia has a right to be proud of the work of a single generation."[18]

FROM THE TALENTED TENTH TO THE GUIDING HUNDREDTH

During the early twentieth century, Du Bois believed that a pragmatic educational approach was needed to address the complexity and breadth of the so-called "Negro problem." He therefore called on the talented tenth to lead African Americans in their struggle for equality. The talented tenth would be classically educated and would eliminate racial inequalities in the courts and in education.

At the end of World War II, the social, economic, and political conditions of African Americans had become much more complex than they were when Du Bois began addressing them during the 1890s and early 1900s. Non-Western countries challenged the new world order of Western dominance around the world; American capitalism continued to expand; and white Southerners hardened their opposition to African American social, economic, and political advancement.[19]

To Du Bois's dismay, the talented tenth had failed to effectively address demands for social justice by African Americans. Moreover, they had not adequately challenged the expansion of American imperialism and capitalism at the expense of Africans and other oppressed groups. Instead, Du Bois argued, the talented tenth had used their education to advance their own interests and improve their own economic status. As members of this group became upwardly mobile and moved into the American middle and upper classes, they seldom reached back to uplift the African American masses. "I assumed that with knowledge, sacrifice would automatically follow. In my youth and idealism, I did not realize that selfishness is even more natural than sacrifice."[20] Du Bois came to the conclusion that leadership would have to come from the masses and that educating a "thousand times as many Negroes" was a more realistic strategy that would facilitate economic cooperation, effective schooling, and a broadly based educational agenda for African Americans.[21]

Du Bois reconceptualized his notion of the talented tenth before his fraternity, Sigma Pi Phi, in Wilberforce, Ohio, in 1948.[22] He argued that because the social and economic problems of African Americans were so extensive and because the talented tenth had failed in its responsibility of uplifting the masses, a more expansive and inclusive model of leadership was needed. He called this new model the "guiding hundredth":

> Here comes a new idea for a Talented Tenth: The concept of a group-leadership, not simply educated and self-sacrificing, but with clear vision of present world conditions and dangers, and conducting American Negroes to alliance with culture groups in Europe, America, Asia and Africa, and looking toward a new world culture.[23]

Du Bois envisioned an African American community and a new cadre of leaders composed of "educated and specially trained experts in the main branches of science and the main categories of human work."[24] One way to facilitate the development of the guiding hundredth was for existing groups such as fraternities, sororities, and other organizations to diversify their memberships by recruiting and admitting members of the African American working class to their ranks. The Boule, he argued, could not have a great impact on black life if it restricted its membership to the privileged few. Du Bois encouraged the organization to increase its membership from 440 in 1948 to 30,000 by 1960. A larger membership would provide a more representative cross-section of the black populace. Du Bois believed this could be achieved without sacrificing the quality of membership in the organization.[25]

During the 1940s, Du Bois also addressed the struggles of working-class African American women and their role as leaders. For instance, in his 1949 unpublished essay "The American Negro Woman," he argued that black women were forced to work because of the "economic difficulties of Negro men in earning sufficient [income] to support a wife and children." Hard-working black women, Du Bois noted, were often criticized for gaining a degree of economic independence from men. Despite such criticism, Du Bois argued, "the advance among colored women has been spectacular." Working-class women had entered the workplace and were taking leadership roles by supporting their families. Throughout history, Du Bois argued, black women of all classes had risen to leadership roles in society. Du Bois identified Sojourner Truth, an unschooled woman, as an example of a black woman of the proletariat class who rose to lead her people.[26] "The American Negro Woman" further emphasized Du Bois's idea that leadership should come from all classes in the black community.

Perhaps Du Bois saw the manifestation of the guiding hundredth in the leadership of grassroots organizations such as the SNYC, SNCC, Congress of Racial Equality (CORE), and the Southern Christian Leadership Conference (SCLC). These organizations were comprised of educated individuals who believed that they were obligated to train and educate the masses for leadership in their own communities. We cannot be sure whether they viewed themselves as the guiding hundredth, but we do know that many of the individuals in these organizations had great respect for Du Bois and his writings.[27]

AFROCENTRIC, PAN-AFRICAN, AND GLOBAL EDUCATION

As early as the 1890s, Du Bois believed that hundreds of years of miseducation and misinformation had resulted in African Americans possessing negative views of Africa. Such negative views of or ignorance about Africa, along with stereotypes about African "barbarism," prevented African Americans from seeing the similarities between their oppression in the United States and the victimization of Africans under European colonialism.

Du Bois clearly understood these connections and demonstrated his support for African independence movements through his participation in the Pan-African Congresses between 1900 and 1945. At the Congresses he pushed for African solidarity, autonomy, and freedom from imperialism, calling upon Africans to unite and develop their economic and political strength to oppose European imperialism and aggression. Although there was some disagreement among the conferees about the best approaches to Pan-African solidarity, contact between African peoples was established and the fervor for Pan-Africanism was in the air. Du Bois believed firmly that education was the most effective strategy for correcting misinformation about Africa and for helping people of African descent around the world unite politically to overthrow outside oppression.[28]

By the 1940s, Du Bois's call for solidarity among African peoples was heard around the world. African leaders responded to the call for Pan-African unification. Du Bois's own words capture the essence of his views on

Pan-Africanism: "Pan-Africa means intellectual understanding and cooperation among all groups of Negro descent in order to bring about at the
earliest possible time the industrial and spiritual emancipation of the Negro
peoples."[29]

Du Bois sought to develop Pan-Africanism through an Afrocentric approach to history and education. In addition to his many essays and editorials on Africa and its people in *The Crisis*, Du Bois published a number of
books that reflect a Pan-African and Afrocentric perspective. One of the most
important of these works is *The World and Africa* (1947). In this treatise,
Du Bois described the contributions of Africa and its peoples to world history and showed Africa's connection to other peoples and places. Integrating Marxist analysis and Afrocentric historiography, Du Bois discussed the
contributions of African labor and natural resources to the world. He argued that ancient Egypt was a "Negro civilization" that influenced Greek,
Roman, and other civilizations of Europe, and called on the oppressed of all
the laboring classes to unite against European colonialism. An overarching
theme of the text is that African peoples should unite politically and economically to resist European and American imperialism.[30]

The teaching that focused on Africa in public schools and even in African American colleges, Du Bois noted, too often "belittled and sneered at
Africa." Schools also taught that "Africa had no history and no culture."
Collaboration and intellectual synergy between African scholars and intellectuals, Du Bois believed, would provide an intellectual knowledge base for
African peoples to draw upon in educating the world about Africa and its
peoples.[31]

Du Bois believed that black intellectuals worldwide should take an active role in disseminating knowledge about Africa and African peoples. In
1955, he published an essay in *Presence Africaine*, a journal founded and
edited by Senegalese intellectual Alioune Diop. The purpose of the journal
was to distribute scholarship and information about African peoples throughout the diaspora. Du Bois's essay, entitled "Africa and the American Negro
Intelligentsia," called on black intellectuals to collaborate on scholarship and
disseminate knowledge of Africa and its people throughout the African diaspora
and the world. Du Bois believed that such knowledge was necessary not only
for the black proletariat, but also for black leaders who were "widely igno-
rant of the history and present situation in Africa and indifferent to the fate
of African Negroes."[32]

Perhaps the most important scholarly endeavor to reflect Du Bois's
Afrocentric perspective was his attempt to publish an encyclopedia of Africa
and its peoples. In 1961, Du Bois accepted an invitation and funding from
Ghanian President Kwame Nkrumah to move to Accra, Ghana, to work on
his *Encyclopedia Africana*. Although he died before it came to fruition, the
prospectus for the project clearly outlined a Pan-African perspective that was

Afrocentric. For instance, Du Bois proposed that the encyclopedia "should basically concern itself with the African continent as such: the geographical entity. It must be unashamedly Afro-centric, but not indifferent to either the impact of the outside world upon Africa, or to the impact of Africa upon the outside world."[33] Du Bois's statement emphasizes the centrality of Africa and African peoples while also acknowledging the importance of European or "outside" influences. Du Bois's proposal reflects his dialectical approach to transcending double-consciousness, in which knowledge and education are grounded in the black experience, but at the same time engage the outside world.[34]

It should be noted that in the course of Du Bois's work on the *Encyclopedia Africana* he had contact with a number of African scholars throughout the diaspora, as well as with scholars who contributed to the history of Pan-Africanism. Du Bois also corresponded with African scholars and intellectuals such as Alioune Diop. On February 25, 1961, Diop wrote Du Bois to inform him that a group of historians was meeting at the University of Ibadan, Nigeria, to discuss methodologies for studying African history. Sensing that Diop might also be considering developing an encyclopedia about African peoples, Du Bois responded:

> I beg to remind you that the Ghana Academy of Learning, under the Presidency of His Excellency, Kwame Nkrumah, has undertaken the compilation and publication of an Encyclopedia Africana. I have already brought this to your attention. . . . Other African institutions and scholars are working with us. I trust you will keep this in mind and that our efforts will not be divided.[35]

Du Bois corresponded with scholars such as Diop, Basil Davidson, Melville Herskovits, and others who would eventually become recognized as major contributors to an Afrocentric worldview through their historical work on Africa and its importance to civilization.

Du Bois's advocacy of Afrocentric and Pan African education was a result of his ongoing efforts to combat white supremacist ideas and to address blacks' "warring souls" or double-consciousness. Throughout his life, Du Bois had argued that black children needed a strong grounding in their culture and history to protect them from the psychological damage caused by white supremacy. An incident involving his daughter, Yolande, is reflective of his ongoing concern. One evening Yolande consulted her father about a problem she was having with a dark-complexioned student in her classroom. Du Bois's granddaughter recounts the conversation between Yolande and Du Bois:

> She [Yolande] said [to Du Bois]: I have this youngster and she has behavioral problems that I don't really know how to address. . . . this youngster is named Lillie White and she is extremely dark and everybody teases her about it, and

it is completely coloring all aspects of her life. She is not a happy student, she's not a happy person. I don't know as a teacher, how I should get into this or if I should. . . . My grandfather's response to that, by the way, was Yolande, if you were black as the ace of spades and your name was Lillie White, how would you feel? That was his answer. My mother just completely withdrew and started to imagine what an experience that would be.[36]

The exchange between Yolande and Du Bois reveals Du Bois's understanding of psychic duality among black children. For Du Bois, the situation of Lillie White must have represented the personification of the "warring souls" of black people and the veil of race through which blacks saw themselves. The episode also provides another example of why Du Bois believed that Afrocentric and Pan-African education and curricula were important in the education of black children.

From 1940 to 1963, Du Bois also vigorously encouraged African Americans to conceptualize their social, economic, and political conditions as connected to those of other oppressed people around the world. Extending his idea of Pan-Africanism, he hoped to bring the plight of all oppressed people before the eyes of the world by calling attention to worldwide racism and classism. Wilson Moses points out the duality in Du Bois's thinking by noting that Du Bois could "be a spirited advocate for Pan Africanism, while insisting that African peoples were members of a world community centered in universal values."[37] In conceptualizing the nexus of the Pan-African and global struggle, Du Bois stated: "This is the firing line not simply for the emancipation of the American Negro but for the emancipation of the African Negro and Negroes of the West Indies; for the emancipation of the colored races; and for the emancipation of white slaves of modern capitalist monopoly."[38]

Du Bois had long hoped for African peoples of the world to unite and join forces with oppressed people of all races and classes. During the last three decades of his life he worked feverishly toward this goal. His ideas and efforts would resonate with and become part of the platform of other leftist revolutionary groups of the 1940s, 1950s and 1960s.

EDUCATION IN *THE BLACK FLAME*

During the final decade of his life, Du Bois took the opportunity to reflect on the social and educational issues of his lifetime. In his late eighties, he knew he did not have much time or energy remaining to conduct the type of empirical social science and historical research he had carried out in his younger years. However, Du Bois still had much to say. As a result, between 1957 and 1961 Du Bois produced three novels, collectively called *The Black*

Flame. The novels were titled *The Ordeal of Mansart* (1957), *Mansart Builds a School* (1959), and *Worlds of Color* (1961). The topics addressed in *The Black Flame* trilogy span Du Bois's lifetime and include many of the social and educational problems confronting blacks in the late nineteenth century and the first half of the twentieth century.

In conceptualizing *The Black Flame*, Du Bois used the methodological approach of "historical fiction," noting that his novels for the most part were historically accurate. Du Bois believed that historical and fictional writing both required imagination and creativity to construct narratives of events that were not entirely clear. Historical fiction, he argued, was a methodologically valid approach as long as the writer acknowledged its use and limitations.

While some scholars view *The Black Flame* trilogy as poorly written and among Du Bois's least significant works, the trilogy provides insight into Du Bois's thinking on a plethora of social and educational issues during his lifetime. The novels also provide a retrospective and kaleidoscopic view of black history and the black experience through a number of characters that mirror Du Bois's own life experiences and his contemplation of black education. Though the writing is at times cumbersome, *The Black Flame* shows that Du Bois's mind was still sharp in his final years and that his views had moved to the far political left.

The Black Flame centers on the character of Manuel Mansart, a black educator who struggles to find his place in a white-dominated and capitalistic society. Mansart's struggles begin as a child, when his mother fights to provide him with a good education in the midst of Jim Crow society. An important component of Mansart's education, however, is the informal education he receives from his mother and her advice on how to navigate white society. She provides such a lesson after Mansart beats up a white boy for picking a fight with him. Knowing that Mansart does not understand the social ramifications of striking whites, Mansart's mother admonishes him and instructs him in the social mores of the white world: "Manuel, don't you never strike a white boy. Take what they give, bow, run away. Don't hit 'em. Don't fight. You can't. They'se got the power. We got to wait."[39] Mansart's mother's words reflect the survival techniques that many blacks of his era advocated in their relationships with whites. Her words also resonate with Booker T. Washington's idea that blacks must be patient in their struggle for equality.

In *The Black Flame*, social context is connected to the educational dilemma of blacks. As Mansart struggles to fit into the white world, he, like Du Bois, commits himself to surpass whites in his school. Du Bois reinforces Mansart's mission by stating that if "given freedom of opportunity they [black students] would prove to have as much brains, energy and determination as whites."[40]

Du Bois also engages the vocational versus classical education debate in the trilogy. In one passage, for instance, a young Mansart engages in conversation with Colonel Breckenridge, who believes blacks should focus on obtaining vocational education. The exchange between Breckenridge and young Mansart is telling:

"Well, well, and what are you studying?"
"Reading Arithmetic and Geography,"
"And what are you going to be; a farmer, a carpenter, or a minister?"
"No, Sir, I am going to be a lawyer."
"A lawyer? Well, well; where did you get that idea?"
"My mammy says that she wants me to be a lawyer."[41]

Mansart's discussion with Breckenridge reflects the choices that black youth faced during the years of the Washington and Du Bois debates. Du Bois uses Mansart and Breckenridge to show how the white establishment attempted to push blacks into industrial education. The fact that Mansart's mother wants him to become a lawyer may indicate that she supported the idea of a talented tenth and saw Mansart as part of it.

At age fourteen, Mansart attends a high school on campus at Atlanta University, where his eyes are opened to the world. "Here he came into contact with a new kind of white folks; Northerners, both men and women, as teachers. It was both astonishing and disconcerting. They were different in speech and manners."[42] Mansart's experience at AU mirrors Du Bois's experience at Fisk, where Du Bois was also introduced to a black world with white professors committed to helping black people. Like Fisk, AU had poor equipment and few resources, but "high ideals." Just as Mansart is enlightened by a German instructor, Miss Freiburg, as a student Du Bois was enlightened by German idealism and social science. One can easily see this as a metaphor for Du Bois's own enlightenment experience in Germany.

One of the most insightful chapters in the trilogy, titled "The New Education," is found in *Mansart Builds a School*. In this chapter, Mansart is a grown man and has been appointed president of Georgia State Colored Agricultural and Mechanical College in Macon, Georgia. As president he quickly learns about the relationship between money and education, as white businessmen in Macon demand a cut of almost all the revenue from services to the college and black workers will not benefit from work at the school. Mansart also learns that white labor unions exclude blacks, and demand that he was not to provide education to blacks that would provide them with skills in occupations such as carpentry, masonry, and plastering. One labor official tells Mansart that "The skilled trades hereafter in the South are going to be confined to white men. No matter what Booker Washington or anyone else said, we are not going to have our wages dragged down by cheap 'niggers.'"[43]

The "New Education" of the chapter's title refers to blacks' mounting awareness of how education had been used by whites to control blacks' economic situation. It also refers to blacks' growing understanding of the power of economic cooperation among themselves and the poor and the need for unification of the proletariat class.

In *Worlds of Color*, Du Bois addresses the implications of *Brown v. Board of Education* and takes a global perspective on the conditions of African Americans. After the *Brown* decision, Mansart states: "By force and cheating, separate Negro schools will persist for a generation in many areas. If I had the power, I would postpone this disappearance of the separate Negro school. It was a noble institution with an heroic history. It could rebuild a people and a history."[44]

Despite the pragmatic legacy of separate schools for blacks, however, Mansart believes that blacks have progressed to a point where it is necessary to focus on integrating themselves into the global community. Mansart's viewpoint is consistent with Du Bois's during his final years. Mansart also notes that "Our great task now begins—the education of our children not as a group separate from the world but as an integral part of it."[45]

The focus on global education emerges through Mansart as well as other characters in the novels. Mansart, for instance, becomes enlightened through his travels to France, England, Russia, China, and Japan. As Du Bois had encouraged students at Fisk, his daughter Yolande, and his granddaughter Du Bois, through Mansart he illuminates the importance of attaining knowledge of other cultures around the world. Moreover, the characters in most of his novels are not fully liberated until they have experienced the world.

The Black Flame illuminates the major themes in Du Bois's educational thought and provides insight into Du Bois's most recent thinking on the educational issues he grappled with over the course of his lifetime. Through the characters in *The Black Flame*, Du Bois highlighted the importance of liberal education while also acknowledging the role of industrial and technical education as part of a larger educational plan. He also highlighted the importance of racial identity by showing his characters gaining greater psychological stability after returning to their own cultural grounding and after being exposed to global perspectives.

CONCLUSION

On August 27, 1963, Du Bois summoned Shirley to his bedside and took her hand to let her know that his long journey of nearly a century had come to a close. The weary traveler had lived a long life, had sought to educate his people, and had learned much himself along the way. Now it was time to rest and let others continue the struggle. The day after Du Bois died, a quarter of a million people descended on Washington, D.C., for the March on Washington to call attention to the problems of racism and discrimination that Du Bois had fought so hard to eradicate throughout his life. On that special day of August 28, 1963, the marchers recognized the importance of Du Bois to their movement, and a young charismatic Martin Luther King Jr. reminded the world that blacks were still not free, although he dreamed of a day when they would be free and a part of a multicultural America.

Five years after his March on Washington speech and only a few weeks before his assassination, Dr. King delivered a speech at Carnegie Hall honoring Du Bois and his contributions as an educator. King noted, "Dr. Du Bois was not only an intellectual giant exploring the frontiers of knowledge, he was in the first place a teacher. He would have wanted his life to teach us something about our tasks of emancipation."[46] King's words cogently summed up Du Bois's legacy as an educator and thinker, particularly during the last two decades of Du Bois's life. Education that sought the truth; placed the conditions of blacks in a Pan-African and global context; challenged established historical, economic, and political canons; encouraged free thought and the "freedom to learn"; and sought to emancipate all oppressed peoples were the hallmarks of Du Bois's educational and intellectual legacy from the 1940s through the 1960s. As the civil rights movement progressed, movement leaders would embrace many of Du Bois's social and educational ideas and witness many of his objectives and predictions coming to fruition.

Conclusion: Du Bois's Legacy for the Education of African Peoples and the World Community

In his unpublished novel *A.D. 2150*, Du Bois envisioned a world in which color and caste were irrelevant, and poverty and segregation had been eliminated. In Du Bois's twenty-second-century world, cities were very navigable and transportation was quick, allowing people great mobility and numerous opportunities to interact with one another. On the surface, the world was a much better place in the twenty-second century than it had been in the twentieth. Despite the social and technological advancements, however, Du Bois saw that immorality, death, lack of faith, and resistance to socialism persisted. He therefore concluded that between the twentieth and twenty-second centuries much had improved, but much had stayed the same.[1]

Many of Du Bois's predictions about the improvements in black education have come to fruition. In the twenty-first century, African Americans complete high school at high rates, African Americans' access to higher education have significantly improved, de jure segregation and Jim Crow laws have been eliminated, and African Americans have greater social mobility. Despite these advancements, however, much more must be done to improve the education not only of African Americans, but of all Americans.

DU BOIS'S LEGACY FOR AFRICAN AMERICAN EDUCATION

Despite the lack of attention given to Du Bois as an educational thinker, some scholars have acknowledged Du Bois's influence on their work, and a new generation of scholars has begun to embrace Du Boisian educational thought. Perhaps the most evident legacy of Du Bois's educational thought is the development of Black Studies as a field of scholarly research since the 1960s. Du Bois's scholarship on the black experience, including *The Suppression of the African Slave Trade, The Philadelphia Negro, The Atlanta University Studies, The Souls of Black Folk, Black Reconstruction*, and *The World and Africa*—to name just a few of his significant works—provided the social and political foundation upon which Black Studies emerged in the 1960s. In addition, Du Bois's interdisciplinary approach to the study of the black experience was a precursor to the interdisciplinary approach that has emerged in Black Studies' four decades of existence. Given these contributions, many consider Du Bois a founder of Black Studies.[2]

137

Economist and Black Studies scholar James B. Stewart has been at the forefront of utilizing Du Boisian educational ideas to conceptualize Black Studies as a viable field of study. Stewart's treatise *Flight: In Search of Vision* is a compilation of previously published and new essays covering Stewart's thirty-plus years of writing about Black Studies. Employing a similar trope to Du Bois's in *The Souls of Black Folk*, Stewart uses poetry to hold the chapters together in a coherent narrative. Moreover, in his chapters "The Field and Function of Black Studies" and "The Legacy of W.E.B. Du Bois for Contemporary Black Studies," two previously published works, Stewart utilizes Du Boisian educational ideas to frame a vision and mission for Black Studies.[3] Other Black Studies scholars who identify Du Bois as a precursor or framer of the field include Delores Aldridge, Lucius Outlaw, Manning Marable, Henry Louis Gates, James Turner, Molefi Asante, Maulana Karanga, and Lewis Gordon.

Du Bois's Afrocentric educational perspective has also influenced theories and contemporary ideas in Black Studies. For instance, Black Studies scholar Molefi Asante's concept of Afrocentricity and his ideas about Afrocentric education are genealogical descendants of Du Bois's commitment to developing an Afrocentric historical worldview. In his major treatise *The Afrocentric Idea*, Asante writes that Afrocentricity means "placing African ideals at the center of any analysis that involves African culture and behavior." He further notes that "the Afrocentric analysis reestablishes the centrality of the ancient Kemetic (Egyptian) civilization and the Nile Valley cultural complex as points of reference for an African perspective in much the same way that Greece and Rome serve as reference points for the European world."[4]

Asante asserts that "Du Bois, of course, was not an Afrocentrist; he was, preeminently, a Eurocentrist."[5] At the same time, Asante contends that Du Bois "remains the major pre-Afrocentric figure in the philosophical and intellectual history of African people." Asante further notes that Du Bois and Cheik Anta Diop "had prepared an entire generation of African intellectuals to examine Africa by listening to the African world voice."[6] Regardless of where Du Bois might be placed in the pantheon of Afrocentric thought, it is undeniable that his proposed Afrocentric historical worldview both predates and reflects contemporary ideas about Afrocentricity and Afrocentric education.

While Asante conceptualized the contemporary notion of Afrocentricity, social scientist Asa G. Hilliard III is the most renowned theorist of Afrocentric education or what many also call African-centered education. Citing Du Bois as an influence on his ideas of African-centered education, Hilliard argues that black children experience a double-consciousness when educated outside their cultural frame of reference. As such, Hilliard has consistently argued that historical and cultural grounding in the black experience should be a critical part of black children's education. African-centered education,

Hilliard argues, helps blacks guard against the detrimental psychological effects of white supremacy embedded in school curricula.[7]

Like Du Bois, Hilliard has also challenged notions of black mental inferiority. In some of his recent work, for instance, he problematizes the notion of "black academic underachievement" and concludes that the idea of the academic achievement gap is not based on blacks' intelligence compared to whites', but on how academic excellence is defined. Hilliard also argues that tests do not actually measure intelligence. Du Bois made similar arguments regarding various tests throughout his life.[8]

Afrocentric and African-centered education developed alongside multicultural education during the 1980s and 1990s. James Banks, the foremost authority in the area of multicultural education, identifies Du Bois as a major influence on his conceptualization of multicultural education. For Banks, multicultural education is an attempt to examine the world through the lenses of multiple groups, which mirrors Du Bois's idea that societies improve for the better when they are exposed to the culture and history of all peoples.[9] On the importance of Du Bois's work in his conceptualization of multicultural education, Banks notes that in addition to Carter G. Woodson's *Mis-Education of the Negro*, Du Bois's *The Souls of Black Folk* influenced his thinking:

> Another really important book is by W. E. B. Du Bois, "The Souls of Black Folk," published in [1903]. In this collection of essays, Du Bois talks about having a "double consciousness," meaning having to fit into one's own ethnic community and also fit into the wider mainstream culture. This condition extends beyond African Americans, and to groups such as Native Americans and Asian Americans as well as to immigrants coming from Africa, Asia, and Mexico. I'm an avid reader who has many favorite books, but these two books have stood the test of time.[10]

In 1994, Mwalimu Shujaa published an important volume on black education inspired by Du Bois's educational thought, entitled *Too Much Schooling, Too Little Education: A Paradox of Black Life in White Societies* (1994). The book is composed of essays by some of the leading scholars in the field of black education. Authors in the volume cite Du Bois and Carter G. Woodson, among other African American educators, as influential in shaping the idea that schools for black children should be African-centered. One of the most direct linkages to Du Bois in this volume is Violet Harris's essay, "Historic Readers for African-American Children (1868–1944): Uncovering and Reclaiming a Tradition of Opposition." Extending her previous scholarship on Du Bois and the *Brownies' Book*, Harris uses Du Bois to frame her historical analysis of curricular materials for black children.[11]

Another Du Boisian-inspired work in Shujaa's volume is Ronald Butchart's essay, "Outthinking and Outflanking the Owners of the World," previously published in the *History of Education Quarterly*. Butchart draws from

Du Bois's own words in choosing his title. The phrase alludes to the agenda of African American educators who challenged white supremacist beliefs that blacks did not value education. Butchart shows that Du Bois was significant in framing the discourse on black education during the late nineteenth century and much of the early twentieth century. Thus, Butchart illuminates Du Bois's legacy for African American education.

In the past few years, several scholars who situate their work within the fields of critical race theory, critical theory, and critical pedagogy have identified Du Bois as an influence on their work. Philosopher Lucius Outlaw, for instance, has identified Du Bois among the pantheon of thinkers who influenced his work in critical theory. Derrick Bell, a pioneer in the field of critical race theory, identifies Du Bois as a major influence on his thinking. Gloria Ladson-Billings and William F. Tate identify Du Bois, along with Carter G. Woodson, as influences on their conceptualization of critical race theory in education. Likewise, in a recent study Terry Oatts has utilized Du Bois's educational ideas and critical race theory to develop a theoretical framework for African American education. Finally, Reiland Rabaka has also offered noteworthy scholarship on Du Bois in his construction of an Africana philosophy of education, and Susan Searls Giroux and Joe Kincheloe have consulted Du Bois's educational thought and proposed a racial and critical pedagogy to address racism and classism in contemporary society.[12]

In another important study, womanist education scholar Cynthia Dillard identifies Du Bois as an influence on her recent book *On Spiritual Strivings: Transforming an African American Woman's Academic Life*. Borrowing from Du Bois's 1897 essay "Of Our Spiritual Strivings," Dillard notes that her book "explicates Du Bois's spiritual strivings and firmly characterizes and resonates with 'The Souls of Black Folk,' specifically the Souls of Black womanfolk." Dillard draws on Du Bois's ideas of Pan-Africanism to show how black women's conscious centering in African ideals provides a heuristic for addressing black women's multiple identities in the academy and in their lives.[13]

Du Bois's work as a social scientist has also influenced thinking and research in the field of African American history of education. One of the first studies that comes to mind is V. P. Franklin's seminal work, *The Education of Black Philadelphia: A Social and Educational History of a Minority Community, 1900–1950*. Franklin's study extends the work of Du Bois's *The Philadelphia Negro: A Social Study*. Like Du Bois, Franklin argues that the lowly social conditions of blacks in Philadelphia were partially a function of racism and discrimination.[14]

Likewise, historian James Anderson's classic *The Education of Blacks in the South: 1860–1935* extends some of ideas about education in Du Bois's work, particularly Du Bois's *Atlanta University Studies* and *Black Reconstruction*. A premise of Anderson's work is captured in a quotation at the beginning of his study: "W.E.B. Du Bois was on the mark when he said: 'Public education for all at public expense was, in the South, a Negro idea.'"[15] Anderson extends Du Bois's idea of black agency in education by identifying numerous examples of blacks starting their own schools in the midst of oppression. Like Du Bois, Anderson also shows how white philanthropists and industrialists attempted to control black education and schooling. As historians of education, Franklin and Anderson embody the legacy of Du Bois's sociohistorical work on black education.[16]

Historian and ethnographer Vanessa Siddle Walker's work has also been influenced by Du Boisian educational thought and methods. For instance, in her classic study *Their Highest Potential: An African American School Community in the Segregated South*, Siddle Walker draws on historical and sociological methods to offer a nuanced and complicated understanding of school desegregation. Siddle Walker points out, for example, that not all schools were inherently unequal as a result of being all black. In making her case, she tells the story of all-black Caswell County Training School in North Carolina, a school that was academically superior to white schools in the district and provided a culturally enriching environment for black children. The description of Caswell County Training School reflects precisely the type of black school that Du Bois argued would be best for African Americans in a society that he believed was not ready to offer good mixed education to blacks. Siddle Walker notes that Du Bois's ideas influenced her interpretations in her work on *Their Highest Potential*.[17]

In the area of black women and education, historian Linda Perkins's scholarship has been at the forefront of chronicling and analyzing the role that black women played in race uplift during the nineteenth and twentieth centuries. Perkins notes that while Fanny Jackson Coppin, Anna Julia Cooper, Nannie Helen Burroughs, and other African American women educators have provided her with insight on black women educators, Du Bois also tremendously influenced her understanding of the nature of women's leadership roles in the Black Freedom Struggle. Other historians of black education whose work has been influenced by Du Bois's educational ideas include Ronald Butchart, Michael Fultz, Christopher Span, Joy Williamson, Katrina Sanders-Cassell, and Marybeth Gasman.[18]

Du Bois's educational thought has also influenced social science research on African American education. For instance, in an interview, renowned social scientist Edmund Gordon identified Du Bois as having influenced his conceptualization of "knowing and understanding." He noted that "It was from [Du Bois] that I first learned the importance of looking at the source of what you know because of what he called the knowledge interests and knowledge producer."[19] In his essay "Production of Knowledge and Pursuit of Understanding," Gordon noted that "The production of knowledge and the pursuit of understanding must be guided by a cultural history that informs our understanding of individual learners, social groups, and the social contexts in which all exists." From his concept of knowing and understanding, Gordon believes that all individuals should critique the facts that they are given and that they know, and try to comprehend the social and historical contexts within which they know those facts. He points out that he would later encounter this philosophy in his readings of critical theorists and the Frankfurt School.[20]

Psychologist Aaron D. Gresson has also extended Du Bois's ideas in his work on African American education and psychology. In *The Dialectics of Betrayal: Sacrifice, Violation, and the Oppressed*, Gresson uses Du Bois's concept of psychic duality to explain the psychological dilemma of twoness experienced by African Americans in contemporary society. In a subsequent work, *The Recovery of Race in America*, Gresson extends Du Bois's ideas to understand the nature of racism in U.S. society.[21]

Social scientist Jerome Morris likewise conceptualizes his sociological work on black education and academic achievement within a Du Boisian framework. Drawing from Du Bois's notions of community and communal education for blacks, Morris has coined and explicated the phrase *communal bonds*, which purports that the ideal schooling environment for black children is one in which the school and community are intricately connected. In his ethnographic studies, Morris argues that communally bonded schools provide the best environment to foster black children's academic success. Morris directly links his work to a Du Boisian tradition of social science scholarship.[22]

While Du Bois has yet to secure a place in the canon of higher education scholarship, his ideas have clearly begun to influence this field. For instance, historian of higher education Marybeth Gasman echoes Du Bois's concerns about white philanthropists' engagement with black colleges and universities. While Du Bois welcomed support and funding from white philanthropists, he was also cautious and critical of the role of philanthropy in African American higher education. Gasman whose work explores the relationship between philanthropy and African American higher education, notes that Du Bois's work has helped her to remain critical of this relationship. With access to numerous records and archives, Gasman has extended some of Du Bois's views and argued that some white philanthropists were self-serving while others were altruistic.[23]

Another Du Boisian-inspired example of scholarship in higher education may be found in the work of Larry L. Rowley. Over the past decade, Rowley's work in the sociology of knowledge in higher education has drawn on Du Bois's educational ideas to formulate theories about the role of higher education in the lives of African Americans and to construct empirically based models of African American leadership.[24] For example, in a recent study entitled *Higher Education and African American Civic Participation: An*

Empirical Analysis of Du Bois's "Talented Tenth" Concept, Rowley and his co-authors, Nathan Daun-Barnett and Venice Thandi Sulé, use National Educational Longitudinal Statistics (NELS) data to empirically examine the relationship between African Americans, higher education, and civic participation. They conclude that college-educated African Americans are "more politically and civically engaged than their non-college peers." Rowley and colleagues also note that college-educated blacks are "more likely to engage in community and youth organization volunteerism," which they argue is "highly consistent" with Du Bois's ideas about higher education and leadership among African Americans. To date, this study is the only robust empirical study of Du Bois's concepts of leadership and the talented tenth.[25]

The brief examples discussed above offer just a glimpse of the existing and emerging scholarship in black education that has been inspired by the ideas of W.E.B. Du Bois. Moreover, the legacy of Du Bois's educational thought for African American education presented here is by no means comprehensive. Beyond the fields of Black Studies and African American education, however, Du Bois's educational ideas remain largely unknown or underutilized despite their tremendous potential for helping educators understand the significance of education and schooling in the black experience. Many opportunities remain for exploring the relevance not only of Du Bois, but also of other African American educators and intellectuals, to gain insight into the education of African Americans. It is my hope that a new generation of scholars, not only in education but in other fields as well, will continue to engage more frequently and more substantively with the ideas of Du Bois and other African American educators. In so doing, they will assuredly benefit from the vast knowledge, inspiration, and insight such work may provide.

A DU BOISIAN VISION

Du Bois did not see education as a panacea for the ills in U.S. society, nor did he see it as the sole means for eliminating the negative impact of white racism and discrimination in African American life. Instead, his educational thought was always buttressed by a belief that alleviating African Americans' oppression must be accomplished through social, economic, and political struggle. Though he acknowledged this reality, particularly during his later years, he promoted the value of education as a powerful tool for improving society for all citizens.

Du Bois's writings on education are valuable not only for African Americans but also for many others in the contemporary world. Indeed, they are perhaps more relevant to people today than ever before, given the challenges that African American and other students face in modern and postmodern global society. In light of the achievement gap between white and black students; the inequities in the resources and quality of education available to schools with predominantly minority or poor populations; the increasing economic challenges faced by many black colleges and universities; the shortage of black teachers; and the need to make educational curricula more relevant to all children, Du Bois's educational ideas have much cogency.

As we move further into this new century, Du Bois's educational thought can help us reconsider the challenges in black education and map out a new plan for improving the education of African Americans and all people. Such a venture requires educators to move beyond merely studying Du Bois and proclaiming to be Du Bois scholars; it requires action. In a special issue of the *Annals of the American Academy of Political and Social Science*, historian Mary Frances Berry challenged scholars to embrace a Du Boisian vision that moves beyond discussion into the realm of commitment and action:

> If we have any interest in being like Du Bois, instead of just writing and talking about Du Bois, we must understand that following his example means much more than being a public intellectual who writes for mainstream publications and graces an occasional meeting or dinner at the White House. It means a commitment to act for social change, to rub shoulders with activists on a regular basis, and to rejoice when attacked for being too radical.[26]

In our efforts to improve education for all people in this new century, we must heed Berry's call and promote the Du Boisian ideals that we must all have the freedom to learn and must use our education to promote democracy. Du Bois's intention in providing quality education for African Americans and others was to make the world a better place. The purpose of education, he believed, was to help democratize society, enlighten individuals and groups, eradicate poverty and class distinctions, erase the color line, and emancipate the oppressed. Du Bois's vision, he realized, was ambitious. Thus, he put forth pragmatic and flexible educational ideas that could be readily revised to meet the changing conditions of a rapidly changing world.

It has been my intention in writing this history of Du Bois's educational thought to provide a better understanding of Du Bois's ideas and illuminate the cogency of these ideas for a modern and postmodern society. It is my hope that such understanding will encourage us to create and foster educational ideas that will enlighten individuals, peoples, and communities to build a more democratic society in this new century.

Notes

Introduction

1. W.E.B. Du Bois, *The Autobiography of W.E.B. Du Bois: A Soliloquy on Viewing My Life from the Last Decade of Its First Century* (New York: International Publishers, 1968), 25.

2. Clarence Karier has written perhaps the most definitive intellectual history of American educational thought. Unfortunately, his classic book does not mention Du Bois's contributions to the history of American educational ideas. See Karier, *The Individual, Society, and Education: A History of American Educational Ideas* (Chicago: University of Illinois Press, 1986). Another classic work is Merle Curti's *The Social Ideas of American Educators* (1935; reprint, Totowa, NJ: Littlefield, Adams, and Co., 1974). Surprisingly, Curti does not examine Du Bois's social thought as a prominent educator, although he does devote a chapter to analyzing Booker T. Washington's educational thought.

3. My claim to place Du Bois and other African American educators within an African American intellectual tradition may invite criticism that I am engaging in identity politics and vindicationist scholarship. Clearly, black educators drew from the language, ideology, and perspectives of the dominant white European and American ideas and culture during their lifetime. However, I do assert that the educational ideas of Du Bois and other African American educators were gestated within a social milieu in which black educators proposed ideas to ameliorate the conditions of black people and that collectively, their ideas comprise an African American intellectual tradition

4. See Earl E. Thorpe, *The Mind of the Negro: An Intellectual History of Afro-Americans* (1961; reprint, Westport, CT: Negro Universities Press, 1970); Harold Cruise, *The Crisis of the Negro Intellectual: A Historical Analysis of the Failure of Black Leadership* (1967; reprint, New York: Quill, 1984); V. P. Franklin, *Living Our Stories, Telling Our Truths: Autobiography and the Making of the African-American Intellectual Tradition* (New York: Scribner, 1995); Linda M. Perkins, *Fanny Jackson Coppin and the Institute for Colored Youth, 1865–1902* (New York: Garland, 1987); August Meier, *Negro Thought in America: Racial Ideologies in the Age of Booker T. Washington* (1963; reprint, Ann Arbor: University of Michigan Press, 2002); Wilson Jeremiah Moses, *Alexander Crummell: A Study of Civilization and Discontent* (New York: Oxford University Press, 1989); Jerry Watts, *Heroism and the Black Intellectual: Ralph Ellison, Politics, and Afro-American Intellectual Life* (Chapel Hill: University of North Carolina Press, 1994); and Sterling Stuckey, *Slave Culture: Nationalist Theory and the Foundations of Black America* (New York: Oxford University Press, 1987).

5. I have borrowed the concept that "ideas have consequences" from Southern historian Richard Weaver. While I certainly do not identify with Weaver's nostalgia for the Old South or agree with his ideas of Southern morality, I find cogent his concept that ideas as much as actions propel history. See Richard M. Weaver, *Ideas Have Consequences* (Chicago: University of Illinois Press, 1948).

6. Francis L. Broderick, *W.E.B. Du Bois: Negro Leader in a Time of Crisis* (Stanford, CA: Stanford University Press, 1959); Elliot Rudwick, *W.E.B. Du Bois: Voice of the Black Protest Movement* (Urbana, IL: University of Illinois Press, 1960); David Levering Lewis, *W.E.B. Du Bois: Biography of a Race, 1868–1919* (New York: Henry Holt and Co., 1993) and *W.E.B. Du Bois: The Fight for Equality and the American Century, 1919–1963* (New York: Henry Holt and Co., 2000); Manning Marable, *W.E.B. Du Bois: Black Radical Democrat* (1986; reprint, Boulder, CO: Paradigm Publishers, 2005).

7. For an excellent discussion of intellectual history and literary analysis, see Richard E. Beringer, *Historical Analysis: Contemporary Approaches to Clio's Craft* (Malabar, FL: Robert E. Krieger Publishing Co., 1968).

8. W.E.B. Du Bois, *The Education of Black People: Ten Critiques 1906–1960*, ed. Herbert Aptheker (New York: Monthly Review Press, 1973).

9. W.E.B. Du Bois, *Du Bois on Education*, ed. Eugene Provenzo (Walnut Creek, CA: AltaMira Press, 2002).

10. In 1999, I published two essays that explicated themes in Du Bois's educational thought. See Derrick P. Alridge, "Conceptualizing a Du Boisian Philosophy of Education: Toward a Model for African American Education," *Educational Theory*, vol. 49, no. 3 (1999): 359–379 and "Guiding Philosophical Principles for a Du Boisian-Based African-American Educational Model," *Journal of Negro Education*, vol. 68, no. 2 (1999): 182–199.

11. Wilson J. Moses to Derrick P. Alridge, personal e-mail correspondence, July 20, 2001.

12. W.E.B. Du Bois, "Education and Work," in *The Education of Black People: Ten Critiques 1906–1960*, ed. Herbert Aptheker (New York: Monthly Review Press, 1973), 61–82. Also see Wilson Jeremiah Moses, *Creative Conflict in African American Thought: Frederick Douglass, Alexander Crummell, Booker T. Washington, W.E.B. Du Bois, and Marcus Garvey* (Cambridge, UK: Cambridge University Press, 2004). Historian Richard Hofstadter has aptly noted that contradictions and attempts to reconcile them are common in the thought of American intellectuals. See Richard Hofstadter, *The American Political Tradition and the Men Who Made It* (New York: Vintage, 1948).

13. W.E.B. Du Bois, "The Talented Tenth: Memorial Address," *Boule Journal*, vol. 15, no. 1 (October 1948): 13.

14. Presentism is the act of generalizing about the present and future based on the past or forcing present values and views onto the past. For further discussion regarding presentism and my approach to dealing with the issue as an African American historian of education, see Derrick P. Alridge, "The Dilemmas, Challenges, and Duality of an African American Educational Historian," *Educational Researcher*, vol. 32, no. 9 (December 2003): 25–34.

Chapter 1

1. Rayford Logan, *The Betrayal of the Negro: From Rutherford B. Hayes to Woodrow Wilson* (1965; reprint, New York: Da Capo Press, Inc., 1997), 9; Joe William Trotter Jr., *The African American Experience* (Boston: Houghton Mifflin, 2001), 274–275.

2. Ronald E. Butchart, *Northern Schools, Southern Blacks, and Reconstruction: Freedmen's Education, 1862–1875* (Westport, CT: Greenwood Press, 1980), 99–101.

3. Ibid, 107–114.

4. John Hope Franklin and Alfred A. Moss, Jr., *From Slavery to Freedom: A History of African Americans* (1947; reprint, Boston, MA: McGraw Hill, 2000). Fourth edition. 250–253.

5. Leon F. Litwack, *Been in the Storm So Long: The Aftermath of Slavery* (1979; reprint, New York: Vintage Books, 1980), 384–386.

6. Franklin and Moss, *From Slavery to Freedom*, 252–291.

7. See Wyn Craig, *The Fiery Cross: The Ku Klux Klan in America* (New York: Simon and Schuster, 1987).

8. Trotter, *The African American Experience*, 282.

9. Thomas A. Bailey, David M. Kennedy, and Lizabeth Cohen, *The American Pageant: A History of the Republic* (Boston: Houghton Mifflin Company, 1998), 520.

10. Roy Harvey Pearce, *Savagism and Civilization: A Study of the Indian and the American Mind* (Baltimore, MD: The Johns Hopkins Press, 1967). George M. Fredrickson, *The Black Image in the White Mind: The Debate on Afro-American Character and Destiny, 1817–1914* (1971; reprint, Hanover, NH: Wesleyan University Press, 1987): p. xvii.

11. Charles Darwin, *On the Origin of Species: By Means of Natural Selection of the Preservation of Favoured Races in the Struggle for Life* (1859; reprint, New York: Washington Square Press, Inc., 1963); Herbert Spencer, *Principles of Biology* (New York, Appleton, 1893); Robert C. Bannister, *Social Darwinism: Science and Myth in Anglo-American Social Thought* (Philadelphia: Temple University Press, 1979): 44–46.

12. Daniel W. Crofts, "The Black Response to the Blair Education Bill," *Journal of Southern History*, vol. 37, no. 1 (February, 1971): 41–65.

13. Donald Spivey, *Schooling for the New Slavery: Black Industrial Education, 1868–1915* (Westport, CT: Greenwood Press, 1978): 16–38; James D. Anderson, *The Education of Blacks in the South, 1860–1935* (Chapel Hill, NC: University of North Carolina Press, 1988), 33–78.

14. Ibid.

15. Ibid. Also, see William H. Watkins, *The White Architects of Black Education: Ideology and Power in America, 1865–1954* (New York: Teachers College Press, 2002).

16. Du Bois, *Autobiography*, 83–91.

17. Du Bois, *Autobiography*, 93.

18. Du Bois, "Democracy in Gr. Barrington," c. 1882; Du Bois, "'Baretown Beebe,' speech to National Council of Arts, Sciences, and Professions, Oct. 1948,"

Francis L. Broderick Collection, Schomburg Collection, New York Public Library (Hereafter cited as *Broderick College*). Also see Du Bois, *Autobiography*, 92. Sometimes Du Bois spelled Mr. Beebe's first name "Beartown" instead of "Baretown."

19. Du Bois, *Autobiography*, 82.

20. W.E.B. Du Bois, *The Souls of Black Folk* (1903; reprint, New York: Bantam Book, 1989), 2.

21. T. Thomas Fortune published several newspapers that were in essence the same paper. The papers included the *New York Globe, the Freeman*, and the *New York Freeman*. The *New York Freeman* eventually changed its name to the *New York Age*.

22. W.E.B. Du Bois, "Great Barrington Notes," *New York Globe*, April 14, 1883.

23. W.E.B. Du Bois, *The Freeman,* December 6, 1884, 4.

24. W.E.B. Du Bois, *New York Globe*, September 8, 1883, 4.

25. W.E.B. Du Bois. Catalogue of Great Barrington High School, 1882–1883. *The Papers of W.E.B. Du Bois, Addendum* (Hereafter cited as *Du Bois Papers, Addendum*).

26. W.E.B. Du Bois, *Dusk of Dawn: An Essay Toward an Autobiography of a Race Concept* (1940; reprint, New Brunswick, NJ: Transaction Publishers, 2000), 20.

27. See Wendell Phillips, *The Scholar in a Republic: Address at the Centennial Anniversary of the Phi Beta Kappa of Harvard College* (Boston: Lee and Shepard Publishers, 1881).

28. Du Bois, *Autobiography*, 108.

29. Ibid., 107.

30. Ibid., 107, 111, 112.

31. Joe E. Richardson, *A History of Fisk University, 1865–1946* (Alabama: The University of Alabama Press, 1980), 2–15.

32. Du Bois, *Autobiography*, 112.

33. Ibid., 112–113.

34. Teacher's certificate, documents dated summer 1886 and 1887, *The Papers of W.E.B. Du Bois*, University of Massachusetts, Amherst (Hereafter cited as *Du Bois Papers*).

35. W.E.B. Du Bois, "A Negro Schoolmaster in the New South," *Atlantic Monthly* (January 1899): 100–101; W.E.B. Du Bois, "A Negro Schoolmaster in the New South," in *Du Bois on Education*, ed. E. G. Provenzo Jr. (Walnut Creek, CA: AltaMira Press, 2002), 24–25.

36. Ibid., 25.

37. W.E.B. Du Bois, "How I Taught School," *The Fisk Herald*, vol. 4, no. 4 (December 1886): 9–10.

38. Ibid.

39. Ibid.

40. W.E.B. Du Bois, "The Hills of Tennessee," *The Fisk Herald*, vol. 4, no. 2 (October, 1886): 7.

41. W.E.B. Du Bois, "Tom Brown," *The Fisk Herald*, vol. 5, no. 4 (December 1887): 5–7; vol. 5, no. 5 (January 1888): 6–7; vol. 5, no. 7 (March 1888): 5–7.

42. W.E.B. Du Bois, "Public Rhetoricals," March 1888, 2–3, *Du Bois Papers*.

43. W.E.B. Du Bois to the Dean of Harvard College, letter dated 1890. Official folder of W.E.B. Du Bois, A.B. 1890, Harvard University.

44. W.E.B. Du Bois, "An Open Letter to the Southern People," in *Against Racism: Unpublished Essays, Papers, Addresses, 1887–1961*, ed. H. Aptheker (Amherst: University of Massachusetts Press, 1985), 4.

45. See "Bismarck," June 1888, *Du Bois Papers*; Du Bois, *Autobiography*, 126.

46. Du Bois, *Autobiography*, 133.

47. Du Bois, *Autobiography*, 143. See William James, *The Principles of Psychology*, vols. 1 & 2 (New York: Henry Holt and Co., 1890). It is impossible to show a direct link between Du Bois's concept of double-consciousness and James's idea. In fact, a case can be made that Du Bois's experiences at Fisk might have led to the initial articulation of Du Bois's concept. However, given the influence that Du Bois himself acknowledged James had on his thinking, it is reasonable to assert that James's ideas likely informed, but may not have initiated, Du Bois's conceptualization of double-consciousness. There is a robust literature that addresses this issue from varying viewpoints. For an excellent discussion of James's influence on Du Bois, see Dickson D. Bruce, "W.E.B. Du Bois and the Idea of Double Consciousness," *American Literature*, vol. 64, no. 2 (June 1992): 300–309. Cornel West similarly suggests the influence of James on Du Bois, calling Du Bois a "Jamesian Organic Intellectual." See Cornel West, *The American Evasion of Philosophy: A Genealogy of Pragmatism* (1982; reprint, Madison: University of Wisconsin Press, 1989).

48. Du Bois, *Autobiography*, 148.

49. William James to Henry James, June 6, 1903, *The Letters of William James, volume II*, ed. Henry James (Boston: The Atlantic Monthly Press, 1920), 196. It should also be noted that James also had respect for Booker T. Washington. In a letter to the editor of *The Republican* in 1909, James stated, "Du Bois and Washington are champions of coordinate [sic] & equally essential interests, in my humble opinion; they are citizens of whom our country may be equally proud; and I should esteem it a national calamity if either of them gave up the cause for which he fights." William James, "The Problem of the Negro (1909)" in *Essays, Comments, and Reviews* (Cambridge, MA: Harvard University Press), 192–193.

50. See Louis Menand, *The Metaphysical Club: A Story of Ideas in America* (New York: Farrar, Straus and Giroux, 2001), xi.

51. Ibid., xii.

52. William James, *Pragmatism and The Meaning of Truth* (1907; reprint, Cambridge, MA: Harvard University Press, 1998), 31. For a handy resource that examines James, pragmatism, and many other ideas in Western thought, see Peter Watson, *The Modern Mind: An Intellectual History of the 20th Century* (New York: HarperCollins Publishers, 2001).

53. Menand, *The Metaphysical Club*, xii.

54. James T. Kloppenberg, "Pragmatism: An Old Name for Some New Ways of Thinking?," *Journal of American History*, vol. 83, no. 1 (June 1996): 119; Nancy Muller Milligan, "W.E.B. Du Bois' American Pragmatism," *Journal of American Culture*, vol. 8 (Summer 1985): 33.

55. G.W.F. Hegel, *The Phenomenology of Mind* (1807; reprint, New York: The MacMillan Co., 1931) and *The Philosophy of History*, trans. J. Sibree (1837; reprint, New York: Willey Book Co., 1944). For a concise description of Hegel's

ideas, see J. Bronowski & Bruce Mazlish, *The Western Intellectual Tradition: From Leonardo to Hegel* (New York: Harper and Row Publishers, 1962), 472–515. For an examination of Hegel and Du Bois, see Odessa M. Weatherford-Jacobs, "Hegel and Du Bois: A Study of the Influence of G.W.F. Hegel on the Early Writings of W.E.B. Du Bois (1896–1903)," (Ph.D diss., Saint Louis University, 2002), 51. For a very insightful essay on Du Bois and Hegel, see Joel Williamson, "W.E.B. Du Bois as a Hegelian," in *What Was Freedom's Price?*, ed. David S. Sansing (Jackson: University Press of Mississippi, 1978), 21–51.

56. See W.E.B. Du Bois, "A Vacation Unique," in Shamoon Zamir, *Dark Voices: W.E.B. Du Bois and American Thought, 1888–1903* (Chicago: University of Chicago Press, 1995), 217–225. Also, see Du Bois, *Dusk of Dawn*, 33–34.

57. Du Bois, "A Vacation Unique," 221.

58. W.E.B. Du Bois, "Does Education Pay?," in *W.E.B. Du Bois: Writings in Periodicals Edited by Others*, ed. H. Aptheker (Millwood, NY: Kraus-Thomson Organization, 1982), 7.

59. Ibid., 2, 7.

60. Ibid., 12–13.

61. Ibid.

62. W.E.B. Du Bois, "Jefferson Davis as a Representative of Civilization," 1890, *Du Bois Papers, Addendum*, 1

63. Du Bois, "Carlyle," c. 1890, *Du Bois Papers*. Thomas Carlyle, *On Heroes, Hero-Worship and the Heroic in History* (1841; reprint, Berkeley, CA: University of California Press, 1993).

64. Du Bois, "Carlyle."

65. Shamoon Zamir makes this point as well. See Zamir, *Dark Voices*, 65.

66. W.E.B. Du Bois, "Harvard and the South: A Commencement Pact, 1891," Student Papers, 1881–1891, 8. *Du Bois Papers*.

67. Ibid., 12.

68. Du Bois, *Autobiography*, 157.

69. See Barrington S. Edwards, "W.E.B. Du Bois Between Worlds: Berlin, Empirical Social Research, and the Race Question," *Du Bois Review*, vol. 3, no. 2 (2006): 395–424.

70. Kenneth D. Barkin, "'Berlin Days' 1892–1894: W.E.B. Du Bois and German Political Economy," *boundary 2*, vol. 27, no. 3 (Fall 2000): 79–101. Sieglinde Lemke, "Berlin and Boundaries: *sollen versus geschehen*," *boundary 2*, vol. 27, no. 3 (Fall 2000): 53. Also see Fritz K. Ringer, *The Decline of the German Mandarins: The German Academic Community, 1890–1933* (1969; reprint, Middleton, CT: Wesleyan University Press, 1990), 143–149. For an excellent discussion on Schmoller and his ideas regarding research-based strategies in German social reform, see Erik Grimmer-Solem, *The Rise of Historical Economics and Social Reform in Germany, 1864–1894* (Oxford: Oxford University Press, 2003), 172–245.

71. Ibid.

72. Francis Broderick, "DuB, Gustav Schmoller," n.d. *Francis Broderick Collection*, Schomburg Center for Research in Black Culture, New York. Broderick Collection.

73. Lemke, "Berlin and Boundaries" 54.

74. W.E.B. Du Bois, "A Fellow of Harvard," December 7, 1892, *Du Bois Papers*.

75. Ibid.

76. Ibid.

77. W.E.B. Du Bois, "A Spring Wandering," March 24, 1893, *Du Bois Papers, Addendum.*

78. W.E.B. Du Bois, "University of Berlin," *The Fisk Herald,* vol. 11, no. 1 (May 1893): 6.

79. W.E.B. Du Bois, "Berlin Germany," Journal Notes, February 23, 1894, *Du Bois Papers.*

80. W.E.B. Du Bois, "Celebration of My Twenty-fifth Birthday," February 23, 1893, *Du Bois Papers.*

81. Du Bois, *Autobiography,* 183.

Chapter 2

1. In his essay (The Negro Question, 1890), American novelist and social critic George Washington Cable defined Negroes' situation as follows:

> Superficially, it [the Negro question or problem] is whether a certain seven millions of the people, one-ninth of the whole, dwelling in and natives to the Southern States of the Union, and by law an undifferentiated part of the Nation, have or have not the same full measure of the American citizen's rights that they would have were they entirely of European instead of wholly or partly of African descent.

George Washington Cable, "The Negro Question" in *The Negro Question: A Selection of Writings on Civil Rights in the South by George Washington Cable,* ed. Arlin Turner (Garden City, New York: Doubleday, 1958), 121.

2. See Richard Hofstadter, *The Progressive Movement, 1900–1915* (Englewood Cliffs, NJ: Prentice-Hall, 1963), 1–15.

3. Ibid.

4. See Lynn D. Gordon, *Gender and Higher Education in the Progressive Era* (New Haven, CT: Yale University Press, 1990), 34.

5. *Historical Statistics of the United States, Volume 1, Population* (New York: Cambridge University Press), 1-541, 1-166.

6. John A. Garraty and Mark C. Carnes, *A Short History of the American Nation* (New York: Longman, 2001), 506.

7. For an excellent discussion of Progressivism and Jane Addams, see Michael McGerr, *A Fierce Discontent: The Rise and Fall of the Progressive Movement in America, 1870–1920* (New York: Free Press, 2003), 53–54.

8. See Upton Sinclair, *The Jungle* (1906; reprint, Boston, MA: Bedford/St. Martin's, 2005); Garraty and Carnes, *A Short History of the American Nation,* 521.

9. Rayford W. Logan, *The Negro in American Life and Thought: The Nadir, 1877–1901* (New York: Dial Press, 1954).

10. Between 1889 and 1918, 2,522 blacks were lynched. Of this number, fifty were black women. See *Thirty Years of Lynching in the United States, 1889–1918* (New York: National Association for the Advancement of Colored People, 1919); Leon Litwack, *Trouble in Mind: Black Southerners in the Age of Jim Crow* (New York: Vintage Books, 1998); Orlando Patterson, *Rituals of Blood: Consequences of Slavery in Two American Centuries* (Washington, DC: Civitas/Counterpoint,

1998), 179–232; William F. Pinar, *The Gender of Racial Politics and Violence in America: Lynching, Prison Rape, & the Crisis of Masculinity* (New York: Peter Lang, 2001), 47–95.

11. Frederick L. Hoffman, *Race Traits and Tendencies of the American Negro* (1896; reprint, Clark, NJ: Lawbook Exchange, 2004); Charles Carroll, *The Negro: A Beast or in the Image of God* (St. Louis, MO: American Book and Bible House, 1900); Robert W. Shufeldt, *The Negro: A Menace to American Civilization* (Boston: Richard G. Badger, 1907).

12. Thomas Dixon Jr., *The Leopard's Spots: A Romance of the White Man's Burden, 1865–1900* (New York: Doubleday, Co., 1902); *The Clansman: An Historical Romance of the Ku Klux Klan* (New York: Doubleday, Co, 1905).

13. See *Birth of a Nation*, prod. and dir. D.W Griffith, David W. Griffith Corp., Republic Picture Home Video, 1991, 1915. Some historians, however, believe that Wilson viewed the film but never made this statement. See also Mary Frances Berry and John W. Blassingame, *Long Memory: The Black Experience in America* (New York: Oxford University Press, 1982), 382.

14. It should be noted that Cremin's characterization of Progressivism has been challenged and that some scholars view it as too broad to provide a meaningful definition. Despite this criticism, his book remains one of the most articulate analyses of the influence of Progressivism on education, and I assert that the characteristics delineated here, broad though they may be, capture the spirit of the movement even as they highlight the difficulty of trying to singularly define Progressivism. See Lawrence A. Cremin, *The Transformation of the School: Progressivism in American Education, 1876–1957* (New York: Alfred A. Knopf, 1961).

15. "Administrative Progressives," as historian David Tyack calls them, responded by calling for greater organization, efficiency, and centralization of school management. In their vision of greater efficiency and more differentiated curricula in American education, administrative Progressives exacerbated the already abysmal educational conditions of blacks by relegating them to lower academic tracks based on "efficient" standardized IQ testing. See David B. Tyack, *The One Best System: A History of American Urban Education* (Cambridge: Harvard University Press, 1974), 128, 217–218.

16. Ibid., 182–191.

17. See Watkins, *The White Architects*.

18. Henry A. Bullock, *A History of Negro Education in the South, from 1619 to Present* (Cambridge, MA: Harvard University Press, 1967), 172–173. Note that Bullock stresses that these were black college students who graduated under a college-level curriculum. Also see Butchart, *Northern Schools, Southern Blacks, and Reconstruction*, 167–179, and Anderson, *The Education of Blacks in the South*, 10–17.

19. As an example, in 1911, *The Common School and the Negro American* reported that in the years 1909–1910 the Negro school term was an average of 101 days a year compared to 128 days for white students. Black students were frequently excused from school to work on farms to help satisfy labor demands during harvest seasons. As a result, the prevalence of sharecropping among blacks played a mitigating role in their negative school attendance. See W.E.B. Du Bois, *The Common School and the Negro American* (Atlanta, GA: Atlanta University Press, 1911). Also, see Bullock, *A History of Negro Education*, 175–177.

20. Bullock, *A History of Negro Education*, 180; Michael Fultz, "African American Teachers in the South, 1890–1940: Powerlessness and the Ironies of Expectations and Protest," *History of Education Quarterly*, vol. 35, no. 4 (Winter 1995): 404.

21. Thomas Jesse Jones, *Negro Education: A Study of the Private and Higher Schools for Colored People in the United States* (1917; reprint, New York: Arno Press, 1969), 81. The tensions between Du Bois and Jones have been thoroughly explicated. See Donald Johnson, "W.E.B. Du Bois, Thomas Jesse Jones and the Struggle for Social Education," *Journal of Negro History*, vol. 85, no. 3 (Summer 2000): 71–95; Herbert M. Kliebard, "'That Evil Genius of the Negro Race': Thomas Jesse Jones and Educational Reform," in *Changing Course: American Curriculum Reform in the 20th Century*, ed. Herbert M. Kliebard (New York: Teachers College Press, 2002), 24–35; William Watkins, *The White Architects*, 114–117.

22. Ibid.

23. W.E.B. Du Bois, "Negro Education," *The Crisis* 15 (February 1918), 173–178.

24. John Dewey, *The School and Society* (1899; reprint, Chicago: University of Chicago Press, 1967), and *The Child and the Curriculum* (Chicago: University of Chicago Press, 1909). See J. Perkinson, *The Imperfect Panacea: American Faith in Education 1865–1990* (New York: McGraw-Hill, Inc. 1991), 83, and Karier, *The Individual, Society, and Education*, 146. At one point in his career, Dewey seemed, however, to reconcile his notion of democratic education with what he believed was sometimes a pragmatic need for a differentiated curriculum. See John Dewey, "Racial Prejudice and Friction," *The Middle Works of John Dewey, 1899–1924*, ed. Jo Ann Boydston (Carbondale, IL: Southern Illinois University Press, 1988), 242–254. See also Urban and Wagoner, *American Education*, 221. Also see Jim Garrison, *Dewey and Eros: Wisdom and Desire in the Art of Teaching* (New York: Teachers College Press, 1997).

25. Dewey, *The School and Society*, 29, 127–130.

26. Joel H. Spring, *Education and the Rise of the Corporate State* (Boston, MA: Beacon Press, 1973), 85.

27. John Dewey, "Industrial Education and Democracy," *The Survey* (March 22, 1913), 870.

28. Ibid.

29. John Dewey, "Address of John Dewey, Proceedings of the National Negro Conference, 1909" in *The American Negro: His History and Literature* (1909; reprint, New York: Arno Press, 1969), 72.

30. In an earlier work, I asserted that Dewey "ignored the salient issues of race and racism that were embedded in the fabric of American society and that impeded American democracy." See Alridge, "Conceptualizing a Du Boisian Philosophy of Education," 368. While Dewey virtually ignored racial issues in his educational philosophy, he did speak out against racism and was a founding member of the NAACP. Dewey also addressed racial prejudice in a controversial essay entitled "Racial Prejudice and Friction," in which he argued that some types of segregation are understandable given society's discriminatory practices toward ethnic minorities. Dewey stated, "The simple fact of the case is that at present the world is not sufficiently civilized to permit close contact of peoples of widely different cultures without deplorable consequences." See John Dewey, "Racial Prejudice

and Friction." For a comparative analysis of Dewey's and Du Bois's educational ideas, see Ben Burkes, "Unity and Diversity through Education: A Comparison of the Thought of W.E.B. Du Bois and John Dewey," *Journal of Thought* (Spring 1997): 99–110.

31. W.E.B. Du Bois to John Dewey, May 15, 1931, *Du Bois Papers*. Du Bois again requested essays from Dewey in June and August of 1931 and January 12 and 13 of 1932.

32. David Levering Lewis brought to my attention that Dewey gave lectures in Harlem on several occasions. Psychologist Edmund Gordon remembers attending lectures given by Dewey in Harlem. Dewey's connections to the African American community is beyond the scope of this study. However, such work would contribute significantly to our understanding of Dewey, education, and race. See Interviews. See David Levering Lewis.

33. W.E.B. Du Bois, *The Suppression of the African Slave Trade to the United States of America, 1638–1870* (1896; reprint, Baton Rouge: Louisiana State University, 1969).

34. Du Bois, *Autobiography*, 186.

35. Yolande Du Bois Williams, interview by author, tape recording, New Orleans, LA, July 19, 2005.

36. W.E.B. Du Bois, "The True Meaning of a University," delivered in the Upper Chapel of Wilberforce University on December 20, 1894, before the Sodalian Literary Society. *Du Bois Collection*, Fisk.

37. Ibid., 20.

38. W.E.B. Du Bois, Review of *Race Traits and Tendencies of the American Negro* by Frederick L. Hoffman, *Annals of the American Academy of Political and Social Science*, vol. 9 (January, 1897): 128–130. See also Katz and Sugrue, "Introduction," in *W.E.B. Du Bois, Race, and the City: The Philadelphia Negro and Its Legacy*, eds. Michael B. Katz and Thomas J. Sugrue (Philadelphia: University of Pennsylvania Press), 21–23.

39. W.E.B. Du Bois, Review of *Race Traits and Tendencies of the American Negro*.

40. Katz and Sugrue, "Introduction," in *W.E.B. Du Bois, Race, and the City*, 13.

41. See Du Bois, *Autobiography*, 194–204; Robert Gregg, "Giant Steps: W.E.B. Du Bois and the Historical Enterprise," in *W.E.B. Du Bois, Race, and the City*, 83.

42. Du Bois, *Autobiography*, 197.

43. W.E.B. Du Bois, *Dusk of Dawn: An Essay Toward an Autobiography of a Race Concept* (1940; reprint, New Brunswick, NJ: Transaction Publishers, 2000), 50–51.

44. W.E.B. Du Bois, *The Philadelphia Negro: A Social Study* (1899; reprint, New York: Schocken Books, 1967), 92.

45. Ibid., 95.

46. Du Bois, *The Souls of Black Folk* (1903; reprint, New York: Alfred A. Knopf, 1993), 165.

47. Du Bois, *Autobiography*, 222.

48. See Lewis, *Biography of a Race*, 333–336.

49. Du Bois, *Autobiography*, 217.

50. W.E.B. Du Bois, *The College-Bred Negro* (Atlanta: Atlanta University Press, 1900), 64.

51. The "slave states" were comprised of all the Southern states, including the District of Columbia, Maryland, West Virginia, Delaware, and Missouri. W.E.B. Du Bois, *The Negro Common School* (Atlanta: Atlanta University Press, 1901), 17.

52. W.E.B. Du Bois, *The Negro Common School*, 105.

53. Ibid., 117.

54. Ibid., 37.

55. W.E.B. Du Bois, "Heredity and the Public Schools," in *Du Bois on Education*, ed. Eugene F. Provenzo (Walnut Creek, CA: AltaMira Press, 2002), 121.

56. W.E.B. Du Bois, "The Development of a People," *International Journal of Ethics*, vol. 14, no. 3 (April 1904): 292–311.

57. W.E.B. Du Bois and Augustus Granville Dill, *The College-Bred Negro American* (Atlanta: Atlanta University Press, 1910), 5.

58. Ibid., 7.

59. W.E.B. Du Bois and Augustus Granville Dill, *The Common School and the Negro American* (Atlanta: Atlanta University Press, 1911), 13–14.

60. Ibid., 104–106.

61. Ibid., 100–101.

62. Ibid., 115–119.

Chapter 3

1. Alexander Crummell, "Civilization, the Primal Need of the Race," in *Destiny and Race: Selected Writings, 1840–1898 Alexander Crummell*, ed. Wilson Jeremiah Moses (Amherst: University of Massachusetts Press, 1992), 285.

2. Alexander Crummell, "The Necessities and Advantages of Education Considered in Relation to Colored Men," July 4, 1844, *Alexander Crummell Papers*, Schomburg Research Center of the New York Public Library.

3. Quoted in Alfred A. Moss Jr., *The American Negro Academy: Voice of the Talented Tenth* (Baton Rouge: Louisiana State University Press, 1981), 40.

4. W.E.B. Du Bois, "The Conservation of Races," in *W.E.B. Du Bois: A Reader*, ed. David Levering Lewis (New York: Henry Holt and Company, 1995), 20–27.

5. For a comprehensive examination of Washington's life and ideas, see Louis R. Harlan, *Booker T. Washington: The Making of a Black Leader, 1856–1901, Volume I* (New York: Oxford University Press, 1972) and *Booker T. Washington: The Wizard of Tuskegee, 1901–1915, Volume II* (New York: Oxford University Press, 1983). While dated, Curti's examination of Washington's educational ideas remains one of the most thorough, concise, and insightful. See Curti, *The Social Ideas of American Educators*, 288–309. For a recent excellent and highly accessible analysis of the Washington and Du Bois debate, see Jacqueline M. Moore, *Booker T. Washington, W.E.B. Du Bois, and the Struggle for Racial Uplift* (Wilmington, DE: Scholarly Resources Inc., 2003).

6. W.E.B. Du Bois to Booker T. Washington, September 4, 1895, in *The Correspondence of W.E.B. Du Bois: Volume I, Selections, 1877–1934*, ed. Herbert Aptheker (Amherst: University of Massachusetts Press, 1973), 39.

7. See W.E.B. Du Bois, "The Evolution of Negro Leadership," *The Dial*, vol. 31, no. 362 (July 1901): 54.

8. Du Bois wrote, "It would be unjust to Mr. Washington not to acknowledge that in several instances he has opposed movements in the South which were unjust to the Negro; he sent memorials to the Louisiana and Alabama constitutional conventions, he has spoken against lynching, and in other ways has openly or silently set his influence against sinister schemes and unfortunate happenings." W.E.B. Du Bois, *The Souls of Black Folk*, 41.

9. Du Bois, *The Souls of Black Folk*, 37.

10. Booker T. Washington to W.E.B. Du Bois, May 9, 1903, *Du Bois Papers*.

11. Booker T. Washington to W.E.B. Du Bois, July 6, 1903, *Du Bois Papers*.

12. Washington to Daniel Merriman, April 25, 1910, *The Booker T. Washington Papers, Volume 10, 1909–11*, ed. Louis R. Harlan, (Urbana: University of Illinois, 1981), 321–322.

13. See Washington to Du Bois, August 24, 1894, *Correspondence*, 38. See also Lewis, *Biography of a Race*, 233–237.

14. W.E.B. Du Bois, interview by Charles H. Thompson, n.d. *Charles H. Thompson Papers*, Moorland-Spingarn Research Center, Washington, DC. For a detailed examination of Washington's episode in New York, see William H. Gatewood, "Booker T. Washington and the Ulrich Affair," *Journal of Negro History*, vol. 55, no. 1 (January 1970): 29–44.

15. See Michael Rudolph West, *The Education of Booker T. Washington: American Democracy and the Idea of Race Relations* (New York: Columbia University Press, 2006).

16. Pero Gaglo Dagbovie, "Exploring a Century of Historical Scholarship on Booker T. Washington," *Journal of African American History*, vol. 92, no. 2 (Spring 2007): 259, 239–264.

17. Alexander Crummell to Anna Julia Cooper, June 3, 1886, *Anna Julia Cooper Papers*, Moorland-Spingarn Research Center.

18. Anna Julia Cooper, *A Voice from the South* (1892; reprint, New York: Oxford University Press, 1988), 50–51.

19. Ibid., 57.

20. *Proceedings of the Second Hampton Negro Conference, May 25, 1894*, in Louis Harlan, ed., *The Booker T. Washington Papers, vol. 3* (Chicago, IL: University of Illinois Press, 1974), 444.

21. For an excellent discussion of the matter, see Charles Lemert and Esme Bhan (eds.), *The Voice of Anna Julia Cooper: Including* A Voice from the South *and Other Important Essays, Papers, and Letters* (Lanham: Rowman and Littlefield Publishers, Inc., 1998), 9–11, and Mary Helen Washington, "Introduction," in Anna Julia Cooper, *A Voice from the South*, xxxiii–xxxix.

22. See W.E.B. Du Bois, "The Damnation of Women," in *W.E.B. Du Bois: A Reader*, ed. David Levering Lewis (New York: Henry Holt and Company, 1995), 304–305. Also see Mary Helen Washington, "Introduction," in Cooper, *A Voice from the South*, xxvii–liv.

23. Anna Julia Cooper to Du Bois, December 31, 1929, *Correspondence, vol. 1*, 411. See Claude G. Bowers, *The Tragic Era: The Revolution after Lincoln* (New York: Halcyon, 1929).

24. For a detailed examination of the contribution of black women educators to African American educational thought, see Stephanie Y. Evans, *Black Women in*

the Ivory Tower, 1850–1954: An Intellectual History (Gainesville: University Press of Florida, 2007).

25. Kelly Miller, "Education for Manhood," *Kelly Miller's Monographic Magazine* (Washington, DC: Murray Bros. Printing Co., 1913), 4.

26. W.E.B. Du Bois to Kelly Miller, "Warns Miller on BW meeting," November 2, 1903, *Broderick Collection.*

27. Kelly Miller, "Surplus Negro Women," in *Race Adjustment: Essays on the Negro in America*, ed. Kelly Miller (New York: The Neale Publishing Company, 1908).

28. For an excellent interpretation of Miller's educational philosophy, see August Meier, "The Racial and Educational Philosophy of Kelly Miller, 1895–1915," *Journal of Negro Education*, vol. 29, no. 2 (Spring 1960): 121–127.

29. See Opal V. Easter, *Nannie Helen Burroughs* (New York: Garland Publishing, Inc., 1995), 30–31.

30. Karen A. Johnson, *Uplifting the Women and the Race: The Educational Philosophies and Social Activism of Anna Julia Cooper and Nannie Helen Burroughs* (New York: Garland Publishing Inc., 2000), 93; and Evelyn Brooks Higginbotham, *Righteous Discontent: The Women's Movement in the Black Baptist Church, 1880–1920* (Cambridge, MA: Harvard University Press, 1993), 212–213. Also see Sharon Harley, "Nannie Helen Burroughs: 'The Black Goddess of Liberty,'" *Journal of Negro History*, vol. 81 no. ¼ (Winter-Autumn, 1996): 62–71; Traki Taylor, "'Womanhood Glorified': Nannie Helen Burroughs and the National Training School for Women and Girls, Inc., 1909–1961," *Journal of African American History*, vol. 87, no. 4 (Autumn 2002): 390–402.

31. Higginbotham, *Righteous Discontent*, 213.

32. Nannie Helen Burroughs, "12 Things the Negro Must Do for Himself." n.d. *Nannie Helen Burroughs Papers*, Library of Congress. Washington, DC.

Chapter 4

1. W.E.B. Du Bois, "The Training of Negroes for Social Power," in *The Oxford W.E.B. Du Bois Reader*, ed. Eric J. Sundquist (New York: Oxford University Press, 1996), 335.

2. The "talented tenth" was Du Bois's view that the most educated blacks should lead the race. See W.E.B. Du Bois, "The Talented Tenth," in *The Negro Problem*, ed. Booker T. Washington et al. (New York: James Pott and Company, 1903), 33.

3. W.E.B. Du Bois, "Strivings of the Negro People," *Atlantic*, vol. 80 (August 1897): 194–198. Du Bois, "Of Our Spiritual Strivings," *Souls*, 1–9.

4. W.E.B. Du Bois to African American High School Girl, December 24, 1904. *Correspondence*, volume 1, 84.

5. W.E.B. Du Bois, "The Work of Negro Women in Society," *Spelman Messenger*, vol. 18 (1902).

6. However, Du Bois also advocated gender-specific roles for black women as mothers, nurturers, and homemakers. Such a view was consistent with the views of many other men, and some women, of the era. Even Cooper, as I have pointed out, preached maternal, gender-specific roles for women. For an excellent analysis of Du Bois and other "race men," see Hazel Carby, *Race Men* (Cambridge, MA: Harvard University Press, 1998).

7. Nina Gomer Du Bois to Du Bois, January 5, 1902, *Du Bois Papers*.

8. African American educators of the period, including black women, conceptualized black women's education and leadership within a Victorian framework. I have addressed this issue elsewhere in a comparative analysis of Anna Julia Cooper's and Du Bois's educational thought. Derrick P. Alridge, "Of Victorianism, Civilizationism, and Progressivism: The Educational Ideas of Anna Julia Cooper and W.E.B. Du Bois, 1892–1940," *History of Education Quarterly*, vol. 47, no. 4 (November 2007): 416–446. Also see Joy James, "The Profeminist Politics of W.E.B. Du Bois with Respect to Anna Julia Cooper and Ida B. Wells Barnett," in *W.E.B. Du Bois: On Race and Culture*, eds. Bernard Bell, Emily Grosholz, and James Stewart (New York: Routledge, 1996), 142–60.

9. Marable, *W.E.B. Du Bois*, 55.

10. W.E.B. Du Bois, "The Niagara Movement: Address to the Country," in *W.E.B. Du Bois: A Reader*, ed. David Levering Lewis (New York: Henry Holt, 1995), 368.

11. W.E.B. Du Bois, "A Rational System of Negro Education." n.d., 2, *Du Bois Collection*. While there is no conclusive date to be found on this essay, the dates 1897–1900 appear in the upper right corner.

12. Ibid., 7.

13. The leading founder of Sigma Pi Phi was pharmacist Henry M. Minton. Du Bois became a charter member of Zeta Boule, founded in 1912. See Charles H. Wesley, *History of Sigma Pi Phi: First of the Negro-American Greek Letter Fraternities*, vol. 1 (1954; reprint, New York: Fred Weidner & Daughter Printers, 2002), 88–89, and *Henry Arthur Callis, Life and Legacy* (1977; reprint, Washington, DC: Foundation Publishers, 1997), 15, 120, 148. Historian Kevin Gaines argues that race uplift ideology was primarily a middle-class agenda promoted by black elites. Gaines also notes, "The limitations of black elites' defensive appropriation of dominant racial theories for the purpose of erecting a supposedly positive black identity resulted from their desperate situation." Elsewhere, I have pointed out that while black educators were limited by the dominant uplift ideologies and discourses of their day, they were very pragmatic in forging race uplift agendas that resonated with both blacks and whites and that ultimately advanced the entire black race. See Kevin Gaines, *Uplifting the Race: Black Leadership, Politics, and Culture in the Twentieth Century* (Chapel Hill: University of North Carolina Press, 1996), xv, and Alridge, "Of Victorianism, Civilizationism, and Progressivism." According to historian Gail Bederman, the establishment of fraternal organizations during the early twentieth century was a response to the "excessive femininity" of Victorian culture and reflected middle-class men's call to revitalize manhood and masculinity. While Bederman appears to be talking about white fraternities, her thesis may be applicable to black fraternities as well. Black fraternities of the period were typically comprised of middle-class black males, and the idea of manhood was a critical element in their mission of race uplift. See Gail Bederman, *Manliness & Civilization: A Cultural History of Gender and Race in the United States, 1880–1917* (Chicago: University of Chicago Press, 1996), 16, 19, 22–23.

14. W.E.B. Du Bois to Yolande Du Bois, October 29, 1914, in *The Correspondence*, 208.

15. W.E.B. Du Bois, "The Hampton Idea," in *The Education of Black People: Ten Critiques, 1906–1960*, ed. Herbert Aptheker (New York: Monthly Review Press, 1973): 14.

16. Ibid., 9–10.

17. Du Bois, "Strivings of the Negro People," 194–198.

18. Shamoon Zamir, for instance, argues that Du Bois was referring primarily to class duality between the black middle and lower classes. See Zamir, *Dark Voices*, 116. Paul Gilroy offers a cosmopolitan and multi-ethnic analysis of Du Bois's idea of double-consciousness and argues that Du Bois's notion should be examined as relevant to all people of color in colonial and post-colonial societies. See Paul Gilroy, *The Black Atlantic: Modernity and Double Consciousness* (Cambridge, MA: Harvard University Press, 1993). Ross Posnock, like Zamir, sees a class dimension in Du Bois's notion of double-consciousness, and like Gilroy, Posnock offers a Du Boisian double-consciousness interpretation that is cosmopolitan. Ross Posnock, *Color & Culture: Black Writers and the Making of the Modern Intellectual* (Cambridge, MA: Harvard University Press, 1998), 3–7, 41–42. Molefi K. Asante dismisses Du Bois's concept as Eurocentric. See Molefi K. Asante, *The Afrocentric Idea*, (1987; reprint, Philadelphia: Temple University Press, 1998), 177. Adolph Reed argues that Du Bois was, in fact, referring to the social realities of black life and the hegemonic nature of white society in his notion of double-consciousness. Adolph L. Reed Jr., *W.E.B. Du Bois and American Political Thought: Fabianism and the Color Line* (Oxford: Oxford University Press, 1997). My point here is not to engage the debate, nor to trace Du Bois's thinking on the matter to a single individual or group. It is perhaps best to state that Du Bois's notion likely resonated with the thinking of his time. I therefore want to offer a straightforward interpretation by stating that when Du Bois spoke of double-consciousness in 1897 and 1903, he was referring primarily to the social conditions of blacks in American and European societies.

19. Du Bois's concept of double-consciousness in *Souls* bears striking similarities to ideas in Hegel's *Phenomenology of Mind*. Zamir provides an excellent analysis of *Souls* and Hegel in Zamir, *Dark Voices*.

20. Historian Daryl Michael Scott has argued that Du Bois's focus on alleviating the psychological tension of double-consciousness reflected the "therapeutic ethos" of the late nineteenth century, which promoted the notion that blacks had a damaged psyche. This idea, Scott argues, was not used only by Du Bois. Scott argues that after Reconstruction white liberals promoted psychological rehabilitation and inclusion into society for blacks, whereas white conservatives pointed out that pathological behavior among blacks justified the exclusion of blacks from the larger society. See Daryl Michael Scott, *Contempt and Pity: Social Policy and the Image of the Damaged Black Psyche, 1880–1996* (Chapel Hill: University of North Carolina Press, 1997).

21. James B. Stewart, "Psychic Duality in the Novels of W.E.B. Du Bois," *Phylon*, vol. 44, no. 2 (1983): 103. Also see Stewart, "Perspectives in Reformist, Radical, and Recovery Models of Black Identity Dynamics from the Novels of W.E.B. Du Bois" in *Flight: In Search of Vision*, ed. James B. Stewart (Trenton, NJ: Africa World Press, 2004), 107–127. Corey D. B. Walker has also identified black identity as the focal point of Du Bois's articulation of double-consciousness. See Corey D. B. Walker, "Modernity in Black: Du Bois and the (Re)Construction of Black Identity" in *The Souls of Black Folk*, *Philosophia Africana*, vol. 7, no. 1 (March 2004): 83–93.

22. W.E.B. Du Bois, "The True Brownies," *The Crisis*, vol. 16, no. 6 (1919): 285.

23. Ibid.

24. Ibid., 286.

25. Du Bois discussed the idea of double-consciousness long after 1903 and 1907 in both fictional and nonfictional writings. In his book *Dusk of Dawn* (1940), for instance, Du Bois discussed the contemporary dilemma of African Americans, stating: "Not only do white men but also colored men forget the facts of the Negro's double environment. The Negro American has for his environment not only the white surrounding world, but also, and touching him usually much more nearly and compelling, is the environment furnished by his own colored group. . . . The American Negro, therefore, is surrounded and conditioned by the concept which he has of white people and he is treated in accordance with the concept they have of him." As an autobiographical work, *Dusk of Dawn* may be construed as Du Bois's own struggle with race and double-consciousness. See W.E.B. Du Bois, *Dusk of Dawn: An Essay toward An Autobiography of a Race Concept* (1940; reprint, New Brunswick, NJ: Transaction Publishers, 2000), 173.

Chapter 5

1. Garraty and Carnes, *A Short History of the American Nation*, 561–566.
2. Ibid.
3. Ibid.
4. W.E.B. Du Bois, "Close Ranks," in *W.E.B. Du Bois: A Reader*, ed. David Levering Lewis (New York: Henry Holt and Co., 1995), 697.
5. Trotter, *The African American Experience*, 375–376; Franklin and Moss, *From Slavery to Freedom*, 359.
6. Trotter, *The African American Experience*, 386.
7. Alain Locke, "The New Negro," in *The New Negro: An Interpretation*, ed. Alain Locke (New York: Albert and Charles Boni, 1925), 3, 11.
8. W.E.B. Du Bois to Cecil B. DeMille, June 8, 1926, *Du Bois Papers*.
9. See Franklin and Moss, *From Slavery to Freedom*, 419–421. See Evelyn Brooks Higginbotham, *Righteous Discontent: The Women's Movement in the Black Baptist Church, 1880–1920* (Cambridge: Harvard University Press, 1993).
10. Franklin and Moss, *From Slavery to Freedom*, 395.
11. David Levering Lewis, *W.E.B. Du Bois: The Fight for Equality in the American Century, 1919–1963* (New York: Henry Holt and Co., 2000), 50.
12. Moses, *Creative Conflict in African American Thought*, 264–267.
13. Ibid., 63–64, and Raymond Wolters, *Du Bois and His Rivals* (Columbia, Missouri: University of Missouri Press, 2002), 143–191; Marable, *Black Radical Democrat*, 120.
14. Quoted in Lewis, *The Fight for Equality*, 81.
15. Amy Jacques Garvey to Du Bois, April 24, 1944, *Correspondence*, vol. 2, 379. For a thorough examination of the life of Amy Jacques Garvey, see Ula Yvette Taylor, *The Veiled Garvey: The Life and Times of Amy Jacques Garvey* (Chapel Hill: University of North Carolina Press, 2002).
16. For an informative essay on black adult education during the Harlem Renaissance, see Juanita Johnson-Bailey, "African Americans in Adult Education: The Harlem Renaissance Revisited," *Adult Education Quarterly*, vol. 56, no. 2 (February 2006): 102–118. Also see David L. Lewis, *When Harlem Was in Vogue* (New York: Oxford University Press, 1980), 157–162.

17. Robert C. Weaver, "The New Deal and the Negro: A Look at the Facts," *Opportunity*, vol. 13, no. 7 (July 1935): 200–203.

18. Gunnar Myrdal, *An American Dilemma: The Negro Problem and Modern Democracy, vol. 1* (1944; reprint, New Brunswick, NJ: Transaction Publishers, 1996), 232–233.

19. Raymond Wolters, *Negroes and the Great Depression: The Problem of Economic Recovery* (Westport, CT: Greenwood Publishing Company, 1970), 7. Gunnar Myrdal points out, however, that while white farm ownership declined between 1920 and 1930, it increased between 1930 and 1940, showing further evidence of the greater negative impact of the Depression on black farmers compared to white farmers. Myrdal, *American Dilemma*, 237–238.

20. See Wolters, *Negroes and the Great Depression*, 96–155.

21. E. Franklin Frazier, *The Negro in the United States* (1949; reprint, New York: The MacMillan Co., 1957), 396.

22. Ibid., 397, 402.

23. See W.E.B. Du Bois, *The Negro Artisan* (Atlanta: Atlanta University Press, 1902).

24. W.E.B. Du Bois, "The Negroes of Farmville, Virginia: A Social Study," *Bulletin of the Department of Labor*, No. 14, Washington, DC (January 1898).

25. Ibid., 17–18.

26. Ibid.

27. W.E.B. Du Bois, "The Upbuilding of Black Durham: The Success of the Negroes and Their Value to a Tolerant and Helpful Southern City," *The World's Work*, vol. 13 (January, 1912): 234.

28. W.E.B. Du Bois, *Economic Cooperation among Negro Americans* (Atlanta: Atlanta University Press, 1907), 8. For further discussion, see Joseph DeMarco, "The Rationale and Foundation of Du Bois's Theory of Economic Cooperation," *Phylon: The Atlanta University Review of Race and Culture*, vol. 35, no. 1 (March 1974): 5–15.

29. W.E.B. Du Bois, "Forum of Fact and Opinion," *Pittsburgh Courier*, June 26, 1937 in *Newspaper Columns by W.E.B. Du Bois, Volume 1, 1883–1944*, ed. Herbert Aptheker (White Plains, NY: Kraus-Thomson, 1986), 213–214.

30. W.E.B. Du Bois to Wilbur K. Thomas, May 3, 1935, *The Correspondence of W.E.B. Du Bois: Volume II Selections, 1934–1944*, ed. Herbert Aptheker (Amherst: University of Massachusetts Press, 1976), 57–58.

31. W.E.B. Du Bois, "Forum of Fact and Opinion," *Pittsburgh Courier*, November 7, 1936, in *Newspaper Columns by W.E.B. Du Bois*, vol. 1, *1883–1944*, ed. Herbert Aptheker (White Plains, NY: Kraus-Thomson, 1986), 132–133.

32. Ibid.

33. Du Bois experienced a different Germany in 1936 than he had during his student years in the 1890s. By 1936, fascism had swept across Germany and anti-Semitism was rampant. Only two years earlier Hitler had eliminated his political rivals in a purge called the Night of the Long Knives. Kristallnacht, Hitler's first pogrom against the Jews, was only two years away. In his columns in the *Pittsburgh Courier* written during and after his stay in Germany, Du Bois spoke out against the anti-Semitism he saw in Germany and warned of the further oppression to come. He noted a sign he saw from his hotel room instructing Germans not to provide winter relief to Jews, so as to prevent Germany from "sink[ing] to the level of the 'Jewish Bolshevist countries of the rest of

the world.'" Du Bois was prophetic in predicting that he was witnessing "an attack on civilization" on the horrific level of the "Spanish Inquisition and African slave trade." See W.E.B. Du Bois, "Forum of Fact and Opinion," *Pittsburgh Courier*, December 19, 1936, in *Newspaper Columns by W.E.B. Du Bois, Volume 1*, 149–150.

34. W.E.B. Du Bois, "Address Delivered by Dr. W.E.B. Du Bois, Tenth Anniversary Conference of the National Association for the Advancement of Colored People," June 25, 1919, *Du Bois Collection*, Fisk.

35. W.E.B. Du Bois as quoted in Vincent P. Franklin, "W.E.B. Du Bois and the Education of Black Folk," essay review in *History of Education Quarterly*, vol. 16, no. 1 (Spring 1976): 113.

36. W.E.B. Du Bois, "The Tragedy of 'Jim Crow,'" *The Crisis*, vol. 26, no. 4 (August 1923): 172.

37. *Report of Debate Conducted by the Chicago Forum: "Shall the Negro Be Encouraged to Seek Cultural Equality?"* March 17, 1929 (Chicago: Chicago Forum Council, 1929), 6.

38. Ibid., 20. Du Bois had little faith that whites would adequately fund black schools. Four years earlier he made this case in an essay entitled "Gifts and Education," in which he argued that blacks had always depended on the benevolence of whites. See W.E.B. Du Bois, "Gifts and Education," in *W.E.B. Du Bois: A Reader*, 270.

39. W.E.B. Du Bois, "Pechstein and Pecksniff," *The Crisis*, vol. 36, no. 9 (September 1929): 313–314.

40. Ibid., 313.

41. W.E.B. Du Bois, "Segregation," *The Crisis*, vol. 40, no. 1 (January 1934): 2.

42. W.E.B. Du Bois to the Board of Directors of the National Association for the Advancement of Colored People, June 11, 1934, *Du Bois Papers*.

43. W.E.B. Du Bois, "Does the Negro Need Separate Schools?" *Journal of Negro Education*, vol. 4, no. 3 (July 1935): 335.

44. Ibid.

45. In 1935, Du Bois further explicated his support of voluntary segregation as a method of gaining social, economic, and political strength. He stated, "American Negroes have got to take refuge in a limited amount of voluntary self-segregation in order to accumulate and apply sufficient strength for self-defense and self-assertion and eventual equality with other men." Through strength facilitated by the communalism of voluntary segregation, Du Bois believed, blacks would gain equality. See Du Bois, "Voluntary Segregation," c. 1935, *Du Bois Papers*.

46. W.E.B. Du Bois, "Race Segregation with Special Reference to Education," c. 1936, *Du Bois Papers*.

47. W.E.B. Du Bois, "The Wharton School," n.d., *Du Bois Collection*, Fisk.

48. Ibid.

49. See Lewis, *The Fight for Equality*, 270; Du Bois to J. W. Studebaker, November 7, 1938, *Correspondence, Volume II*, 175.

50. See Rachel Davis Du Bois, "The Face-to-Face Unit as a Group for a Program of Intercultural Education," *Journal of Educational Sociology*, vol. 19, no. 9 (May 1946): 555–561. Du Bois mentions Rachel Du Bois's contributions to race relations in "Race Relations in the United States, 1917–1947," *Phylon*, vol. 1, no. 2 (2nd Quarter: 1940): 235 and "A Chronicle of Race Relations," *Phylon*, vol. 2, no. 4 (4th Quarter: 1941): 406. See also Lewis, *The Fight for Equality*, 270.

51. Dorothy Cowser Yancy, "William Edward Burghardt Du Bois' Atlanta Years: The Human Side–A Study Based Upon Oral Sources," *Journal of Negro History*, vol. 63, no. 1 (January 1978): 59–67.

52. Du Bois, *Autobiography*, 283.

Chapter 6

1. Johnny Washington, "Introduction," in *Alain Locke and Philosophy: A Quest for Cultural Pluralism* (Westport, CT: Greenwood Press, 1986), xvii–xxxii.

2. Alain Locke, "The Role of the Talented Tenth," *Howard University Record*, vol. 9 (December 1918): 15.

3. Ibid., 16.

4. Alain Locke, "Address to the Child Study Association, New York City," November 29, 1932, *Alain Locke Papers*, Moorland-Spingarn Research Center, Washington D.C. For excellent analyses of Locke's philosophy of education, see Talmadge C. Guy, "Alain Locke and the AAAE Movement: Cultural Pluralism and Negro Adult Education," *Adult Education Quarterly*, vol. 46, no. 4 (Summer 1996): 209–223, and Talmadge Guy, "Adult Education and Propaganda: Alain Locke's Views on Culture, Propaganda, and Race Progress," *The Langston Hughes Review*, vol. 13, no. 2 (1995): 68–76.

5. See Alain Locke, "The New Negro," in *The New Negro*, ed. Alain Locke (1925; reprint, New York: Atheneum, 1968), 3–16; W.E.B. Du Bois, "Criteria of Negro Art," in *The Oxford W.E.B. Du Bois Reader*, ed. Eric J. Sundquist (New York: Oxford University Press, 1996), 324–328; and W.E.B. Du Bois and Alain Locke, "The Younger Literary Movement," *The Crisis*, vol. 27, no. 5 (February 1924): 161–162.

6. Alain L. Locke, *Race Contacts and Interracial Relations: Lectures on the Theory and Practice of Race*, ed. Jeffrey C. Stewart (Washington, DC: Howard University Press, 1992).

7. Historian Manning Marable provides a thorough investigation of the events surrounding Locke, Du Bois, and the *Bronze Booklets* in Manning Marable, "Alain Locke, W.E.B. Du Bois and the Crisis of Black Education during the Great Depression," in *Alain Locke: Reflections on a Modern Renaissance Man*, ed. Russell J. Linneman (Baton Rouge, LA: Louisiana State University, 1982), 63–76. Also see Du Bois, *Dusk of Dawn*, 320–322.

8. W.E.B. Du Bois, "The Passing of Alain Locke," *Phylon* (1954): 252.

9. Du Bois notes that he had "toyed with" the idea of writing an *Encyclopedia Africana* in 1909. See W.E.B. Du Bois, "A Portrait of Carter G. Woodson," *Masses and Mainstream* 3 (June 1950): 24.

10. Carter G. Woodson, "Encyclopedia Africana," n.d., *Carter G. Woodson Collection* (Washington, DC: Library of Congress, Photoduplication Service, 1997).

11. W.E.B. Du Bois to Carter G. Woodson, January 29, 1932, *Woodson Collection*.

12. In recent years, Henry Louis Gates has accused Woodson of playing a decisive role in convincing the GEB not to fund the *Encyclopedia of the Negro*. At the time of this writing, Gates has not produced documentation to support this claim. The episode, however, is well documented in Kenneth Robert Janken, *Rayford W. Logan and the Dilemma of the African American Intellectual* (Amherst, MA: University of

Massachusetts, 1993), 89–97, and Lewis, *The Fight for Equality*, 427–433; 444–447. References to this episode may also be found in both the *Du Bois Papers* and the *Woodson Papers*. The Association of the Study of African American Life and History has also responded to Gates's claims. See "Open Letter to Dr. Henry Louis Gates, Jr., Harvard University from The Executive Council-Association for the Study of African American Life and History," *Journal of African American History*, vol. 88, no. 3 (March 28, 2003). Also see W.E.B. Du Bois and Guy B. Johnson, *Encyclopedia of the Negro: Preparatory Volume with Reference List and Reports* (New York: The Phelps-Stokes Fund, 1946).

13. W.E.B. Du Bois, "A Portrait of Carter G. Woodson," 23–24.

14. Carter G. Woodson, *The Mis-Education of the Negro* (1933; reprint Washington, D.C.: ASALH Press, 2005).

15. Ibid., 23.

16. Ibid., 5.

17. Audrey T. McCluskey, "Multiple Consciousness in the Leadership of Mary McLeod Bethune," *NWSA Journal*, vol. 6, no. 4 (Spring 1994): 69–81.

18. See Audrey Thomas McCluskey, "In Pursuit of Unalienable Rights: Mary McLeod Bethune in Historical Perspective (1875–1955)," eds. Audrey Thomas McCluskey and Elaine M. Smith, *Mary McLeod Bethune, Building a Better World: Essays and Selected Documents* (Bloomington, IN: Indiana University Press, 1999), 3–27.

19. See "School Founder, Letter to Booker T. Washington, November 3, 1902," eds. Audrey T. McCluskey and Elaine M. Smith, *Mary McLeod Bethune, Building a Better World*, 75.

20. McCluskey, "Multiple Consciousness," 69–81.

21. Ibid.

22. Mary McLeod Bethune, "The Association for the Study of Negro Life and History: Its Contribution to Our Modern Life," *Journal of Negro History*, vol. 20, no. 4 (October 1935): 407.

23. Ibid.

24. Du Bois to Arthur B. Spingarn, May 30, 1945, *Du Bois Correspondence*, vol. 3, 14.

25. Charles H. Thompson, "The Educational Achievements of Negro Children," *Annals of the American Academy of Political and Social Science*, vol. 140 (November 1928): 194.

26. Ibid., 193–208.

27. Ibid., 208.

28. See Thompson to Du Bois, November 1, 1934, *Du Bois Collection*, Fisk.

29. Du Bois to Thompson, November 5, 1934, *Du Bois Collection*, Fisk.

30. Du Bois to Thompson, February 14, 1935, *Du Bois Collection*, Fisk.

31. Thompson to Du Bois, February 16, 1935, *Du Bois Collection*, Fisk.

32. Wayne Urban, *Black Scholar: Horace Mann Bond, 1904–1972* (Athens, GA: University of Georgia Press, 1992), 10.

33. Horace Mann Bond, "Intelligence Tests and Propaganda," *The Crisis*, vol. 28 (1924): 63.

34. Ibid., 24.

35. Horace Mann Bond, "The Curriculum and the Negro Child," *Journal of Negro Education*, vol. 4, no. 2 (April 1935): 164, 159–168.

36. Horace Mann Bond, *The Education of the Negro in the American Social Order* (New York: Prentice-Hall, Inc., 1934), 12–13.

37. Bond was a charter member of Chi Boule, founded in Nashville, Tennessee, in 1939. See Charles H. Wesley, *History of Sigma Pi Phi: First of the Negro-American Greek-Letter Fraternities* (1954; reprint, New York: Sigma Pi Phi Fraternity, Fred Weidner & Daughter Printers, 2002), 88–89, 237–238.

38. Julian Bond, telephone interview with author, January 25, 2005.

39. For a thorough explication of Counts's educational thought, see Gerald L. Gutek, *The Educational Theory of George S. Counts* (Columbus, Ohio: Ohio State University Press, 1970).

40. George S. Counts, "Dare Progressive Education Be Progressive?," *Progressive Education*, vol. 4, no. 4 (April 1932): 261.

41. Counts, "Dare Progressive Education Be Progressive?," 261.

42. Quoted in David Richard Sumpter, "A Critical Study of the Educational Thought of W.E.B. Du Bois" (Ed.D diss., Peabody College, Vanderbilt University, 1973), 51.

43. Soren A. Mathiasen to Du Bois, January 6, 1931, *Correspondence, Volume II*, 433. Du Bois to Lillian A. Alexander, January 10, 1930, *Correspondence, Volume II*, 415. Mathiasen was director of the Pocono People's College in Henryville, Pennsylvania. Du Bois had expressed interest in the concept of a People's College before receiving correspondence from Counts. For instance, in 1930 he wrote a letter to a Harlem resident and NAACP supporter expressing his desire to establish a People's College:

> With regard to the People's College that I have in mind, it will, of course, be opened to students of every color and race. At the same time, its object would be to realize democracy in the United States by the education of human beings in liberal lines, but I am proposing to do the educating, with such help that I can get, and there is not much chance that many white students would apply. If they did, they would be welcomed just as white persons with the proper point of view would be welcomed on the faculty.

44. George S. Counts, Reinhold Niebuhr, and Elmer Rice to W.E.B. Du Bois, February 7, 1936, *Du Bois Papers*. For an excellent discussion of Du Bois as a social reconstructionist edu-cator, see William H. Watkins, "Reclaiming Historical Visions of Quality Schooling: The Legacy of Early 20th Century Black Intellectuals," in *Beyond Desegregation: The Politics of Quality in African American Schooling*, ed. Mwalimu J. Shujaa (Thousand Oaks, CA: Corwin Press, Inc., 1996). For a very informative essay on Progressive educators and the issue of race, see Ronald K. Goodenow, "The Progressive Educator, Race, and Ethnicity in the Depression Years: An Overview," *History of Education Quarterly* (Winter 1975): 365–394.

45. While Curti may not be considered by historians to be a Social Reconstructionist in name, his ideas are in agreement with many of those proposed by George Counts. Like Counts in the 1930s, Curti questioned the individualistic ethos of capitalism and business in controlling schools. See Curti, *The Social Ideas of American Educators*, 581–591. It should also be noted that *The Social Ideas of American Educators* was published in the same series as Counts's *The Social Foundations of American Education*.

46. Merle Curti to Du Bois, December 5, 1932, *Du Bois Papers*.

47. Ibid.

48. Du Bois to Curti, December 9, 1932, *Du Bois Papers.*

Chapter 7

1. W.E.B. Du Bois, *Black Reconstruction in America* (1935; reprint, New York: Touchstone, 1995). Du Bois's analysis of the public and psychological wages of being white was a point that he had made almost two decades previously when he stated, "The discovery of personal whiteness among the world's peoples is a very modern thing, a nineteenth and twentieth century matter." See W.E.B. Du Bois, *Darkwater: Voices within the Veil* (1920; reprint, New York: Dover Publications, 1999), 29. For a classic analysis of whiteness, see David R. Roediger, *The Wages of Whiteness: Race and the Making of the American Working Class* (1991; reprint, New York: Verso, 1993).

2. Du Bois, "Segregation," in *W.E.B. Du Bois: A Reader*, 558.

3. Du Bois, "The Field and Function of the Negro College," in *The Education of Black People: Ten Critiques, 1906–1960*, ed. Herbert Aptheker (New York: Monthly Review Press, 1973), 84.

4. W.E.B. Du Bois, "The Negro College," *The Crisis*, vol. 40, no. 8 (August 1933): 175; Du Bois as cited in Marable, "Alain Locke, W.E.B. Du Bois and the Crisis of Black Education during the Great Depression," 6.

5. Ibid.

6. W.E.B. Du Bois, "Curriculum Revision," n.d., *Du Bois Papers.*

7. Ibid.

8. "The People's College Opens," *The Atlanta University Bulletin*, December 1942. Lists of courses for The People's College may be found in the Rufus Clement Presidential Records, Robert W. Woodruff Library, Clark Atlanta University.

9. W.E.B. Du Bois and Ira De A. Reid, "Africa and World Freedom," *Phylon*, vol. 4 (1943): 8–12.

10. W.E.B. Du Bois, "Education and Work," in *The Education of Black People: Ten Critiques, 1906–1960*, 76–80.

11. Du Bois, *Darkwater*, 122–123.

12. Ibid., 123.

13. Du Bois, "Diuturni Silenti," 41–60.

14. W.E.B. Du Bois, "The Revelation of Saint Orgne the Damned," in *The Education of Black People: Ten Critiques, 1906–1960*, ed. Herbert Aptheker (New York: Monthly Review Press, 2001), 140.

15. W.E.B. Du Bois, "Curriculum Revision," 9.

16. W.E.B. Du Bois to Yolande Du Bois Williams, October 9, 1939, *Du Bois Papers.*

17. Yolande Du Bois Williams interview.

18. *The Crisis*, vol., 1, no. 5 (March 1911). Also see Richard Cullen Rath, "Echo and Narcissus: The Afrocentric Pragmatism of W.E.B. Du Bois," *Journal of American History*, vol. 84, no. 2 (September 1997): 461–495.

19. *The Crisis*, vol. 5, no. 6 (April 1913): 312.

20. W.E.B. Du Bois, *The Negro* (1915; reprint, Amherst, NY: Humanity Books, 2002).

21. It should be noted that a number of other scholars also contributed to Afrocentric history. One such scholar was Drusilla Dunjee Houston. Houston dedi-

cated her life to illuminating the contributions of ancient African civilizations to the world. Houston's greatest contribution to Afrocentric history was her book, *Wonderful Ethiopians of the Ancient Cushite Empire*, which has recently been edited and republished by historian Peggy Brooks-Bertram. Brooks-Bertram notes that Du Bois ignored Houston's letters to him to review *Wonderful Ethiopians* in *The Crisis*. See "Introduction" in Drusilla Dunjee Houston, *Wonderful Ethiopians of the Ancient Cushite Empire, Book II: Origin of Civilization from the Cushites* (Buffalo: NY: Peggy Bertram Publishing, 2007), vi–lvii.

22. W.E.B. Du Bois, "The Field and Function of the Negro College," 125.

Chapter 8

1. Ronald E. Powaski, *The Cold War: The United States and the Soviet Union, 1917–1991* (New York: Oxford University Press, 1998), 6–7.

2. Andrew Cayton et al., *America: Pathways to the Present* (Needham, MA: Prentice Hall, 2000), 741.

3. Ibid., 742.

4. See Paul Robeson, *Here I Stand* (1958; reprint, Boston: Beacon Press, 1988).

5. For a comprehensive examination of the decline of Progressive education, see Diane Ravitch, *The Troubled Crusade: American Education, 1945–1980* (New York: Basic Books, 1985), 43–80.

6. For an excellent examination of the anti-intellectual climate of the Cold War era, see Richard Hofstadter, *Anti-Intellectualism in American Life* (New York: Vintage Books, 1962).

7. See Mary L. Dudziak, *Cold War Civil Rights: Race and the Image of American Democracy* (Princeton, NJ: Princeton University Press, 2000).

8. W.E.B. Du Bois, "Behold the Land," *The AME Review*, vol. 83, no. 224 (April–June, 1965), 31.

9. Ibid.

10. Ibid., 33.

11. Donald L. Hollowell, interview with Maurice C. Daniels, tape recording, Atlanta, Georgia, May 15, 2002.

12. To date, the most informative work on Du Bois and the civil rights movement may be found in Gerald Horne, *Black and Red: W.E.B. Du Bois and the Afro-American Response to the Cold War, 1944–1963* (New York: State University of New York Press, 1986), 223–253.

13. Du Bois, "I Bury My Wife," in *W.E.B. Du Bois: A Reader*, 142. Also see Joy James, "The Profeminist Politics of W.E.B. Du Bois with Respect to Anna Julia Cooper and Ida B. Wells Barnett," in *W.E.B. Du Bois: On Race and Culture*, 141–160.

14. See Shirley Graham Du Bois, *His Day is Marching On: A Memoir of W.E.B. Du Bois* (Philadelphia: J. B. Lippincott Company, 1971); Gerald Horne, *Race Woman: The Lives of Shirley Graham Du Bois* (New York: New York University Press, 2000).

15. Du Bois, *Autobiography*, 361–395.

16. Ibid. Also, see Horne, *Black and Red*, 125–127.

17. W.E.B. Du Bois, *Autobiography*.

18. W.E.B. Du Bois, "'We rejoice and tell the world . . . but we must go further,'" *National Guardian*, May 31, 1954, 5.

19. W.E.B. Du Bois, "Does 'all deliberate' mean 338 years?" *National Guardian*, November 4, 1957, 4.

20. W.E.B. Du Bois, "Schools for Minorities," June 27, 1954, 879, *Du Bois Papers*.

21. W.E.B. Du Bois, "Wither Now and Why?," in *The Education of Black People: Ten Critiques, 1906–1960*, ed. Herbert Aptheker (New York: Monthly Review Press, 1973), 151.

22. Du Bois's letter to King has not been located. King's letter to Du Bois, however, can be found in the *Du Bois Papers*. See Martin Luther King Jr. to Du Bois, October 20, 1960, *Du Bois Papers*.

23. W.E.B. Du Bois, "Will the Great Gandhi Live Again?" *National Guardian*, February 11, 1957, 6–7.

24. Ibid., 360.

25. W.E.B. Du Bois, "Gandhi and American Negroes," in *W.E.B. Du Bois: A Reader*, 92.

26. W.E.B. Du Bois, "Crusader without Violence," *National Guardian*, November 9, 1959, 8.

27. Du Bois, "Will the Great Gandhi Live Again?," 6.

28. Edmund W. Gordon, telephone interview with author, January 19, 2007.

29. Howard Zinn to Du Bois, April 5, 1960, *Du Bois Papers*. In his letter Zinn speaks of a phone conversation that he had earlier with Du Bois.

30. Howard Zinn to Derrick P. Alridge, personal e-mail correspondence, June 8, 2006.

31. W.E.B. Du Bois, interview with Moses Asch, 1961, *Smithsonian Folkways Recordings*.

32. Letter to J. Edgar Hoover, October 6, 1950, *The FBI Files on W.E.B. Du Bois* (Wilmington, DE: Scholarly Resources, 1996), microform.

33. W.E.B. Du Bois, "Petition of Right to the President, the Congress and the Supreme Court of the United States of America," c. 1957, *Du Bois Papers*, and "A Petition to the President of the United States, The Honorable John F. Kennedy," February 1961, *Du Bois Papers*.

34. W.E.B. Du Bois to Grace Goens, September 13, 1961, *Du Bois Papers*.

35. In an interview with former SNCC program director Cleveland Sellers, he pointed out that Du Bois and other African American educators had a great influence on the civil rights movement and helped frame civil rights activists' thinking. See Cleveland Sellers, interview with author, tape recording, Columbia, SC, December 16, 2004.

36. Septima Clark with LeGette Blythe, *Echo in My Soul* (New York: Dutton, 1962), 13–20.

37. Tomiko Brown-Nagin, "The Transformation of a Social Movement into Law? The SCLC and NAACP's Campaigns for Civil Rights Reconsidered in Light of the Educational Activism of Septima Clark," *Women's History Review*, vol. 8, no. 1 (1999): 87.

38. Septima Clark, interview with Eliot Wigginton, June 20, 1988. *Septima Clark Collection*, Avery Institute, College of Charleston.

39. See Myles Horton, "Educational Theory," in *The Myles Horton Reader*, ed. Dale Jacobs (Knoxville: The University of Tennessee Press, 2003), 211–216.

40. "Highlander Folk School Citizenship Training Program," *Septima Clark Papers*, Avery Institute, College of Charleston.

Chapter 9

1. Historian Gerald Horne has noted scholars' failure to acknowledge Du Bois's contributions to the modern civil rights movement of the 1950s and 1960s. He has also cogently chronicled Du Bois's engagement with the movement. See Gerald Horne, *Black and Red: W.E.B. Du Bois and the Afro-American Response to the Cold War, 1944–1963* (Albany: State University Press of New York, 1986).

2. Du Bois, "Education and Negroes," n.d., 11–14, *Du Bois Collection*, Fisk.

3. Ibid., 17.

4. Du Bois, "The Public School," n.d., *Du Bois Collection*, Fisk.

5. Du Bois, "The Problems of the High School and the Junior College," 1947, *Du Bois Papers*.

6. Ibid., 4.

7. Du Bois, *Black Reconstruction*, 638.

8. Du Bois, *Black Reconstruction*, 711–730. In a recent work, curriculum historian Haroon Kharem extends Du Bois's argument and argues that white supremacy and repressive ideologies toward nonwhites continues to exist in the curricula in the United States. See Haroon Kharem, *A Curriculum of Repression: A Pedagogy of Racial History in the United States* (New York: Peter Lang, 2006).

9. W.E.B. Du Bois, "Should Negro History Be Taught As a Separate Subject?," n.d., *Du Bois Papers*.

10. W.E.B. Du Bois, "The Freedom to Learn," *Midwest Journal*, 2 (Winter 1949): 11.

11. Ibid.

12. W.E.B. Du Bois, "Is It Democracy for Whites to Rule Dark Majorities?" May 15, 1945, *New York Post*, p. 8.

13. W.E.B. Du Bois, "Economic Illiteracy," November 19, 1947, *Du Bois Collection*.

14. W.E.B. Du Bois, "Speech Delivered by W. E. Burghardt Du Bois at the California Labor School's Second Annual Banquet," March 7, 1948, *Du Bois Collection*, Fisk.

15. W.E.B. Du Bois, "A Program for the Land Grant Colleges," in *Writings in Non-Periodical Literature Edited by Others*, ed. Herbert Aptheker (Millwood, New York, 1982), 201.

16. For a detailed discussion of the Marxist influences on Du Bois's educational thought, see Stanley L. Goldstein, "The Influence of Marxism on the Educational Philosophy of W.E.B. Du Bois, 1897–1963" (Ph.D. diss., University of Texas, Austin, 1972).

17. W.E.B. Du Bois, "Elementary Education and War," April 10, 1950, *Du Bois Papers*.

18. W.E.B. Du Bois, "Russia—An Interpretation," *Soviet Russia Today*, October 1949, *Du Bois Papers*.

19. Mary Frances Berry and John W. Blassingame, *Long Memory: The Black Experience in America* (New York: Oxford University Press, 1982), 328–329.

20. W.E.B. Du Bois, "The Talented Tenth Memorial Address," *Boule Journal*, vol. 15 (October 1948): 4.

21. Ibid., 12.

22. Ibid., 3–13.

23. Ibid., 8.

24. Ibid.

25. Ibid., 11.

26. W.E.B. Du Bois, "The American Negro Woman," c. 1949, *Du Bois Papers*.

27. Cleveland Sellers, interview by author, tape recording, Columbia, SC, December 16, 2004.

28. See Du Bois, "Pan-Africa and the New Racial Philosophy," *The Crisis*, vol. 40, no. 11 (November 1933): 247.

29. Ibid.

30. W.E.B. Du Bois, *The World and Africa: An Inquiry into the Part Which Africa Has Played in World History* (New York: International Publishers, 1947), 99.

31. Ibid.

32. W.E.B. Du Bois, "Africa and the American Negro Intelligentsia," *Présence Africaine*, no. 5–7 (December 1955–January 1956): 34–51.

33. W.E.B. Du Bois, "For Cooperation toward an Encyclopedia Africana," Info. Report #2, Accra, Ghana (September 1962). Also see "Provisional Draft: Proposed Plans for an Encyclopedia Africana," Rare Books Room: Pennsylvania State University, 1961; Wilson Jeremiah Moses, *Afrotopia: The Roots of African American Popular History* (Cambridge, UK: Cambridge University Press, 1998), 1–17.

34. An examination of Du Bois's "Proposed Plans for an *Encyclopedia Africana*" provides further insight into Du Bois's ideas about the contents of such an encyclopedia and outlines an ideal "Afro-centric" curriculum. Du Bois proposed that several subjects must first be covered that would provide the historical foundation for the encyclopedia. The subjects he proposed for study in the introduction included:

1. African Origins (a survey of the present state of our knowledge of African prehistory down to about 5,000 B.C.).
2. The Geography of Africa and Its Historical Significance.
3. Africa's Place in the Birth of Civilization.
4. Africa during the Middle Ages (a survey of the levels of political and cultural development achieved).
5. Trade Routes across the Sahara and across the Seas.
6. The Significance of the European Trade in African Slaves (its origins and consequences).
7. The European Economy and Euro-African Relations since the 18th Century (changes in relationship resulting from the transition from European mercantilism to industrial capitalism and then to imperialism).
8. The Social and Economic Consequences of Colonialism.
9. The Achievement of African Liberation.

See Du Bois, *Proposed Plans for an Encyclopedia Africana*, 3.

35. W.E.B. Du Bois to A. Diop, March 7, 1961, *Du Bois Papers*.

36. Yolande Du Bois Williams, interview by author, tape recording, New Orleans, La., July 19, 2005.

37. Moses, *Afrotopia*, 136.

38. W.E.B. Du Bois, "Behold the Land," *The AME Review*, vol. 83, no. 224 (April–June 1965): 31.

39. W.E.B. Du Bois, *The Ordeal of Mansart* (New York: Mainstream Publishers, 1957), 118. For excellent analyses of *The Black Flame*, see Arnold Rampersad, *The Art and Imagination of W.E.B. Du Bois* (Cambridge, MA: Harvard University Press, 1976) and Jack B. Moore, *W.E.B. Du Bois* (Boston, Twayne Publishers, 1981).

40. Ibid., 125.

41. Ibid., 114–115.

42. Ibid., 122.

43. W.E.B. Du Bois, *Mansart Builds a School* (New York: Mainstream Publishers, 1959), 105.

44. W.E.B. Du Bois, *Worlds of Color* (New York: Mainstream Publishers, 1961), 306.

45. Ibid., 308.

46. Martin Luther King Jr., "Honoring Dr. Du Bois" in *Freedomways Reader: Prophets in Their Own Country*, ed. Esther Cooper Jackson with Constance Pohl (Boulder, Colorado: Westview Press, 2000).

Chapter 10

1. W.E.B. Du Bois, *A.D. 2150*, c. 1950, *Du Bois Papers*.

2. For an excellent examination of Du Bois's contributions to Black Studies, see Nagueyalti Warren, "The Contributions of W.E.B. Du Bois to Afro-American Studies in Higher Education." Ph.D. diss., University of Mississippi, 1984.

3. James B. Stewart, *Flight: In Search of Vision* (Trenton, NJ: Africa World Press, Inc., 2004).

4. Asante, *The Afrocentric Idea*, 11.

5. Ibid., 136.

6. Ibid., xv–xvi, 138.

7. Asa G. Hilliard III, *SBA: The Reawakening of the African Mind* (Gainesville, FL: Makare Publishing, 1998). Like Du Bois, Hilliard also hails Egypt as a great African civilization.

8. See Asa G. Hilliard III, "No Mystery: Closing the Achievement Gap between Africans and Excellence," in *Young, Gifted, and Black: Promoting High Achievement Among African-American Students*, eds. Theresa Perry, Claude Steele, and Asa G. Hilliard III (Boston: Beacon Press, 2003), 131–165.

9. See James Banks, "African American Scholarship and the Evolution of Multicultural Education," *Journal of Negro Education*, vol. 61, no. 3 (Summer 1992): 273–286.

10. James A. Banks, "News & Events Faculty Spotlight," http://depts.washington.edu/coe/news/fac_spotlight/banks.html.

11. See Violet J. Harris, "Historic Readers for African-American Children (1868–1944): Uncovering and Reclaiming a Tradition of Opposition," in *Too Much Schooling, Too Little Education: A Paradox of Black Life in White Societies*, ed. Mwalimu Shujaa (Trenton, NJ: Africa World Press, 1994), 143–175.

12. See Lucius Outlaw, *Critical Social Theory in the Interests of Black Folk* (Lanham, MD: Rowman and Littlefield, 2005); Derrick Bell, *And We Are Not Saved: The Elusive Quest for Racial Justice* (New York: Basic Books, 1987). Gloria Ladson-Billings and William F. Tate IV, "Toward a Critical Race Theory in Education," *Teach-*

ers College Record, vol. 97, no. 1 (Fall 1995): 47–68; Terry Oatts, *W.E.B. Du Bois & Critical Race Theory: Toward a Du Boisian Philosophy of Education* (McDonough, GA: Exceptional Publications, 2006); Reiland Rabaka, "W.E.B. Du Bois's Evolving Africana Philosophy of Education," *Journal of Black Studies*, vol. 33, no. 4 (2003): 399–449; Susan Searles Giroux, "Reconstructing the Future: Du Bois, Racial Pedagogy and the Post-Civil Rights Era," *Social Identities*, vol. 9, no. 4 (2003): 563–598; Joe L. Kincheloe, *Critical Pedagogy Primer* (New York: Peter Lang, 2005), 59–64.

13. Cynthia B. Dillard, *On Spiritual Strivings: Transforming an African American Woman's Academic Life* (New York: State University of New York Press, 2006), x.

14. V. P. Franklin, *The Education of Black Philadelphia: A Social and Educational History of a Minority Community, 1900–1950* (Philadelphia: University of Pennsylvania Press, 1979).

15. Anderson, *The Education of Blacks in the South*, 6.

16. Also see Franklin and Anderson's collaborative volume on African American education, V.P. Franklin and James D. Anderson, eds., *New Perspectives on Black Educational History* (Boston: G. K. Hall, 1978).

17. Vanessa Siddle Walker to Derrick P. Alridge, e-mail correspondence, January 7, 2007. Also, see Vanessa Siddle Walker, *Their Highest Potential: An African American School Community in the Segregated South* (Chapel Hill, NC: University of North Carolina Press, 1996).

18. The work of these historians extends Du Bois's ideas and arguments on African American education, teachers, and teacher education in his *AU Studies*.

19. Edmund W. Gordon, phone interview with author, January 19, 2006.

20. Edmund W. Gordon, "Production of Knowledge and Pursuit of Understanding," in *Edmund W. Gordon: Producing Knowledge, Pursuing Understanding*, ed. Carol Camp Yeakey (Stamford, CT: JAI Press Inc., 2000), 301–318.

21. See Aaron D. Gresson, *The Dialectics of Betrayal: Sacrifice, Violation and the Oppressed* (Norwood, NJ: Ablex Publishing Corporation, 1982) and *The Recovery of Race in America* (Minneapolis: University of Minnesota Press, 1995).

22. Jerome E. Morris, "Can Anything Good Come from Nazareth? Race, Class, and African-American Schooling and Community in the Urban South and Midwest," *American Educational Research Journal*, vol. 41, no. 1 (2004): 69–112.

23. See Marybeth Gasman, *Envisioning Black Colleges: A History of the United Negro College Fund* (Baltimore: Johns Hopkins Press, 2007).

24. Larry L. Rowley, Nathan Daun-Barnett, and Venice Thandi Sulé, *Higher Education and African-American Civic Participation: An Empirical Analysis of Du Bois's "Talented Tenth" Concept*. Paper presented at annual meeting of the Association for the Study of Higher Education, November 4, 2006, Anaheim, California. Larry L. Rowley, "The Rise of Du Boisian Studies in the American Academy: Implications for 21st Century Scholarship on Race," *African American Research Perspectives* (Fall 2005), 138–150. Larry L. Rowley, "W.E.B. Du Bois: Role Model and Mentor for African American Undergraduate Men," *About Campus*, vol. 6, no. 5 (November–December 2001): 20–25.

25. For another notable assessment of the talented tenth, see Juan Battle and Earl Wright II, "W.E.B. DuBois's Talented Tenth: A Quantitative Assessment," *Journal of Black Studies*, vol. 32, no. 6 (2002): 654–672.

26. Mary Frances Berry, "Du Bois as Social Activist: Why We Are Not Saved," *Annals of the American Academy of Political and Social Sciences*, vol. 568 (March 2000): 109.

Selected Bibliography

This bibliography includes manuscript collections consulted and selected primary and secondary sources cited. Full citation information for items not included in this bibliography may be found in the endnotes.

MANUSCRIPT COLLECTIONS

ATLANTA UNIVERSITY, ROBERT W. WOODRUFF LIBRARY
Rufus E. Clement Records, 1939–1969.

AVERY INSTITUTE, COLLEGE OF CHARLESTON, CHARLESTON, SC
Septima Clark Papers

FISK UNIVERSITY, NASHVILLE, TN
W.E.B. Du Bois Collection

HOWARD UNIVERSITY, MOORLAND-SPINGARN RESEARCH CENTER, WASHINGTON, DC
The Anna Julia Cooper Papers
The Kelly Miller Papers
The Alain Locke Papers
The Charles H. Thompson Papers (unprocessed)

LIBRARY OF CONGRESS, WASHINGTON, DC
The Carter G. Woodson Collection
Nannie Helen Burroughs Papers

SCHOMBURG RESEARCH LIBRARY, NEW YORK
Alexander Crummell Papers
Francis Broderick Collection

UNIVERSITY OF MASSACHUSETTS, AMHERST
The Papers of W.E.B. Du Bois
The Papers of W.E.B. Du Bois, Addendum

COLLECTED PAPERS IN PRINT

The Booker T. Washington Papers, ed. Louis R. Harlan (Urbana: University of Illinois Press, 1972–1984)
The Middle Works of John Dewey, ed. Jo Ann Boydston (Carbondale: Southern Illinois University Press, 1976–1983)

INTERVIEWS

Edmund W. Gordon, January 19, 2007 (phone)
Julian Bond, January 2005, Charlottesville, Virginia (phone)
David Levering Lewis, October 2005, New York (phone)
Cleveland Sellers, December 2004, Columbia, South Carolina
Yolande Du Bois Williams, July 19, 2005, New Orleans

GOVERNMENT COLLECTIONS, DOCUMENTS, AND PUBLICATIONS

Federal Bureau of Investigation Files
    W.E.B. Du Bois
    Martin Luther King Jr.
U.S. Bureau of Census
U.S. Department of Education
U.S Department of Labor

PUBLISHED WORKS

Primary Sources

Clark, Septima Poinsette with LeGette Blythe. *Echo in My Soul*. New York: E.P. Dutton & Co., Inc., 1962.

Darwin, Charles. *On the Origin of Species: By Means of Natural Selection of the Preservation of Favoured Races in the Struggle for Life*. New York: Washington Square Press Inc., 1963. Originally published in 1859.

Dewey, John. *The Child and the Curriculum*. Chicago: University of Chicago Press, 1909.

———. *The School and Society*. Chicago: University of Chicago Press, 1967. Originally published in 1899.

Du Bois, W.E.B. *The Autobiography of W.E.B. Du Bois: A Soliloquy on Viewing My Life from the Last Decade of its First Century*. New York: International Publishers, 1968.

———. *Black Reconstruction in America, 1860–1880*. New York: Simon & Schuster, 1995. Originally published in 1935.

———. *Dark Princess: A Romance*. Jackson, MS: University Press of Mississippi, 1995. Originally published in 1928.

———. *Darkwater: Voices within the Veil*. New York: Dover Publications, 1999. Originally published in 1920.

———. "Diuturni Silenti." *The Education of Black People: Ten Critiques, 1906–1960*, edited by Herbert Aptheker, 41–69. New York: Monthly Review Press, 1973.

———. *Dusk of Dawn: An Essay toward an Autobiography of a Race Concept*. New Brunswick, NJ: Transaction Publishers, 2000. Originally published in 1940.

———. "Education and Work." *The Education of Black People: Ten Critiques,*

1906–1960, edited by Herbert Aptheker, 61–82. New York: Monthly Review Press, 1973.

———. "How I Taught School." *The Fisk Herald*, vol. 4, no. 4 (December 1886): 10.

———. *The Negro*. Amherst, New York: Humanity Books, 2002.

———. "A Negro Schoolmaster in the New South." *Atlantic Monthly*, vol. 83 (January 1899): 100–101.

———. "An Open Letter to the Southern People." In *Against Racism: Unpublished Essays, Papers, Addresses, 1887–1961*, edited by Herbert Aptheker, 1–4. Amherst: University of Massachusetts Press, 1985.

———. *The Philadelphia Negro: A Social Study*. New York: Schocken Books. Originally published in 1899.

———. *The Quest of the Silver Fleece: A Novel*. College Park, MD: McGrath Publishing Co., 1969. Originally published in 1911.

———. "The Revelation of Saint Orgne the Damned." *The Education of Black People: Ten Critiques, 1906–1960*, edited by Herbert Aptheker, 83–102. New York: Monthly Review Press, 1973.

———. *The Souls of Black Folk*. New York: Bantam Books, 1989. Originally published in 1903.

———. *The Suppression of the African Slave Trade to the United States of America, 1638–1870*. Baton Rouge: Louisiana State Press, 1969. Originally published in 1896.

———. "Tom Brown." *The Fisk Herald*, vol. 5, no. 4 (December 1887): 5–7.

———. "Whither Now and Why?" *The Education of Black People: Ten Critiques, 1906–1960*, edited by Herbert Aptheker, 149–158. New York: Monthly Review Press, 1973.

———. *The World and Africa: An Inquiry into the Part Which Africa Has Played in World History*. New York: International Publishers, 1996. Originally published in 1946.

Galton, Francis. *Hereditary Genius: An Inquiry into its Laws and Consequences*. New York: Appleton & Co., 1887.

Giddings, Franklin. *Civilization and Society: An Account of the Development and Behavior of Human Society*. New York: H. Holt and Co., 1932.

———. *The Principles of Sociology: An Analysis of the Phenomena of Association and of Social Organization*. New York: The Macmillan Co., 1896.

Highlander Folk School Citizenship Training Program. Septima Clark Papers, Avery Institute, College of Charleston, Charleston, SC.

James, William. *Pragmatism*. Cambridge, Massachusetts: Harvard University Press, 1998. Originally published in 1907.

———. *The Principles of Psychology*. New York: Henry Holt and Co., 1890.

Jones, Thomas Jesse. *Negro Education: A Study of the Private and Higher Schools for Colored People in the United States*. New York: Arno Press, 1969. Originally published in 1917.

Phillips, Wendell. *The Scholar in a Republic: Address at the Centennial Anniversary of the Phi Beta Kappa of Harvard College, June 30, 1881*. Boston: Lee and Shepard Publishers, 1881.

Prosser, Charles A., and Charles R. Allen. *Vocational Education in a Democracy*. New York: The Century Co., 1925.

Schultz, Alfred P. *Race or Mongrel*. New York: Arno Press, 1977. Originally published in 1908.

Thirty Years of Lynching in the United States, 1889–1918. New York: National Association for the Advancement of Colored People, 1919.

Washington, Booker T. *Up from Slavery*. New York: Avon Classics, 1965.

Woodson, Carter G. *The Education of the Negro Prior to 1861*. Washington, D.C.: Associated Publishers, 1919.

———. *The Mis-Education of the Negro*. Washington, DC: ASALH Press, 2005. Originally published in 1933.

Secondary Sources

Alridge, Derrick P. "The Dilemmas, Challenges, and Duality of an African American Educational Historian." *Educational Theory*, vol. 32, no. 9 (2003): 25–34.

———. "Of Victorianism, Civilizationism, and Progressivism: The Educational Ideas of Anna Julia Cooper and W.E.B. Du Bois." Paper presented at the annual meeting of the American Education Research Association, New Orleans, 2002.

Anderson, James D. *The Education of Blacks in the South, 1860–1935*. Chapel Hill: University of North Carolina Press, 1988.

Banks, William M. *Black Intellectuals: Race and Responsibility in American Life*. New York: W.W. Norton & Co., 1996.

Bederman, Gail. *Manliness and Civilization: A Cultural History of Gender and Race in the United States*. Chicago: University of Chicago Press, 1995.

Beringer, Richard E. *Historical Analysis: Contemporary Approaches to Clio's Craft*. Malabar, FL: Robert E. Krieger Publishing Co., 1968.

Berry, Mary Frances. "Du Bois as Social Activist: Why We Are Not Saved." *The Annals of the American Academy of Political and Social Science*, 568 (March 2000): 100–110.

Burstyn, Joan N. *Victorian Education and the Ideal of Womanhood*. Totowa, NJ: Barnes & Noble Books, 1980.

Butchart, Ronald E. *Northern Schools, Southern Blacks, and Reconstruction: Freedmen's Education, 1862–1875*. Westport, CT: Greenwood Press, 1980.

Craig, Wyn. *The Fiery Cross: The Ku Klux Klan in America*. New York: Simon and Schuster, 1987.

Cremin, Lawrence A. *The Transformation of the School: Progressivism in American Education, 1876–1957*. New York: Alfred A. Knopf, 1961.

Curti, Merle. *The Social Ideas of American Educators*. Totowa, NJ: Littlefield, Adams, and Co., 1974.

De Marco, Joseph. *The Social Thought of W.E.B. Du Bois*. New York: University Press of America, 1983.

Dillard, Cynthia B. *On Spiritual Strivings: Transforming an African American Woman's Life*. Albany: State University of New York Press, 2006.

Dmytryshyn, Basil. *USSR: A Concise History*, 2nd ed. New York: Charles Scribner's Sons, 1971.

Dudziak, Mary L. *Cold War Civil Rights: Race and the Image of American Democracy*. Princeton, NJ: Princeton University Press, 2000.

Evans, Stephanie Y. *Black Women in the Ivory Tower, 1850–1954: An Intellectual History*. Gainesville: University Press of Florida, 2007.

Foner, Eric. *Reconstruction: America's Unfinished Revolution, 1863–1877*. New York: HarperCollins Perennial Classics, 2002. Originally published in 1988.

Franklin, John Hope, and Moss, Alfred A. Jr. *From Slavery to Freedom: A History of African Americans*, 4th ed. Boston: McGraw Hill, 2002.

Franklin, V. P. *Black Self-Determination: A Cultural History of the Faith of the Fathers*. Westport, Connecticut: Lawrence Hill & Co., 1984.

———. *Living Our Stories, Telling Our Truths: Autobiography and the Making of the African American Intellectual Tradition*. New York: Scribner, 1995.

Frazier, E. Franklin. *The Negro in the United States*. New York: The MacMillan Co., 1957.

Fredrickson, George. *The Black Image in the White Mind: The Debate on Afro-American Character and Destiny, 1817–1914*. Hanover, NH: Wesleyan University Press, 1987.

Fullinwider, S. P. *The Mind and Mood of Black America: 20th Century Thought*. Homewood, IL: The Dorsey Press, 1969.

Gaither, Milton. *American Educational History Revisited: A Critique of Progress*. New York: Teachers College Press, 2003.

Garraty, John A., and Mark C. Carnes. *A Short History of the American Nation*. New York: Longman, 2000.

Gasman, Marybeth. "W.E.B. Du Bois and Charles S. Johnson: Differing Views on the Role of Philanthropy in Higher Education." *History of Education Quarterly*, 42, no. 4 (2002): 493–516.

Gilroy, Paul. *The Black Atlantic: Modernity and Double Consciousness*. Cambridge, MA: Harvard University Press, 1993.

Gordon, Lynn D. *Gender and Higher Education in the Progressive Era*. New Haven, CT: Yale University Press, 1990.

Harlan, Louis R. *Booker T. Washington, The Making of a Black Leader, 1856–1901, Volume I*. New York: Oxford University Press, 1972.

———. *Booker T. Washington, The Wizard of Tuskegee, 1901–1915, Volume II*. New York: Oxford University Press, 1983.

———. *Separate and Unequal: Public School Campaigns and Racism in the Southern Seaboard States, 1901–1915*. New York: Atheneum, 1969.

Higginbotham, Evelyn Brooks. *Righteous Discontent: The Women's Movement in the Black Baptist Church, 1880–1920*. Cambridge: Harvard University Press, 1993.

Historical Statistics of the United States, Volume 1, Population. New York: Cambridge University Press, 2006.

Hofstadter, Richard. *Anti-Intellectualism in American Life*. New York: Vintage Books, 1962.

Horne, Gerald. *Race Woman: The Lives of Shirley Graham Du Bois*. New York: New York University Press, 2000.

Johnson, Karen A. *Uplifting the Women and the Race: The Educational Philosophies and Social Activism of Anna Julia Cooper and Nannie Helen Burroughs*. New York: Garland Publishing, Inc., 2000.

Karier, Clarence. *The Individual, Society, and Education: A History of American Educational Ideas*. Chicago: University of Illinois Press, 1986.

Kharem, Haroon. *A Curriculum of Repression: A Pedagogy of Racial History in the United States*. New York: Peter Lang, 2006.

La Faber, Walter. *America, Russia, and the Cold War, 1945–1984*. New York: Alfred A. Knopf, 1985.

Lewis, David Levering. *When Harlem Was in Vogue*. New York: Oxford University Press, 1989. Originally published in 1981.

———. *W.E.B. Du Bois: Biography of a Race, 1868–1919*. New York: Henry Holt, 2000.

Litwack, Leon F. *Been in the Storm So Long: The Aftermath of Slavery*. New York: Random House Vintage Books, 1980.

Logan, Rayford. *The Betrayal of the Negro: From Rutherford B. Hayes to Woodrow Wilson*. New York: Da Capo Press, Inc., 1997. Originally published in 1965.

Marable, Manning. *W.E.B. Du Bois: Black Radical Democrat*, 2nd ed. Boulder: Paradigm Publishers, 2005.

McGerr, Michael. *A Fierce Discontent: The Rise and Fall of the Progressive Movement in America, 1870–1920*. New York: Free Press, 2003.

Menand, Louis. *The Metaphysical Club: A Story of Ideas in America*. New York: Farrar, Straus, and Giroux, 2001.

Moore, Jacqueline M. *Booker T. Washington, W.E.B. Du Bois, and the Struggle for Racial Uplift*. Wilmington, DE: Scholarly Resources Inc., 2003.

Moses, Wilson J. *Alexander Crummell: A Study of Civilization and Discontent*. New York: Oxford University Press, 1989.

———. *Creative Conflict in African American Thought: Frederick Douglass, Alexander Crummell, Booker T. Washington, W.E.B. Du Bois, and Marcus Garvey*. Cambridge, UK: Cambridge University Press, 2004.

Patterson, Orlando. *Rituals of Blood: Consequences of Slavery in Two American Centuries*. Washington, DC: Civitas/Counterpoint, 1998.

Pearce, Roy Harvey. *Savagism and Civilization: A Study of the Indian and the American Mind*. Baltimore: John Hopkins Press, 1967.

Perkinson, J. *The Imperfect Panacea: American Faith in Education, 1865–1990*. New York: McGraw Hill, Inc., 1991.

Pinar, William F. *The Gender of Racial Politics and Violence in America: Lynching, Prison Rape, and the Crisis of Masculinity*. New York: Peter Lang, 2001.

Posnock, Ross. *Color and Culture: Black Writers and the Making of the Modern Intellectual*. Cambridge, MA: Harvard University Press, 1998.

Powaski, Ronald E. *The Cold War: The United States and the Soviet Union, 1917–1991*. New York: Oxford University Press, 1998.

Reed, Adolph L. Jr. *W.E.B. Du Bois and American Political Thought: Fabianism and the Color Line*. New York: Oxford University Press, 1997.

Richardson, Joe E. *A History of Fisk University, 1865–1946*. Alabama: University of Alabama Press, 1980.

Ross, Barbara Joyce. *J. E. Spingarn and the Rise of the NAACP, 1911–1939*. New York: Atheneum, 1972.

Rudwick, Elliot. *W.E.B. Du Bois: A Study in Minority Group Leadership*. Philadelphia: University of Pennsylvania Press, 1960.

Scott, Daryl Michael. *Contempt and Pity: Social Policy and the Image of the Dam-*

aged Black Psyche, 1880–1996. Chapel Hill: University of North Carolina Press, 1997.

Sinclair, Upton. *The Jungle*. Boston: Bedford/St.Martin's Press, 2005. Originally published in 1906.

Spivey, Donald. *Schooling for the New Slavery: Black Industrial Education, 1868–1915*. Westport, CT: Greenwood Press, 1978.

Spring, Joel H. *Education and the Rise of the Corporate State*. Boston: Beacon Press, 1973.

Stewart, James B. *Flight: In Search of Vision*. Trenton, N.J.: Africa World Press, 2004.

Thorpe, Earl E. *The Mind of the Negro: An Intellectual History of Afro-Americans*. Westport, CT: Negro Universities Press, 1970.

Trotter, Joe William Jr. *The African American Experience*. Boston: Houghton Mifflin, 2001.

Tyack, David B. *The One Best System: A History of American Urban Education*. Cambridge, MA: Harvard University Press, 1974.

Watkins, William H. *The White Architects of Black Education: Ideology and Power in America, 1865–1954*. New York: Teachers College Press, 2001.

Watson, Peter. *The Modern Mind: An Intellectual History of the 20th Century*. New York: HarperCollins, 2001.

Watts, Jerry Gafio. *Heroism and the Black Intellectual: Ralph Ellison, Politics, and Afro-American Intellectual Life*. Chapel Hill: University of North Carolina Press, 1994.

West, Cornel. *An American Evasion of Philosophy: A Genealogy of Pragmatism*. Madison: University of Wisconsin Press, 1989. Originally published in 1982.

West, Michael Rudolph. *The Education of Booker T. Washington: American Democracy and the Idea of Race Relations*. New York: Columbia University, 2006.

Wolters, Raymond. *Negroes and the Great Depression: The Problem of Economic Recovery*. Westport, CT: Greenwood Publishers, 1970.

———. *Du Bois and His Rivals*. Columbia: University of Missouri Press, 2002.

Zamir, Shamoon. *Dark Voices: W.E.B. Du Bois and American Thought, 1888–1903*. Chicago: University of Chicago Press, 1995.

THESES AND DISSERTATIONS

Goldstein, Stanley. "The Influence of Marxism on the Educational Philosophy of W.E.B. Du Bois, 1897–1963." Ph.D. diss., University of Texas, Austin, 1972.

Sumpter, David Richard. "A Critical Study of the Educational Thought of W.E.B. Du Bois." Ph.D. diss., George Peabody College for Teachers, Vanderbilt University, 1973.

Warren, Nagueyalti. "The Contributions of W.E.B. Du Bois to Afro-American Studies in Higher Education." Ph.D. diss., University of Mississippi, 1984.

Weatherford-Jacobs, Odessa. "Hegel and Du Bois: A Study of the Influence of G.W.F. Hegel on the Early Writings of W.E.B. Du Bois (1896–1903)." Ph.D. diss., Saint Louis University, 2002.

Index